Leadership and Learning

Helping Libraries and Librarians Reach Their Potential

Lyndon Pugh

The Scarecrow Press, Inc.
Lanham, Maryland, and London
2001

SCARECROW PRESS, INC.

Published in the United States of America
by Scarecrow Press, Inc.
4720 Boston Way, Lanham, Maryland 20706
www.scarecrowpress.com

4 Pleydell Gardens, Folkestone
Kent CT20 2DN, England

Copyright © 2001 by Lyndon Pugh

All rights reserved. No part of this publication may be reproduced, stored in a retrieval system, or transmitted in any form or by any means, electronic, mechanical, photocopying, recording, or otherwise, without the prior permission of the publisher.

British Library Cataloguing-in-Publication Information Available

Library of Congress Cataloging-in-Publication Data

Pugh, Lyndon.
    Leadership and learning : helping libraries and librarians reach their potential / Lyndon Pugh.
      p. cm.
    Includes bibliographical reference and index.
    ISBN: 0-8108-4146-0 (alk. paper)
    1. Library employees—In-service training. 2. Librarians—In-service training. 3. Library employees—Effect of technological innovations on. 4. Librarians—Effect of technological innovations on. 6. Organizational change—Management. 6. Career development. I. Title.

Z668.5 .P84 2001
020'.71'55—dc21   200134856

∞™ The paper used in this publication meets the minimum requirements of American National Standard for Information Sciences—Permanence of Paper for Printed Library Materials, ANSI/NISO Z39.48-1992.
Manufactured in the United States of America.

Contents

List of Figures v
Acknowledgments vii
Introduction ix

Part 1: Learning, Development, and the Organization

Chapter 1   The Organizational Background   1
Chapter 2   Creating a Learning Structure in Libraries 31
Chapter 3   Managing Learning in Libraries   57

Part 2: Self-Development

Chapter 4   How Librarians Learn   77
Chapter 5   Thoughts on Self-Development   97
Chapter 6   Self-Development at Work   105

Part 3: Some Key Techniques and Issues

Chapter 7   Coaching   131
Chapter 8   Mentoring   159
Chapter 9   Learning in Teams   185
Chapter 10   Motivation   205
Chapter 11   Epilogue: Some Issues for Learning   223
Bibliography   229
Index   235
About the Author   241

List of Figures

1.1	Organizational Complexity and Changes in Training Styles	13
2.1	A Two-Layer Team Structure	43
2.2	A Team Structure around a Permeable Core	44
2.3	A Model of the Learning Library	50
3.1	The Place of Learning and Development in the Structure	66
3.2	The Management Process for Learning and Development	67
4.1	The Original Ground Floor Plan	89
4.2	The Original First Floor Plan	90
4.3	The Expansion into the Faculty Office	91
4.4	The Library Extension Mark One	91
4.5	The Library Extension Mark Two: Ground Floor	93
4.6	The Library Extension Mark Three: First Floor	94
5.1	Preparing for Self-Development	103
6.1	The Process of Learning from Work	123
7.1	The Manager–Coach Shift	132
7.2	The Roles of the Coach	143
7.3	Coaching Behavior	149
7.4	The Coaching Process	150
8.1	The Mentoring Process: Key Features	172
9.1	The Team Learning Process	195

Acknowledgments

A number of writers have had a seminal influence on this book. The marks of their ideas and ways of thinking can be found in many passages, and they demand a separate acknowledgment. Work by the Centre for Labour Studies at the University of Leicester, United Kingdom, has influenced the sections on the development of training theories. The treatment of educational psychology has benefited enormously from my reading and interpretation of material on curriculum studies from the Faculty of Education at the University of New England, Australia. I am indebted to Dennis and Valentina McInerney for their work in the same area. Peter Senge has influenced the chapters on self-development and learning in teams, as well as the general concept of the learning organization. The structure of the learning subsystem in chapter 2 is based on work on learning organizations by Pearn, Roderick, and Mulrooney. Peter Honey, alone and with Alan Mumford, has directed the thoughts on self-learning and learning from work. Case study 3 draws for background on a modification of information taken from separate papers by Barbara Allan and Clive Field, but the events analyzed did not take place in either of their institutions.

On a practical level, Jennifer Welsh and colleagues at the University of Wales Institute in Cardiff have helped in providing the necessary resources. My thanks are owed to them all.

Introduction

Hilarie Owen (2001) wrote that the two key issues for today's organizations are leadership and learning. The two themes are related. This book tries to make some points about learning, and the implicit links with leadership, or with new forms of management. First, the most important form of learning that takes place in libraries is work-based and goes on outside formal staff development structures. Second, this learning has to be encouraged through the creation of organizations that will support it. Third, there are also some important techniques that have to be deployed: coaching, mentoring, group learning, and motivation. Last, this workplace-based self-development must be systematically managed. These final two points begin to touch on the connection between learning and leadership.

Part 1 considers the organizational features that are felt to be essential for self-development through work-based learning. Richard Heseltine (2000) said, "I find it hard to take the imaginative leap to envisage what the Web equivalent of the future will look like". The question posed, of what things are going to be like in an age of new technology, is a very important one. It can be expanded: What will libraries look like when they combine data and metadata in ways that are really convenient for users, when we truly and organically integrate all forms of data at the point of use? How will we organize from a human point of view when we have real hybrid librarians? What challenges, other than the obvious technological ones, lie in a future where large areas of our resource collections have no physical entity, where libraries have no walls, and when collections need not be accessed through libraries? What will we do as other professionals claim some of the territory once exclusively held by librarians? How will we handle our affairs if our best talents increasingly move into other areas where there is a better market for the skills of organizing information in a new environment?

Electronic developments, as Heseltine pointed out, are creating a community of shared interests. They are improving communications among the knowledge creators, and between the knowledge creators and those who wish to use the knowledge. At the same time they are creating the possibility of new roles for librarians. If we are going to answer Heseltine's question, we first of all need creativity in the context of organizational development. Creativity in this situation is the ability to deal with problems like the ones Heseltine described—problems that are not easy to define and that require long-term effort. They will also need a different kind of thinking that will question conventional wisdom and will craft some solutions from traditions, disciplines, and ways of working which might not normally have a lot to do with conventional librarianship.

If we are going to develop this kind of thinking in libraries we will need people with the confidence to take risks and to break with convention. Our staff will want to take more responsibility. They will be people with good skills in communication and social interaction; these skills will equip them to work with information workers who come from different traditions and have different ways of looking at things. In turn, this will support innovation and novel solutions to problems.

We will also need to give them the scope to use their talents: this means more responsibility. This is a particularly relevant point in view of the fact that creativity of the kind this book champions comes from everywhere in the organization, not just the top. To paraphrase Branden (1998), who spoke of organizations in general, libraries will no longer be run by a few thinkers, and a lot of doers. Part 1 looks at the need for new thinking and proposes some structural changes that will help to create and manage an environment that supports learning.

Part 2 offers a more personal solution. The other key part of the argument is that work-based individual learning is now the most prevalent and potent force for development. This is because individual learning influences all of the key issues:

- Job satisfaction and the ability to retain staff
- Performance improvement

- Laying the foundation for continuous learning
- Skills improvement
- Behavior change and subsequent attitude change
- Motivation and organizational health

(Whetherly, 2001)

Part 3 considers some of the training behavior which supports the idea of individual learning in the workplace. Parsloe and Wray (2000) support the view that coaching and mentoring are the vital techniques for underpinning the one-to-one learning for which Whetherley argues. To this I add team learning, because it links learning to structures and turns individual learning into true organizational learning. Chapter 10 looks at motivation, which in some respects is a summary of all that has gone before.

Use is made of terms like "training," "learning," and "development." There is a continued argument about the use and meaning of these terms. I have tried to be consistent, and in this book learning occurs when a new skill, or piece of knowledge, is absorbed and applied. Development is the long-term cumulative effect of these experiences, and involves attitude change. This is what this book is about. I may not have achieved my objective of consistent use, but I hope the context makes the meaning clear in all cases. I have also on occasions used the word "facilitator" to describe once again a broad spectrum of roles, which could include trainers, coaches, mentors, and enablers. In any case, I apologize to the purists, who are usually right in the end.

The case studies in the book all actually happened. They did not happen in the institutional contexts in which they are reported and analysed here, and the personalities have obviously been disguised. While they are therefore real events, which took place in real libraries, they cannot be linked to specific institutions or individuals. Any similarity to colleagues or former colleagues is therefore coincidental.

Lyndon Pugh
Mabws Fawr
Pembrokeshire, Wales
February 2001

Part 1
Learning, Development and the Organization

Chapter 1

The Organizational Background

The background to training and development in information services has altered considerably over the last ten years. Organizational change should lead to a revision of skills requirements. Theoretically, this in turn should have an indirect effect on the approaches to training, on the ways in which training is managed, and how it is generally delivered in libraries. Changes in the practice of management might also follow. The growth of interest in knowledge management, and the learning organization theory which predates this, are two of the developments that have given the issue of learning greater prominence in organizational life. It should therefore be possible to identify a number of trends, both internal and external, that are influencing training and development in information services. This chapter looks at those influences.

New Management Theories

In the 1960s and 1970s the Organization Development school was taking the first tentative steps that eventually led to the emergence of ideas about learning organizations. None of these mainstream management theories really had much impact on library organizations, probably because many librarians have a healthy distrust of theory. Conscious projects aimed at turning libraries into learning organizations, with an overt awareness of what organizational learning actually is, and promoting the deliberate use of learning as a tool for growth and change, have not been all that common. Certainly, there are few libraries that would be recognised as learning organizations by Attwood and Beer (1988), or Beard (1993), two writers who reported on practical implementation, nor by Pearn, Roderick, and Mulrooney (1995), who set out a blueprint for the development of learning organizations.

Knowledge management, on the other hand, caught our imagination, if not our widespread active commitment to it. These theories, together with other theories like "Open Book Management," underlie the argument that there are some organizational characteristics that are essential if learning is to be properly supported.

Knowledge-Based Theories

For the sake of clarity, I have grouped these theories together under the heading of "Knowledge-Based Theories." In short, they say that learning and development depends on:

- Flatter Structures
- Genuinely empowered staff
- A people-centered approach
- Encouraging the questioning of conventional wisdom
- Participative management
- Open communication
- The accessibility of all organizational data

Flatter Structures

Structural flexibility is a significant feature that has an impact on training and development. Moves toward flatter structures usually occur for other reasons than to support learning. Pugh (1997), for example, found a complex mix of motivation behind the integration of academic support services in British universities and less practical alteration to structures than might have been expected. The same phenomenon may be occurring in public library systems, for whatever reasons, as they merge with other public service departments. Even so, better learning can be a by-product of flexibility.

Real learning in libraries is tied to structural change. Building organizations that maximize the knowledge of all our staff depends on flexibility. This is important to encourage a broad approach to learning and to create sufficient opportunities to apply this learning. As well as flexible structures, if all the knowledge we create in libraries is to be applied to organizational and individual development, it also calls for empowerment.

Empowerment

We should clarify what empowerment actually is. Although the high watermark for empowerment seems to have passed for now in many sectors (see also page 21), it still seems to me to be of fundamental importance to learning in information services. It means moving power, decision making, and responsibility to as low a point in the organization as it can realistically and practically go. This has to be supported by resources, access to information, training, leadership, and managerial backing. In return it demands responsibility and accountability from workers, and it is a process of development and growth.

People-Centered Organizations

People-centered organizations will require an emphasis on individual learning. Organizations will have to develop the skills needed to help people learn from experience and put in place all the support systems such as self-study facilities, open learning, learning groups, and learning facilitators. Building development around learning will lead to a reappraisal of the way the training function is managed. Conventionally, this is a low-priority issue in libraries, and its customary place in the organizational structure might not be appropriate. In short, as library organizations become more flexible it might be more sensible to decentralize the training function. Traditionally, our information services have consistently put more effort into group or whole-organization training events. There will need to be more of an emphasis on learning that actually takes place below this formal level, that is, in the workplace. For training, the consequences of all of this are:

- Learning is work-based
- Learning is part of strategic planning
- There should be a balance of self-development and other learning
- Creating a learning organization is a practical and deliberate act:
    - It involves collaboration between trainers and learners
    - It requires a behavior change on the part of all involved
    - It is learner-driven, not trainer-controlled
    - It calls for new skills for trainers

Chapter 2 explains why these organizational characteristics are important for learning. It also looks at why hierarchical organizations, with a number of layers, long chains of command, vertical communication, and a great deal of specialization, create blocks to learning.

Technological Change

Flatter structures, and people-centered learning organizations, are linked to technology. Here, the picture again seems to be a slightly confusing one for libraries. We have not yet been able to make the best use of technology in the service of flexible organizations. Technological change in libraries has not had the same effects as in many other professions. Perhaps partly as a result of this, it presents particular problems, as well as opportunities, for trainers. Hendry (1991) explored the impact of technology and product development on training. I would argue that both these characteristics are seen at work in today's information services. Technological change is widespread, and product development is clearly taking place through the growth of electronic and digital information sources, hybrid libraries, and virtual libraries. These factors, according to Hendry, invariably produce a shortfall in skills and knowledge.

The General Impact of Technology

We have known for a long time (Perrow, 1967) about the link between organizational structure and the type of technology used in organizations. If the technology used is routine, the organization will be highly structured. Sophisticated technologies require greater structural flexibility, and the more sophisticated they are, the greater the need for flexibility. Within the same organization, it is also to be expected that different types of technology will be employed in different departments or sections, and by implication these can be supported by different structures.

What constitutes routine and nonroutine, or sophisticated, technology? Withey (1983), considered that a technology was routine if: for most of the time, most of the tasks were the same from day to day; the same job was to a great extent done in the same way; most of the jobs involved repetitive tasks. Other factors were: the extent to which work was based on established procedures and practices; whether there was a generally accepted way of dealing with the major aspects of the work; the existence of an agreed sequence of steps to follow in the main tasks; a foundation of a defined body of knowledge on which the work was based.

It could be argued that the effect of technology on librarianship is to reduce a number of tasks to routine activities. If so, hierarchical structures might be expected and could be the norm in areas of routine technology. The most appropriate kind of training for what might, a little inaccurately, be called "low technology" would be centralized, trainer-driven, and, in many cases, behavioristic. This book is far from making the argument that this is right—it is simply suggesting that a great deal of our training might have fitted this description in the past.

The Technological Mix in Libraries

It is more realistic to say that libraries at present reflect the use of both routine and nonroutine technology. As a result, they should also reflect a mix of both highly structured and flexible forms of training. For example, we can see that a whole panoply of processes and tasks, even sometimes in middle and senior management, are clerical, administrative, or routine. They might not be managed without a professional input, yet they only require a minimal amount of it. These activities may not involve totally predictable tasks, but they would not score highly on most of Withey's tests of routine technology (1983). In these areas we might identify a need for structured, on-the-job training. On the other hand, the electronic library is producing a new breed of information workers, whose portfolio of new skills will be deployed alongside more traditional skills for some time to come. This mix will demand a much more sophisticated approach to training.

Technology in Support of Self-Development

When technology is introduced into other organizations, a number of things have usually happened: there has been both skills improvement and de-skilling; organizational layers have been reduced; managerial roles have altered; the labor force has shrunk. We have seen only part of this in libraries, and there has been an unexpected benefit. In chapters 4, 5, and 6, there is some discussion of the idea of self-direction, where staff draw esteem from work itself, and from the way library management views their contribution. Their self-esteem increases if they have some control over how they carry out their jobs. This freedom and responsibility puts them in a position to engage with the idea of self-development. A virtuous cycle of increased self-esteem, performance improvement, and further development is therefore created. The introduction of automation into libraries has helped all of this, by reducing the amount of routine tasks in the work. This provides more time and opportunity for other developments, and contributes to the creation of the conditions described earlier. Learning based on self-development, and learning from experience, is now feasible for staff who, because they were once bogged down with routine tasks, might have been locked into activities at the lower end of on-the-job training. For example, Edwards (1998) describes the use of self-service technology to release clerical assistants from "clerical drudgery," to strengthen reader services, to "facilitate staff development," and to "offer our students a degree of autonomy." What is unfortunate is that we do not yet appear to have maximized the potential effects of this technology on training. We have mainly ignored the computer's capacity for helping to create flexible organizational forms that facilitate job enrichment and job enlargement.

Specialization and Self-Development

Other more obvious consequences of automation for the trainer will be found in the issue of specialization. Many electronic and digital developments come from high quality, in-house, practitioner-based research. They have resulted in the creation of a group of staff with distinctive technological skills, well-honed small scale research experience, and project management experience. Professionals with these characteristics tend to be self-directed, and in most respects tend to work better in small, self-regulating groups. All these factors influence the training approach. They suggest a trend toward self-learning, self-development, and team learning. This again calls for flexible structures.

Technology and the Need for New Management

Automation at the moment is also doing something else. Our technological development is naturally at the stage where we are showing signs of the adroit development of expertise in electronic and digital libraries. Although this expertise is breaking out in patches, it is there in increasing quantities. We are also very good at making links——across library service boundaries and between libraries and the wider community——which enhance the role of librarians and bring an added diversity to the connections between libraries and the societies they serve. We are less adept at learning ways of managing these new libraries, or of devising appropriate structural forms for them, because we do not have to be yet. We tend to look to history and redeploy the techniques we used to deal with other forms of special materials in the past. This need for learning ways of managing and organizing hybrid and electronic libraries will sooner or later be articulated more strongly and will have to be met. At the moment, as Dempsey (1998) pointed out, we do not have many electronic or digital libraries in a form that makes much sense to a user. We are still constrained by a conventional way of looking at how these new resource forms are managed. We are inclined to rely on precedent and organize, for example, into divisions of electronic information, electronic information resources teams, electronic information managers, and the like. This runs the risk of perpetuating the traditional vertical organizational divisions. It reflects a process of thinking that is locked into the old context. What we need is to learn how to think within a new context and with new insights that will create new organizational forms. These forms will integrate the electronic specialists with conventional library operations, and allow their expertise and knowledge to be more widely applied in the service of users. If it is genuine, this bringing together of technologists, Web specialists, multimedia experts, and mainstream librarians will encourage a new synthesis of ideas and experience. It will open up the prospect of a more rounded professional grounding for everyone.

It is crucial also because there are still comparatively limited opportunities in conventional librarianship for the new specialists. One way or another we run the risk of losing these skills either to commercial information services or to other professions. It is only necessary to consider the current state of business information (see, for example, Burke and Hall, 1998) to see how powerful the impetus of specialization can be, and how fast it moves. Introduce an element of competition into this situation, in the form of better salaries, higher prestige, and better working conditions outside the public and education sectors, and the potential for a skills shortage looks even greater. Many directors of cash-strapped library services will be familiar with the need to do something about their inability to pay a competitive rate for the skills they want. Some of them have tried to respond to this by creating environments that empower staff and emphasize a balanced personal and professional development. This compensates to some extent. There might be a greater need in the future for the kind of learning systems that support this sort of initiative—personalized, self-directed, holistic, all-embracing, and linked to formal systems.

On the other hand, for a long time to come, there will be a majority of traditionally trained library staff whose personal and professional development, if they want it, will grow through absorbing and deploying some of the new skills of the electronic world alongside their existing talents. Johnson (2000) has asked where these skills will come from, and sees part of their answer in changing library school curricula. The other part of it has to come from in-house provision, because this is where the new knowledge is being created. At the same time, the interests of the traditional professional will also need to be sustained.

The implications of technological developments for training in modern information services are therefore reasonably clear:

- Cutting routine tasks aids self-development
- Upskilling professionals aids self-development
- Complexity means decentralizing the management of training
- Workplace diversity is significant for learning

Social Forces

We live in an age when the educational policy of many governments is heavily skewed toward usefulness, and winning and holding a competitive edge. Johnson (2000) predicts a situation in which we will be educating information workers almost exclusively for business, commerce, and industry. The technological skills referred to previously may attract a premium in these sectors. Meanwhile, universities, colleges, and public libraries will find it more difficult to recruit and retain specialists who command the broad expanse of modern information services. In-house training efforts will have to be directed at the development of these hybrid librarians, and hybrid managers, because the supply of recruits via the education system may be sparse for a number of reasons explored by Johnson.

Educational Change

Information services are now contemplating, and planning for, the effects of educational change. The growing support for lifelong learning, the increasing significance of distance learning, and other initiatives, like the British UfI (University for Industry), mean that we are having to learn about new ways of delivering information and support outside the physical confines of our universities, colleges, business information units, and public libraries. As more and more students make bigger and bigger financial contributions to their education, the situation in the United Kingdom will resemble that of America and other countries where study has long been combined with work. Improving off-site access to support services is something that demands new thinking similar to that advocated in the examination of the impact of technology on learning. We are moving into the development of services tailored to the delivery of individually designed information packages, which are provided outside the library. These need new skills, new behaviors, and new organizations.

Entrepreneurialism

Much of what has been said in this chapter is in favor of a shift in attitudes, systems, and processes. This shift is based on a new type of behavior. Working with stable systems in conditions of relative stability hardly encourages a widespread ability to identify opportunities, take advantage of them, and generally develop a risk-taking culture. There are signs that some individuals in the profession might be good at this, and they are fast learners. In the United Kingdom at least, we sometimes tended to regard entrepreneurialism exclusively as an income generation issue. This is another thing we need to unlearn, for it is much wider than that. It is about growth in the organization, its people, and its services. It is as much about harnessing talent and making the best of everything. To spot these opportunities, particularly where they involve cross sectoral provision, and then take them, we need to learn how to become entrepreneurs. This a vital part of the learning of different habits of thinking.

User Perceptions

Users in all libraries are increasingly sharing control of their own environments. They are now stakeholders. The developments referred to on page 10 place an emphasis on services for learners (in the broad sense of the word), and will lead to stronger links between all kinds of libraries. If learners are controlling their own learning, and are seen more and more as stake holders, then we need to develop a new partnership with them as users. The concept of customer care needs to be refined, along with the development of more user-friendly processes and systems. The growth of organizational forms that stress participation, and the sharpening of decision making by locating the focus of it closer to the user, must also involve that user. Empowerment has to embrace everyone in the equation, not only staff. This is another example of a behavior shift tied to the development of new processes and systems.

One of the best illustrations of this is the way we currently obtain access to resources in our developing hybrid libraries. Sometimes, it is very much a matter of repeating a number of procedures, perhaps in physically separate locations, and often in exchanges with different staff members. There is sometimes communication with other libraries and usually a great deal of duplicated effort. Our users will increasingly want to occupy what Dempsey (1998) called "digital spaces"; that is, the point where all the forms, all the processes, all the knowledge, and all the access procedures come together. In other words we need to be able to demonstrate the unsutured nature of both modern information sources and the specialisms that help to exploit them. This is very much a question of management approaches that will overcome the fractured and fissured landscape of most library services. It is also a question, again, of inculcating new attitudes, and here the trainer can intervene once more.

Cross Sectoral Forces

Collaboration, networking, and alliances are part of the new vocabulary of information services. Although there has always been cooperation between library services, perhaps more successfully within sectors, the kind of cooperation developing in the new electronic world is going to be different in degree and in kind. It is not only between library sectors, but is also based on public and private partnerships, and there are more and more examples of this. Collection management, as another example, will reach new levels of sophisticated interaction between institutions, thanks to technological advances. New ways of working will bridge the chasms that once existed between services. Constructing and maintaining these forms of collaboration, which will lead to new fashions in organizational structures, will place, on managers and trainers, an onus to develop new skills. These will be novel kinds of leadership, negotiation, collaboration, and working with diversity. The emphasis in management will change to encompass new thinking about these ideas. We will need to develop management styles that are relaxed about the contradictions of organizations entering into partnerships yet retaining their independence. We will see a need for behavior that tolerates differences. We will need followers, and leaders, who are at ease with ambiguity and uncertainty, and feel comfortable with empowerment. We will all work with less reliance on formal structures. In essence we are talking about:

- The learning of new behaviors by everyone in our organizations

Change and Continuity

There will be few who disagree with the proposition that, at the beginning of the new century, library services are going through what is the most significant period of transformation since the invention of movable type. Technology, social, cultural, and political change, as well as new management theories, are combining to create novel internal and external circumstances for libraries. Change itself is the most important learning experience, and trainers will be involved in facilitating the organizational and personal development that comes from it. They will also be totally involved in the effort to assist in learning about change as a phenomenon and how it can be handled inside organizations.

At the same time, some of the things trainers have always done, and have always been good at, will need to continue. Even though we are looking at discontinuous change, some aspects of training and development will remain constant. There will still be a need for the basic competencies in communication, key skills, and key knowledge bases. The relevance of what we already do will not diminish, but will be complemented by other innovative and imaginative approaches. Balancing these needs will call for a holistic and undogmatic approach.

Organizational Change and the Skills Issue

A previous section of this chapter suggested that the de-skilling consequence of technology is actually a positive force in libraries. It has created the circumstances in which personal development can be extended to a group of people who might traditionally have been exposed to a comparatively restricted process of conventional training. Allan (1998), for example, describes the main elements of a developmental process that is now becoming more typical. It is also changing the skills balance and, consequently, the training emphasis.

The literature indicates an agreement that the level of skill in any job is dependent on: how much professional training is needed to do it; how much unskilled repetition there is; the amount of real freedom of action allowed to those who do the job; the status that is granted to the job by managers and by workers. Routine tasks, and some not so routine, are now done by machines. This can only increase, and as it does so it will increase the opportunity for development. This is provided that structures and management attitudes permit this to happen.

As stated, technology, partly because it reduces the routine element of work, is creating conditions in which self-directedness (see chapters 4, 5, and 6) can be a significant feature of organizational life. Flexible organizations are being created in response to a number of stimuli, and together with other managerial or administrative initiatives (see chapters 2 and 3), these are opening the way to job enrichment and job enlargement. All of this is naturally and rightly helping to blur some distinctions between professional and nonprofessional jobs. It is leading to a new emphasis on certain skills that trainers include in their portfolios. To return to the example described by Allan (1998), her library had a process that allowed staff to move through an organization according to the rate of their development. The main elements reported by Allan were:

- Bringing together different skills, traditions, and backgrounds
- Multiskilling for individuals and teams
- Empowerment—decision making was devolved
- The formal linking of progression through the organization to personal and professional development
- Cultural change

The definition of skills in any organization is a complex matter. It is influenced not only by some of the issues referred to previously, but also by other things such as the way in which the workers are organized and how much power they can exert over management. It is also influenced by how much power they exert over the ways they discharge their duties. In some countries, particularly those with undeveloped economies, libraries are a good example of how gender affects the status attached to a job or profession. From time to time all these factors, and more, have

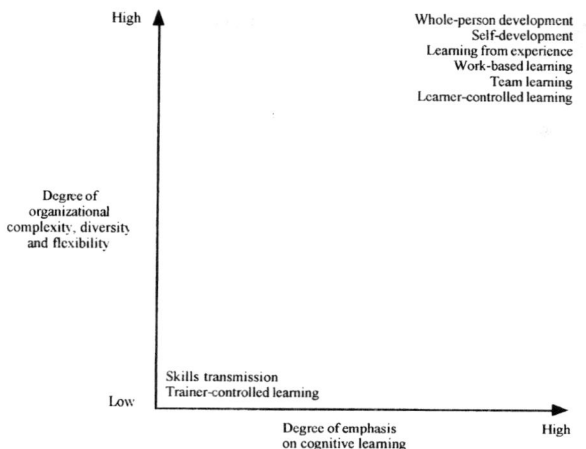

Figure 1.1 Organizational Complexity and Changes in Training Styles

wielded an influence. I am not really brave enough to attempt a detailed justification here, but it might be useful to consider as a general rule that, as organizations respond to the forces discussed here, they will become both more complex and more flexible. While still maintaining the need to develop technical and, in some cases, mechanical skills, this will direct the training effort more toward the transmission of skills that have to do with thinking, working with others, and intellectual and personal development. Figure 1.1 shows how organizational complexity shifts the balance of the training effort toward training that is based on less tangible and more flexible principles.

Change Management and Training

Looking across the corpus of general training literature over the last few years, there is still evidence of considerable uncertainty about the skills and processes to do with managing change. In particular, there are references to confusion over personal roles, as well as the responsibilities and functions of change agents. Many of the skills of change management are generic to the approach to training advocated in this book, and will be learned as a natural consequence. The main learning theories and techniques advocated give weight to working with diversity, to new forms of thinking, behavioral and attitude change, collaboration, and communication skills. Prominence is given to learning to learn, work-based learning, continuous learning, the development and application of intuition, self-directed learning, and problem solving. The learning environment that supports these talents and forms of learning is described throughout this book. Managing change is itself one of the most important components of any development program in the current organizational climate, and there will be a need to give attention to specific skills related to change projects. Pugh (2000) summarized these requirements for each stage of the change process:

- Awareness raising
- Communication skills
- Project management
- Team skills, including team learning
- New operational skills
- Motivation
- Handling resistance and conflict

The Answer: Creativity in the Workplace

We could say that libraries are increasingly involved in new situations, and are beginning to face up to issues that cannot be met by the usual way of thinking. The problems to be solved are new, and we need to devise new ways of dealing with them. The answer lies in learning to be creative.

What Is Workplace Creativity?

Creativity in the workplace is about finding solutions to problems by developing a particular way of thinking. It is about meeting the peculiar organizational needs of information services by applying thinking that is different from the norm, and establishing learning systems that encourage those forms of thinking. Allan (1998) and Edwards (1998) have been cited as two examples of the results of a different way of thinking about development.

We can find the essence of our likely training needs if we start by taking a broad view of the forces that are influencing library services today. Look in particular at the potential of technology as a significant and all-embracing defining agent that is shaping information services for the future. Relate this to some of the emerging management theories. Connect these strands to the organizational forms that are being carved out in response. We can then see the outlines of learning characteristics we will need to nurture and supporting features we will need to put in place.

Solving Imprecise Problems

The position we have reached with technology, and the link between this and the need for creativity in organizational life, is perhaps one of the most intriguing factors. Smith (1982) in considering creativity and learning in organizational behavior, stated that the creative process is solving imprecise problems, Part of this definition of creativity is applicable to the situation in libraries. This is the creation of new conditions of working, based on ideas that are new or original, at least to the host organization.

Finding Creative Ideas for Managing

It can be argued that all the various forms of electronic information provision have succeeded in creating what MacKinnon (1978) would identify as a "creative product." He would say that what we now need is a means of "maintaining, elaborating, evaluating, developing"—in other words, a "creative idea" to manage the resulting information services. Elsewhere in this book the comment has been made that we are at the stage of developing superb electronic services without having much of a feel yet for how we should manage them. Other writers have said that we are not yet able to do this. I believe the problem arises in part because of our reluctance to apply the creative process, and this is a key to our present and future training needs.

We might be able to find some support for this proposition—that we need to learn, or relearn, creativity, by looking at how some libraries have actually approached the issue of new organizations. In the United Kingdom there are some bizarre results, such as the grouping together of public library services and environmental services. Looking at situations like this, it is clear that the wrong question was asked at the start of the process, and the result was a mind-boggling piece of bureaucratic thinking. This approach was also reflected in some, but not all, of the approaches to the reorganization of academic support services in higher education. Contrast this with the emergence of the "Library College" movement in America in the 1960s, where a radical repositioning of some library services was achieved because the right question created the right kind of issue and was met with the right kind of response. What happened afterwards is, of course, another matter.

Solving Wicked Problems

The problem of how libraries are structured and managed when they are subject to the influences described in this chapter, and when they have to deliver a mix of electronic and conventional services, is what MacKinnon, drawing on Rittel and Webber (1973), described as a "wicked" problem. This is like Buttrick's (1997) "closed" and "open" change projects. A wicked problem is imprecise; there are no right or wrong answers. The solution cannot be tested, except over a long period of time. There might be only one opportunity to get it right, and it can be considered to be "a symptom of another problem" (Rittel and Webber 1973). The management of our services in a changing context is being wrongly approached as a closed problem. Therefore, the solution appears deceptively predictable. It looks superficially as if it is amenable to a measured process, can be based on existing templates in past experience, and results can be assessed rather quickly. None of this is true. This is why some of the converged academic support services in the United Kingdom were undone. We might not have asked the right questions, and we might not have given all of the ideas enough implementation time to find out whether or not they were going to work. So, for example, we are still treating new information forms as specialized formats, as we have done historically with every other nonbook format when it first appeared. We appoint managers to manage these formats in a specialized way in a special section. By doing so we ring-fence expertise, and weld another girder into our bureaucratic structures. What we have is a lack of creativity.

Uncertainty demands creative responses to problems and a creative approach to developing organizations. The drive of current management theories should be toward organizations that are imbued with ideas about the primacy of learning. They should be about communication and open information systems. Empowerment and new compacts with users are equally important. We also need to understand that there are significant changes taking place in our workforces. Because of the influences outlined earlier, they are acquiring more high-order skills and specializations. They will become more used to self-direction and to having a say in how they apply their skills and talents. These knowledge workers will need a different form of organization, based on a form of learning that fosters creativity. Above all, our organizations will be about change.

The Characteristics of Workplace Creativity

Hirshberg (1998), in his exposition of strategies for developing creativity, argues that innovative organizations will be based on a kind of creativity that comes from: "opposites, inconsistencies, discontinuities and ambiguities that ignite the creative spark." Our traditional library organizations are monoliths erected on the principles of abolishing inconsistencies and creating uniformity and certainty. Yet within them, we can now see the opposites, inconsistencies, discontinuities, and ambiguities. Hirshberg might say we need a reworking of "what constitutes appropriate, responsible and reliable thought beyond the strictures of the scientific method." We talked earlier of asking the right questions. To Hirshberg, this is concerned "with questions of why, and how questions themselves are asked." He also considered the need to make use of the interplay between different approaches, philosophies, personalities, and skills, acknowledging that "Creative activity . . . comes to life at the edges, whether by blurring, abrading, overlapping or breaking through the partitions." This leads to integration: "creativity is the impulse to integrate, unify and bring together. It tolerates (and at the early stages even prefers) higher levels of disorder . . . so that it can reorder at newer and higher levels of integration." This can all be wrapped up in Hirshberg's key words:

- Polarity
- Questioning
- Unprecedented thinking
- Boundaries
- Synthesis

And it is worth repeating again that the organizational characteristics listed by Hirshberg are those of today's libraries:

- Operating in uncertain conditions
- Past experience offers less help than hitherto
- Ambiguous, inconsistent, and diverse
- Working across boundaries, sectors, expertise, and professions
- Attempting to create unity from this diversity

Hirshberg sees an organization with these characteristics as possessing "creative abrasion . . . it opens the corporate arteries to a flow of new thoughts." The difficulties lie first in creating a form of learning that fosters this creative abrasion and exploits it.

Next is the problem of putting in place a structure that makes this kind of learning all-inclusive. To Hirshberg (1998), it was axiomatic that these creative talents were to be found in all places in an organization. There was, therefore, a need for a learning system that included everybody and allowed for creative friction: "Having struggled to do my job under a system of management based on a profound misunderstanding of the way people actually use their minds, my paramount motivation was to structure an organization around a more realistic assessment of the intrinsic ways we are all wired." Applied to libraries, it might be suspected that this would be a fairly unusual view to take of the personnel.

Translating these thoughts into training and development needs is not difficult. Putting the principles into practice is, and we will look at this later. For now, we need to identify the implications of these ideas for our approach to developing learning:

- Creativity is obviously work-based
- Work-based learning includes
    - Self-development
    - Learning from others
- Creativity is linked to boundary-spanning structures
- These structures support creative friction
- Creativity has to do with helping people to challenge things

Creative Thinkers

Smith (1982) proposed that creative thinkers are characterised by the depth and appropriateness of their knowledge, the ability to apply knowledge, and the willingness to do so. They are dissatisfied with conventional situations and solutions and skeptical about the status quo. They have the ability to produce a range of ideas quickly, to assess the practicality of proposals, and to think in new ways or envision unusual and different solutions to problems.

Workplace Creativity: What it Takes

Leahy and Harris (1993) identified two ways of thinking creatively:

- Divergent: looking at information in several different ways
- Convergent: finding connections between disparate things

They also emphasized the process:

- Prioritizing: selecting what is crucial
- Comparing and combining new information with existing information
- Managing learning

By extension, there is a method that can be learned. Creativity can be applied to problem solving, and again there is a method and skills to be included in development programs. Managing Hirshberg's creative friction calls for skills that might not be part of the conventional repertoire or natural style of managers.

Workplace Creativity and Knowledge

Pasternak and Viscio (1998) took up the issue of knowledge. What follows is my interpretation of their position, and it might be arguable. They describe a context in which a particular form of learning has to take place if organizations are to survive. At the risk of boring repetition, they might well have been talking about libraries:

- They are highly dependent on technology
- There is a degree of doubt and uncertainty about the skills issue
- There is a high degree of interface with the customer
- There is diversity

This leads to some more training or learning needs:

- Learning is based on open communication
- Learning is again work-based
- People build their own skills and manage their own learning
- Most learning involves collaboration
- Much learning comes from reacting to other people's ideas

There are other implications for management:

- Learning has to be managed positively by managing people
- Learning is tied to standards and performance improvement
- Individuals will have to be made accountable for their learning
- A knowledge or learning infrastructure has to be built up

This last point is often difficult for managers to swallow. It means that all the working information that an organization creates must be made available, with the right connections to the range of training and development strategies and techniques that an organization can deploy. This infrastructure must also tie the learning process inextricably to organizational strategies, strategic planning and structures.

O'Keeffe (1998) also argued for a new way of thinking, which was again based on how organizations acquire and use knowledge. He contends that the problem with organizational learning is "unlearning."

Unlearning

In order to face the challenge of step change, the organizations of today and tomorrow need to break with the past. Institutions that do this are marked by decentralization, openness, empowerment, involvement in alliances, technological power, and complexity. We still have to embrace some of these characteristics (O'Keeffe, 1998).

O'Keeffe's argument develops to consider the type of people who will run these organizations. They are risk takers and they think big. They accept tough targets and learn from past failures. Even so, they are not bogged down by the possibility of failing again. They acquire and disseminate knowledge about how things happen, and accept that there is more than one way of doing things. In fact, they learn to think creatively, and they do so partly by judiciously and selectively jettisoning old ways of thought. In O'Keeffe's terms, they "think outside the box." There is a similarity here with the idea of "double loop learning" (Bateson, 1972), that figures in learning organization theory. Double Loop Learning:

> encourages the questioning of accepted wisdom and it scrutinises the current operational parameters. In this way it is a form of learning that alters the entire culture of organizations. The cultural change occurs because Double Loop Learning fosters originality, risk taking and a multidimensional view of problem solving and development. If it takes root it also drives other changes, because Double Loop Learning, like most behavioral change, can-

not emerge without structural change and a realignment of managerial behavior. Double Loop Learning encourages the creative use of dissent, and there is a mass of information that suggests a link between successful innovation and dissent in the form of a willingness to engage in divergent thinking and challenge norms. (Pugh, 2000).

Add to these requirements the need for a new balance of professional skills and values essential for the running of the sort of organizations described here, and some idea of the training needs of such organizations begins to emerge. Consider also that an already well-educated workforce should, in theory, be exposed to empowerment, even if the jury is still out. Ayres (2000) sums up a prevailing mood of disillusion with empowerment, but goes on to make the point that it is a long-term development process. It involves needs identification, skills and competencies audits, detailed planning, and most of all learning. There is then a gradual process of increasing self-management. Staff accept the need for continuing development and, hopefully, will actually want to learn in ways that they can control. They will be in a learning partnership with managers, trainers, and peers. Viewed in this way, empowerment can be made to work—as a quick fix it does not. These things will give us some idea of the kind of learning environment libraries will need to create, and the learning and development style they will have to nurture. We will be looking to base our training response on those humanistic theories of learning that support circumstances congenial to these ambitions.

Some Conclusions

Old and New Skills

In a study on managing change in the hybrid library, Banwell, Day, and Ray (1999) made a courageous attempt to show us what the future might be like, taking the year 2007 as a benchmark. Although based on academic libraries, some of the issues raised are relevant to a wider audience. While the work is not specifically about training, it is a fitting illustration of the developmental needs that will stem from the current period of change. Some of it is a reaffirmation of older skills and values. Much of it has to do with entrepreneurism; income generation; new operational frameworks; increased collaboration with other institutions, with industry, and the wider community; and with the general need for new skills to "support new working practices" in new-style organizations.

Behavior Change

A great deal of this has to do with creating a behavior change, which means learning that puts the emphasis on individual development and instills new talents: collaboration; accommodation; living with diversity; transformational leadership; coaching and mentoring; learning from change. The basis of this portfolio is already present, but we will need to add to it the obvious requirement to strengthen and propagate information technology skills, and also the knowledge and insight to create the new organizational shapes that will support these characteristics. We are beginning to understand that, like all organizations, libraries run on the knowledge of their staff. This commodity does not self-germinate, but it needs a conscious effort to develop potential.

The Strategic Role of Learning

The interaction between training and the wider organizational environment must be strengthened by trainers who are aware that how they discharge their roles will influence the organizational character. Buckley and Caple (1995) affirm the right of the trainer to work without constraints and with an awareness that particular training approaches can have organizational side-effects that will find their way back into the training process. This places the training and development function at the heart of the organization, linking it to all key characteristics and particularly making the connection with performance and service delivery.

The Strategic Role of the Trainer

Learning must be locked into strategic thinking, with facilitators sharing policy making and accepting a responsibility to bring vision and direction to the learning process. Trainers will be both maintainers and innovators, managers and deliverers of training, facilitators of learning in others, and continuing learners themselves.

The Inclusivity of Learning

Inclusivity has to be a feature of learning. Everyone will be given the opportunity to learn, and learning experiences will be fitted to the ways individuals prefer to learn. This will make inclusivity work in practice. Examples are the preferred learning styles and activities (see chapters 4, 5, and 6), but there will also be the problem of dealing with a differentiated workforce drawn from different cultural backgrounds, with different working practices, ways of making decisions, and different priorities.

Adopting these principles confers rights and responsibilities on everyone involved. For the manager, this means:

- We are involved in a step change, for that there is no blueprint
- It involves changing ideas, perceptions, and behaviors
- It involves thinking differently
- Learning is a principle of organization design

For the trainer, the implications are:

- Trainers have to be proactive
- The approach must be catholic and inclusive

For the individuals, there is the expectation of sharing in a new approach and working in a new environment. This environment will give the opportunities, and the support required, to develop self-learning and to participate in group learning. The expectations of the learner will include:

- A clear commitment to developing learning
- Involvement in a partnership for learning
- A say in how learning is delivered and what is learned
- Self-development, learning from experience, work-based learning
- Encouragement of the growth of individual potential
- Continuing professional development
- The acquisition of learning skills
- The full deployment of the skills and attitudes learned

All this will be in an organization that takes the creative talent of its staff, and the responsibility to nurture that talent, as major responsibilities.

There is some evidence from the wider training world that some of these expectations are apparent on the ground. At their 1999 National

Conference, the Institute of Personnel Development (IPD) heard that the results of a survey of 2000 members, by Leicester University Business School, United Kingdom (Beardwell, 1999), indicated that respondents accepted the need to develop more expansive skills and knowledge bases, and felt that most of their learning was spontaneous (by implication, learning was work-based). A majority were also aware that they each had a particular style of learning, which they felt was more appropriate than any other. This is one of the key principles that chapter 2 of this book sets out. Figure 1.1 showed how the emphasis of the training program alters as organizations evolve to deal with the changes set out in this chapter. The implications of these changes can be broadly summed up as increasing complexity, diversity, and flexibility. There will always be a need for skills transmission, and behavioral theories will influence our practical approach to training in some crucial ways. These also will be investigated in chapter 2. Nevertheless, because of the present influences on the shape and character of our organizations, the bias in the training effort will be toward developmental learning typified by the whole-person approach.

Another way of looking at this is to relate training to what has happened to our organizational forms over the years. In the 1990s, we at last started to consider seriously a shift away from organizations that had served our libraries well for a long time, and we began to move slowly toward more flexible or organic ways of running our services. Our organizations are now beginning to be shaped by the withering of the one-time consensus on what we were doing and how we should do it. This has been replaced by uncertainty, by differentiation, by an influx of new experts bringing new skills, new relationships with users, and the need for new behaviors. We are beginning to understand the implications of what some people conceptualize as our roles as knowledge managers, but we are a little slower to turn the knowledge management theory into a blueprint for actually managing our own organizations. This is one of the challenges facing training and development.

At the same IPD Conference referred to earlier (1999), Peter Honey spelled out the need for a positive attitude to learning in today's organizations. Libraries are no exception to this. Across the board, there is also a wealth of evidence attesting to the link between organizational performance and training, with a higher need for training in those sectors that have a high value-added component (Engineering Employers Federation, 1999). The idea of information services being part of this value-added group is something we have only become conscious of comparatively recently. This view is reinforced by the emergence of knowledge management theories, and given added piquancy by electronic and digital developments. It might be challenged by some older hands in the game, who thought that knowledge management was what we always did, and that we had always added value. We sometimes have to recognize our own reactionary sentiments, and we cannot let these stand in the way of the argument. In any event, the notion of tying training inextricably to organization development, organizational change, and most of all to organizational and individual performance, is a major influence on the contribution of training to personal and professional development.

Our organizations are beginning to change—from case-hardened hierarchical machines to looser and more flexible forms. Training needs also move in step, so we see a shift in emphasis from behaviorism and conditioning toward those approaches that, above all, encourage behavior and attitude change. We can sum all of this up by saying that training for today and for future organizations is about ways in that we use knowledge differently. In our traditional organizations, everything was bound together by vertical divisions. This meant that knowledge, information, and skills were compartmentalized and hemmed in by specialization. Developing the creative approach means new structures, processes, and styles of working. This is "unlearning." It is organic and is woven into the life-support systems of the organization. It is targeted on more diffuse objectives than the transmission of skills alone, although this will still be important. It is based on encouragement, motivation, and support for the growth of individual potential. This comes through forms of development that are focused on the individual. It is constructivist and cognitive, rather than didactic and connective.

Case Study 1
NEW ENTREPRENEURS—OR NOT?

This case study is of value for what went wrong. Learning from mistakes is of course an important part of all learning, but regrettably, in this particular instance, the period of reflection and analysis that followed the experiences recorded in the case study came too late. Also, we should not obscure the obverse lesson—that learning can be based on what went right as well as what went wrong. Sadly for the participants in this drama, they did not have the opportunity to run the project again and make use of the lessons they undoubtedly learned from their errors.

The Situation

A metropolitan-area library, serving a seriously underprivileged community with a number of ethnic minorities, had battled hard to come to grips with the problems of creating educational and social opportunities for its clientele. Links had been developed with other community agencies, schools, organizations concerned with training, self-help groups, and government and private employment agencies. Following the receipt of grant aid from a number of organizations, one of the library buildings had been turned into a state-of-the-art resources center. The center offered access to a range of information technology (IT) services including the internet and e-mail. It provided IT training at various levels. A community television unit, with public broadcasting standard facilities for both video and sound, offered a production service for projects which channeled the energies and developed the skills of a number of local people. This unit also produced a range of material for local schools. An audiovisual unit taught photographic and reprographic skills, as well as running a printing service. Homework groups for the schools were also based in the center, and an advisory service provided help in securing employment and returning to work. A committed and expert group of librarians provided a library service based on a strong multimedia collection.

Two things happened to change this situation. After three years, the grant aid to the center was cut, and the funding was reduced to the basic budget provided by the metropolitan authority. At the same time, the central government altered the regulations controlling the activities of local authorities and allowed them to set up and run profit-making ventures. The library director, who was responsible for managing the center and providing the core services, was faced with a dilemma. The facility had done much to improve the self-esteem of the users. It contributed hugely to an improvement in their marketable skills, as well as assisting a respectable number of them back into employment. It was unable to continue to operate on the same scale without an increase in revenue to replace the grant aid.

The Solution

The options were to reduce the services offered or introduce charges. To the director, both of these were unacceptable. Eventually, after some fruitless meetings with council officials, he began to investigate the possibility of raising money through commercial activities.

Initially, he kept this line of thought to himself. He carried out an assessment of the available skills and equipment within the center, and also systematically collected information about the potential market for the services he felt the center could sell. In time, he identified three areas where profit-generating activities could feasibly be mounted. These were:

- Computer services
- Video programs
- Small-scale publishing of educational material

The first of these activities was designed to provide a constant, basic income for the service. The library had a state-of-the-art automated housekeeping system. Within the immediate area were three small colleges, none of that were automated, and none of that could afford automated systems themselves. A series of meetings with library directors and management soon produced formal agreements to lease the use of the center's system to the three colleges. The network was extended, and additional benefits soon became obvious to everybody involved.

The second activity was based on the existing television service. The personnel involved in this included a producer/director, camera crew, video editor, and sound engineer. They were all experienced professionals. They began to negotiate contracts with local firms who needed video presentations for publicity and training purposes.

The final income stream was based on the audiovisual unit, where there was some considerable expertise in small-scale publishing. Working with some of the lecturers from the colleges now sharing the library computer system, they identified a small number of teaching kits that could be produced simply and sold to local schools. This activity turned out to be a pump-priming exercise, because teachers who saw and used the first kits came forward with their own ideas. A number of these were turned into profitable activities. A deal was done with a small training and publishing company, which already provided staff training for the library, and the publications and video productions were marketed nationally and sold widely.

Within a year, the shortfall in grant aid had been made up. For the three years after this, the center budget was increased as the income from the commercial program grew significantly, and the library service in general also benefited from additional resources funded by income generation activities. In the fifth year, the income slumped, and in the sixth year it ceased altogether. Several factors contributed to this dire situation.

From the outset, a tightly-knit group controlled all the commercial activities. This was drawn from the television crew and the audiovisual specialists, under the control of the library director. Other specializations were brought in from outside as required. No other member of the staff of the library service was involved.

Within the group, everything ran according to guidelines and procedures laid down by the library director. There was some discussion and delegation regarding technical matters, but in general the operation was bureaucratic. There was no debate involving other areas of the center or the wider library service. This was partly because the director knew that, although the benefits were accepted, there were some principled objections to the idea of commercial activities. More important, it was also a sign of his own mind-set at the time.

Even worse, the group running these services became exclusive. They were all roughly of the same generation, and in some cases had worked together for over 20 years. This meant that over the six-year period some of them retired and others left for other reasons. No attempt was made to introduce new talent or to upgrade skills. There was some job enlargement to fill gaps. Much of the commercial work involved overtime payments, that were confined to the same tightly-knit group. Members of staff outside the group felt they had no chance of breaking into this closed circle.

Gradually, the group found they could not cover the same portfolio with the same high-quality work, and they began to turn commissions down. When changing allegiances and greater competition started to alter the nature of college education in the area, the computer network broke up. The colleges also began to develop their own entrepreneurial activities. In the end, the commercial unit atrophied, and the income it had generated was replaced by a combination of charges for some services and cutbacks in other areas.

Comment

The difficulty is where to start. Of course, it was not all bad. For a number of years, the project solved the funding problem. It led to a greater degree of cooperation between local colleges and the public library service. It added a new dimension to the resource center work. Yet the seeds of failure were present from the first day.

The fundamental problem was, obviously, the absence of anything other than the most basic learning experience. The way in that the enterprise was set up meant that it was totally insulated from the wider organizational world. It was structured to be self-contained—a part of the library only in the sense that it was locked into the housekeeping systems that controlled procurement, distribution, and accounting procedures.

Behind this, there lay an undeveloped attitude that did not change throughout the life of the project. Indeed, it is fair to say that those participants who were responsible for the strategy only fully appreciated the enormity of their error with the benefit of hindsight. Earlier in this chapter, there was discussion of the need for an entrepreneurial attitude. This involved identifying opportunities, taking risks, nurturing talent, and making the best of everything available. The initial identification of the opportunities was good, but there was no real development of the portfolio. When the future of some of the basic activities become doubtful, there was nothing to replace them. It must also be acknowledged that the first skills audit was good. After this, the skills were jealously guarded, and there was no dissemination of ideas and no growth. This is only partly explained by the failure to change attitudes. There was a structural failure as well. Creating another part of the existing bureaucracy meant that there was little chance of developing an openness to new ideas. The structure prevented other members of staff from contributing, and the lack of information about what was happening in the unit made this worse. There could be no collaboration, no wide ownership, and no inclusivity. None of the learning was transferred. Instead, the skills were concentrated inside the group. Workplace learning suffered badly. Creativity was also a casualty because the conditions necessary to support it were not present. There was no cross boundary working, no synthesis, no questioning, and no challenging of orthodoxy. Internally, the group never became a real team, but simply applied their own special talents within a structure and guidelines laid down by the director. When the need for change could no longer be ignored, the culture that would have made change possible was not there.

To summarize, this case study shows that the attitude shift on which learning is based depends on creativity and new ways of thinking. To achieve this, you need to implement:

- An enabling structure
- Openness
- Questioning
- Teams
- Entrepreneurial leadership, which is not always to do with profits
- Planned management of information, knowledge, and learning:
    - For self-development
    - For learning from others
    - For transferring skills
    - For encouraging diversity

If the group of people who set up this project were to do the same thing today, it is certain that they would take these principles and set about the redesign of the organization. Their experience shows what can happen in knowledge-based organizations if there is a failure to understand the principles on which learning has to be based.

Key Points

Libraries face a new situation caused by the confluence of a number of forces. They can cope with this situation by developing creativity, or innovative thinking. Innovative thinking depends on individual learning. This can be supported by:

- Creating working conditions that allow individuals to develop and apply their talents wherever appropriate; this means doing away with the organizational characteristics that create learning blocks and replacing them with characteristics that encourage people to broaden their horizons and take a flexible attitude to work.
- Treating learning as a major organizational subsystem
- Taking self-development and learning from work as the key ways in which workplace creativity can be fostered
- Using mentoring, coaching, and group learning as training interventions that will support self-development

Chapter 2

Creating a Learning Structure in Libraries

It seems there has always been a destructive tension between the needs of training and development in libraries on the one hand, and the general direction and life force of the library as an organization on the other. This partly stems from the exigencies of running information services on tight budgets, under resource and time constraints, and with increasingly aware and information-literate users. It is also a consequence of the fact that training events do not always fit with what is believed to be the reality and the priorities dictated by things on the ground. A key reason for the emphasis on individual development is that this is the only sure way that learning can really be made to fit the particular working realities of specific organizations. External training events are fine for sketching in the general points, and formal planning is important for providing coherence, but real development comes from what organizations can do to help individuals become driven, proactive learners. The first step in changing things is to move away from the idea that development is an optional activity or a bolt-on accessory.

In another sense, this tension is evidence of the way in which our own built-in conservatism serves to constrict our organizational development. Strategy, policy, planning, implementation, and operations are for the most part carried out in hermetically sealed compartments. I have seen librarians set out to review the appropriateness of their structures without considering the links between strategy, structure, and process. At the other end of the scale, I have heard library managers say that structure does not matter. In all of this, when strategy and policy are considered, learning and development needs are invariably seen as items that come at the end of a long list of priorities. They are not automatically discussed in a way that counts. Learning is left as an individual, work-based activity; without any sort of positive direction or overview, this is haphazard. Nor will learning be seen as a core strategic issue that shapes everything else. This may be bred in part by our old, built-in tendency to see library organizations as machines. As long as the main components are tended to and small amounts of oil are judiciously applied to other things, all will be well. A stoical assumption that organizations will not change is the result. It breeds a comfortable acceptance of the practical support and security offered by bureaucracies. It ignores the fact that in learning and development we have the most potent force not only for organizational change and development, but also for running our libraries.

In a paper on the relative failure of management development in the United Kingdom, Doyle (2000) made the point that the problem arises because development programs are created inside their own boundaries. They are often out of touch with reality and their impact is subject to interference from organizational imperatives and to opposition from individuals with other priorities. In the experience of this writer, these priorities may sometimes include, in some cases, a determination not to learn. The cure for this may be a systems approach, in which development is seen as a subsystem of the organization. It will have the same kind of links with other subsystems, and crucially the same significance in terms of strategy and management. In this way, it becomes an open process related to the whole organization. From the literature, Doyle draws the evidence that development is open to the charges of being unrealistic and uncoordinated. Experience suggests that these strictures are applicable not only to management development, but to development in general. There are four parts to the solution:

- Make development a strategic issue
- Adopt a "stakeholder" approach (Doyle, 2000)
- Create a structure that allows people to learn
- Treat learning as a subsystem of the organization

This means building a new organization. If we want learning to have a real impact on what we do, then we have to treat it in the same way as we treat other processes, systems, or operations. We manage learning and development with a very broadbrush approach at the organizational level. At the individual level, we often assume that it will look after itself. It is actually going on everywhere, and as managers we often know less about it than we should, and, for once, intervene too infrequently.

Learning as a Subsystem

If we are going to pursue this line of reasoning, we first have to accept the full knowledge management argument, or something like it. We can clearly follow the thesis that librarians have a role as knowledge managers, with a valid interest in the process of making information available to other people, so that they can understand it and apply it. This is the easy part. It is also generally agreed that modern organizations face challenges that require them to make the very best use of all the human talents at their disposal. This demands an organizational philosophy, and a system, that "identifies, stores, disseminates and retrieves the knowledge held within the organization [and which] becomes the life force of the organization." (Pugh, 2000). Information of all kinds is collected from the broad experience of work in organizations, and from what is discovered and absorbed from outside the organization. This becomes knowledge when it is analyzed, reflected on, transferred, and applied through action. This is learning: "the process whereby knowledge is created through the transformation of experience," (Kolb, 1985). The learning process in an organization becomes its life system. If it is to function properly, then our treatment of learning and development has to be brought center stage. When we think about strategies, policies, or the culture and character of our libraries, we would ideally start from the learning process. At the very least, we need to ensure that our other systems and design features actually enhance our learning structures and processes.

Building a Learning Library

The first chapter of this book set the targets for creating an environment that supports learning. We need organizations that will make the learning processes as obvious as possible. They will be organizations that will remove institutional barriers to learning. They will help individuals to overcome their own learning blocks through providing appropriate learning support techniques and resources. This means organizations that:

- Are receptive to new thinking and make it easy to question

- Support self-managed individual and group learning
- Foster leadership that emphasises development
- Manage information, knowledge, and learning
- Empower and encourage participation
- Have open information systems

We know also from chapter 1, and will see again in chapter 4, that the form of learning we should encourage will be:

- Inclusive
- Based on a social process
- A force for equality and unity
- Work-based
- Aimed at improving creativity
- Aimed at developing new skills

In all, it will be a learning system stimulated by the change forces likely to exert an increasing influence on libraries, and it will help libraries to meet the challenges of these forces. It will lead to continuously improving services for users who will have heightened expectations.

Creating an organization based on these ideas means taking a holistic view of all the library life support systems—those we use for planning, operations, delivering services, and managing.

It is a rare luxury to be able to plan a new library service starting from a clean slate, without any of the baggage most managers have to deal with when they consider substantial change in library organizations. The thought that this unfettered freedom could be too much for us, conditioned as we are by the weight of our traditional bureaucracies, might also fleetingly cross our minds. Belbin (1998) wrote, of managers in general:

> Teamwork, or rather lip service to teamwork, had become very fashionable and a number of corporations had adopted this approach at the behest of their training departments, while at the same time their management structures retained their typically authoritarian character. This hybrid can bring about a great deal of wasted effort.

Elsewhere he talks of the situation in education and public services where there might be some favorable circumstances for cooperative forms of working, but in practice the bureaucratic mind-set prevented it. Nevertheless, if development is to play the role advocated for it in this book, then we need nothing short of organizational redesign starting afresh.

Why Some Library Organizations Are Bad for Learning

Poor Strategy Formulation

In conventional organizations, strategy is made at the top. Where there is input from below, it is usually filtered through the hierarchy. The management approach to strategy is naturally one of regulating organizational activity and controlling its direction. Translated into learning and development strategies, this means Staff Development and Appraisal Schemes (SDAS), Learning Contracts, Training Needs Analyses (TNA), Skills Audits, and the like. These features form important parts of the load-bearing structure for learning and development. Unfortunately, this is not an apt metaphor. Learning and development is more like an amoeba—it has little or no fixed shape. Elsewhere in this book there are a few references to the perception that more learning and development is stimulated by peers, line managers, supervisors, and self-direction in the workplace than is fed by formal programs. We need to broaden our perspective on how we establish learning strategy and change its nature.

The Lack of Learning Systems

Organizations can be divided into a number of subsystems. These systems all influence and interact with each other. Working together they account for the way the organization functions as an entity. In libraries, we have tended to base these subsystems on technical functions. Obvious examples are acquisitions, cataloging and classification, reader services, reference, and circulation. The organizational culture is also included. A very strong argument in favor of open systems theory has been made by major figures in management thinking over the last forty years. One of the big criticisms in the context of information services is that in planning our library services we begin in the wrong place, and the emphasis on technical functions is too heavy. We can see this wrong place being revisited when we set up separate electronic information services alongside conventional paper-based services. Learning and development, being a diffuse and elusive activity, with more of it running below the surface, is rarely regarded as a true subsystem in itself. We have little difficulty in accepting that other intangible subsystems such as the psychosocial subsystem that makes up the culture of the library, are important: We have some problems in accepting that a large part of the knowledge-creating subsystem lies outside the formal development subsystem set up by management.

Confusion between Functions and Processes

Linked with our fascination for designing jobs narrowly, we are tied to functionally based organizations. This boosts bureaucracies and hierarchies while putting obstacles in the way of learning. In libraries, as in all organizations, there is a degree of specialization that is not a problem in itself. However, functionally based organizations create vertical divisions that unduly strengthen specialization. This hinders the development of job enlargement, where people can take on responsibilities in related areas, and job enrichment, where they can assume more responsibility for their own jobs. These are two vital aids to organizational learning, which is a process, not a function.

Restrictive Structures

Most library structures are difficult to categorize. The reality is that our organizations are probably still not configured in ways that support learning. It is of course not impossible to have a strong commitment to learning in bureaucracies, and many libraries do. In the same way, it is sometimes argued that there might just possibly be good teams in hierarchies. But the effect is likely to be that learning is nowhere near as potent as it would be if other forms were not only considered, but tried out.

Mintzberg (1979) identified five possible "structural configurations": the simple structure, the machine bureaucracy, the professional bureaucracy, the divisional form, and the adhocracy. Not unlike many organizations, most libraries display some of the characteristics of at least four of these types. Some information units have a simple structure. They are so small that there is no division of labor and no specialization. Control is by direct supervision, and personal or charismatic leadership is important. As with most things to do with simple machines, communication is informal. There might be little thought given to development, but what there is will be work-based and self-managed. Because there is no alternative, job enlargement and job enrichment will often be a fact of life, sometimes under considerable work pressure. Working in these libraries can be extremely difficult.

Machine bureaucracies are highly regulated and managed on the basis of the conventional wisdom of doing what has always been done. There is an emphasis on formality and training rather than learning.

Professional bureaucracies can be equally conservative. They will respect and protect professional standards and encourage specialization. Ideas about job enrichment or job enlargement may be difficult to put into practice. Development processes can be subject to top-down control. There is a general resistance to change, and while there may be a recognition of the need to learn, it may not be based on a systematic effort.

Adhocracies are different again. They are seen in library services in the form of matrix management and special project teams. The latter at least are fertile learning grounds. The adhocracy is good for innovation and is said to be a creative environment in which to work. This is probably true, but they can also be a shambles.

Divisional structures are also common in libraries, where academic and public libraries have a number of units operating in relation to an organizational center. They are by and large machine or professional bureaucracies as well.

If you take a metaphorical walk through the average library you will find the whole range of structures. There will be someone running a simple organization, even as primitive as a one-man band. There will be somebody else operating a professional bureaucracy. There might be areas that try to declare independence, and there will be more than a few individuals who are professional bureaucrats and always want to do their own thing. Professional bureaucrats can also be autocrats of the worst type. There will even be some honest attempts to develop real team organizations within bureaucracies, and it is sobering to remember that Belbin (1998) did not necessarily find any correlation between the absence of hierarchies and effective teams. In the most well-ordered hierarchies there might be one or two individuals going discreetly berserk in the basement. Many people will want to vary the basic bureaucratic ethos, but will be hampered in their efforts to do so by the sheer weight of organizational inertia. The vertical divisions, the nature of the communication system, job design, and management styles will act against them. These features will also inhibit learning of the kind that the theory indicates will be most successful for the support of personal, professional, and organizational development.

Laying the Blame on Somebody

When something goes wrong, inflexible organizations with clear lines of communication, solid hierarchies, and impermeable demarcations in responsibilities and duties make it easy to spot the culprit. At the very least, the usual suspects can be rounded up. This might be enjoyable for managers in some circumstances, but it will not encourage risk taking, trying new ideas, or challenging orthodoxy. It will not support learning.

Some Principles for Creating Learning Libraries

Holistic Strategies

The point that development is a strategic issue has already been made. The reason for this is quite simple—development makes for service improvements so it affects everything a library does. It has to do with:

- Skills development
- The management of knowledge and information
- Performance and continuous improvement
- Career development
- Change management
- Organization development
- Motivation
- Organizational culture
- Creativity

Most libraries now consider income generation and commercial activities to be part of their portfolios. Learning and development play large parts in this. If there are implications for budgeting, there is a further argument for considering these matters as a part of strategy. Hargie and Tourish (2000) suggest that how knowledge and information are organized and disseminated, and how people interact with each other, should be treated with as much solemnity as we treat structure, finance, policy, and planning. Organizational failure occurs because key players fail to communicate and staff cannot apply their creativity as well, or as innovatively, as they would wish to. Crucially, people find it harder to accept or support things they know little about, or accept decisions with which they have had little to do in the formative stages. To ask people to subscribe to learning they cannot apply is pointless. We all need a system that makes the benefits of all learning accessible. "At the core of the philosophy of renewal is the recognition that learning is vital." (Gouillart and Kelly, 1995).

An equally compelling argument emerges when we look at the way in which our strategy is formulated. In all traditional organizations it is confined inside the upper reaches of the hierarchy. One of the problems indicated in the literature is that strategy formers have trouble thinking operationally. The difficulty here is that, while strategies should make library objectives clear, there is such a thing as operational strategy, and it is operational strategies that actually dictate how those objectives will be met in practice. There should be a symmetry between the two strategic forms, and the relationship between them needs to be a strong one.

There are a number of answers. One is that the primary purpose of development is to affect organizational performance. It pervades everything, and putting it into the strategic ambit compels consideration of operational issues in a more directed way than is allowed by strict hierarchical forms. Learning and development are things that can influence the tactics that decide how operations are carried out; they can also link this area to strategy and policy if the organizational structure and the ethos are right.

Strategy formulation also has to be changed. A stronger sense of ownership has to be created by allowing the learners a more direct participation in setting the direction of learning. Shared ownership will increase commitment, and at the other end of the process it will improve the transfer of learning. If the strategy is to pay overt attention to the bulk of development that occurs below the surface, largely untouched by the formal development processes, the participation of the learners who hold the keys to this area is essential.

Taking a Systems View of Learning

Making learning a strategic issue and treating it in the same way as other strategic issues puts things into their proper context. Treating learning and development as a subsystem in itself then accomplishes two other things. Devoting the same resources and planning to development as to any of the technical subsystems is integrative, because it is a subsystem that affects everything else, and it is also dynamic. If it is changing in response to organizational and individual needs, it is also going to change the other subsystems.

Organizing Around Processes, Not Functions

The overall process with which we are concerned is the delivery of information to users. This process is conventionally set up in ways that match the vertical and functional divisions in library organizations. Both the information forms and the users are differentiated, or varied. The content of what we deliver comes from a variety of functional specializations, ranging from traditional librarianship through hybrid libraries and Web-based sources to virtual libraries. The implication is that we need to establish small, multifunctional work units focused on specific groups of users. If we accept learning and development as a subsystem that influences all the others, we can begin to see this as a step in the process of breaking away from functional or narrow job-based organizations that inhibit learning. We can move toward more flexible and organic ways of organizing. This points toward structural change. It will also create development through job enrichment and job enlargement. For example, desirable though it may be, there is only a limited point in simply becoming a better manager of the journals collection or the acquisitions section alone. But engineer a situation where the bibliographic or copyright knowledge of the journals manager, or the project management skills of the acquisitions librarian, can be fused with the work of the electronic database manager or the reader services librarian at the point of service delivery, then you will have development. There will also be a better service to the user. None of this would happen so conveniently if the specialisms were segregated.

Building Radical Structures
Our concern is with:

- Improving skills
- Increasing skills
- Broadening the skills base
- Organization development
- Personal development
- Extending people
- Career development
- Equipping people to play wider roles
- Motivating people to learn
- Using work as a learning experience
- Learning from each other

None of these things will be accomplished in organizations that compartmentalize work, and by doing so compartmentalize learning. They will not happen when jobs are designed on narrow specializations or where parts of the organization command exclusive rights to inputs into parts of the library operation. Hierarchical relationships based on formal authority will not, without intervention, somehow or other metamorphose into peer learning or learning within equal relationships. Group learning will not occur without cohesive working and, hence, learning groups. Learning from mistakes will not take place outside a "no blame" culture. Learning from success will not be accomplished without a communication system that works laterally and vertically, making organizational knowledge available to all. Accepting that all the workforce has the benefit of experience to apply to their jobs is pointless unless that experience can *actually* be broadly applied. There has to be access to the experience of everyone and the knowledge that comes from this experience. People must also be able to move around an organization more easily.

Making learning a strategic issue and treating it as a subsystem that is part of the organizational design process puts things into their proper context: Creating a flexible structure is one of the things that makes learning happen on the ground. An organization that attaches real significance to learning will have a structure that fits with the best ways to learn, and that is in tune with what the library wants to do. This is to provide the information people need in ways that are convenient to them. It so happens that flexibility might also be a desirable characteristic of structures in any case, so it is worth pursuing for that reason also.

The Structural Solution: Teams

The search for flexible structures has generated an increasing number of organizational forms in general management. Libraries themselves have experimented with teams in ways that range from the crude and superficial to the highly sophisticated, and matrix management is a feature of a number of systems. The technology of information delivery is making other forms possible, and with this technology some of the new ideas of mainstream management will find their way into library management. The impetus has been to minimize the negative aspects of hierarchies through flattening the apex and reducing the layers in the organization. The idea that these modified organizational structures will be better at supporting learning has not been a major driving force, often because of our own instinctive retention of the things we know to be safe. Naturally, the old, well-ordered way of running things is comfortable. "Most people agree conceptually that the neat, hierarchical model of the organization has outlived its usefulness, but as practitioners, many hearts still yearn for it." (Gouillart and Kelly, 1995).

Belbin's Trapezium
Belbin (1998) charted his own progress toward the development of

team-based organizations. Early in this process, he investigated the Trapezium structure. Belbin's Trapezium organization has two levels. It is flatter at the top than the bottom, more participative and sharing at the top than the bottom, and more autocratic at the bottom than the top. This, I would argue, applies to library organizations as much as any others. Senior management will inevitably find consensus easier to achieve than other parts of the organization, because the role differentiation at the top is less sharp than lower down. As long as the top of the organization retains strategy and policy as its own preserve, it will inevitably tend to be less autocratic than the remainder of it, because the strategy and policy formulation is arguably more amenable to consensus than some operational issues. This is not to say that operations cannot be run on the basis of consensus. The obvious comments are that the Trapezium structure still preserves a less well-defined hierarchy, and will not create empowerment on its own. The organization has fewer layers, but power is still concentrated at the top. It is easy to remove layers from an organization and as a consequence shift power further up the structure instead of down it. Both libraries and their parent organizations are very capable of demonstrating this.

Library Teams

Libraries have rules-based systems. They need to change to learning-based systems and teams might be the best available way of doing this.

A simple model of a team-based library organization was proposed by Pugh (1990). This was portrayed as a series of interlocking circles around an organizational center that was reduced in size. For a truly learning-based organization, teams have a genuine cachet:

- They are appropriate learning environments. They support job enlargement, job enrichment, learning from work, and effective internal communication.
- They are put together on the basis of what people know and share.
- They facilitate empowerment.
- They are vehicles for new management styles.
- They should be based on processes, not functions or jobs.
- They are vehicles for development.

Belbin also pointed out the difficulties associated with teams, particularly those of communication between teams. He advocated a series of interlocking teams to provide integration. In effect he advocated a team-based hierarchy. The basis of this was process teams delivering effective services. The problem of communication between teams was dealt with by cross functional teams, creating links, and dealing with organization-wide issues. Finally, strategic teams created policy, with inputs from the other teams in the organization.

Belbin also spent some time investigating how other organisms went about developing structures. Two principles of organization design emerged from his study of the social structure of ants and termites:

> If a major decision-making function is needed, it should be based on the idea of a cooperating 'caste.' Members of that 'caste' should be selected and trained for the position . . . the adult contributor needs to be prepared for the position by a personal development coach . . . . Others need to contribute to the caste in accordance with the perception of immediate needs and observed pressures . . . . The second guideline [is that] separate but complementary work activities operate simultaneously, in unison and free from the delays associated with relationships of rank.

As well as being a powerful statement in favor of learning and development, this extract also emphasizes the holistic nature of teams. They can be created from people anywhere in the organization, based solely on the

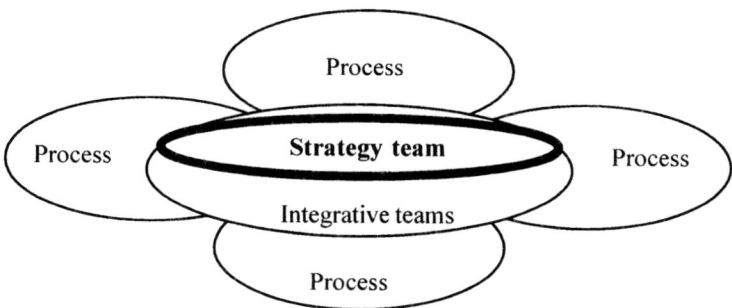

Figure 2.1 A Two-Layer Team Structure

ability to make a relevant contribution. The operation of "separate but complementary work activities . . . in unison . . . " suggests the integrative and communicative power of cross functional teams as shown in figure 2.1. This is my interpretation of Belbin's idea, right or wrong.

The integrative teams are composed, for example, of colleagues who carry out the same or related functions in different process teams. The teams, if they are to have a powerful learning component, are best viewed as small, self-contained units, where people have the opportunity to develop as generalists and learn about several aspects of the work of the team, in addition to a degree of specialization.

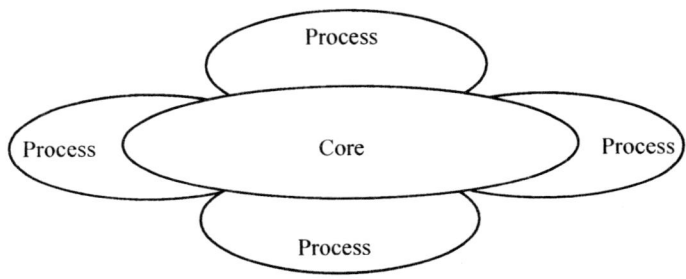

Figure 2.2 A Team Structure around a Permeable Core

Above a first organizational layer of process teams and integrative teams, and drawing some membership from it, would be a layer made up of strategic teams. Learning and development will be the concern of the teams. It will also be the concern of crossorganization learning teams, so will have an integrative function. Teams being structural devices, they will give the necessary strength to the organizational form. They will provide the conditions for learning, and they will integrate.

As shown in figure 2.2, Pasternak and Viscio (1998) see the organizational form in a slightly different way. They build the organization around a core, not a center. The core is a permeable focal point of a network of teams. It contains very few people, but they have a very large responsibility. It gives the organization its direction and its justification for existing.

The core makes things possible—it creates the operating environment, it integrates, and it enables. It helps to create an identity, and it will clarify the strategic mission. It is kept small because the teams that surround it are empowered. The practical creation of organizations like this is covered by Mohrman, Mohrman, and Cohen (1995). This treatment is particularly relevant to educational and public service organizations.

Changing Management Styles

Implementing a structure that supports learning is a step forward only if it is accompanied by a change in behavior. The most important behavior change is the one that has to be made by managers. The organizational conditions proposed in this chapter will compel a change in managerial behavior. The change has already started through the insistence on:

- Making learning a strategic issue
- Creating a learning subsystem
- Devising a structure that facilitates learning

It has to be accompanied by a personal adjustment that managers must make before anyone else can start to change (see chapters 4, 7, 8, and 9).

Unlearning

The technique of unlearning was emphasised in chapter 1, and this is where new management styles begin. The concrete step of altering the library's configuration demands that managers stop thinking about layers. The need is now to think about how things are interlocking across the organization and to concentrate on the relationships between teams.

The Proper Use of Power

Power also has to be used in a different way. The team approach means power centers are diffused and managers have to learn to release their control. If they fail to do this, people will not have the opportunity to stretch themselves by learning to manage some of their own business. As teams assume more responsibility, the managerial role becomes that of a guide, coach, and enabler. It still remains that of the arbiter who will make decisions that teams might not be able to make for a number of reasons, and that of the leader who communicates a view of where the organization should be going and how it should get there. There is also the connective role of unifying the work of all the teams, nurturing a common purpose, and putting the work of the library in the broader institutional and environmental context.

Continuing to Manage

Managers must also remain managers. Total self-management is as mistaken and ill-advised an idea as believing that the machine bureaucracy is good for libraries today. Managerial behavior has to shift to accommodate and foster organizational learning. This happens when managers themselves become learners and facilitators of learning, and when part of that learning includes learning to share power. It depends on developing an authority that comes from leading a common cause, not from rule books or legal power.

Communication

The root of this is something that managers have always been doing. Communication is the key to flexible organizations and to learning. There are a number of studies that have emphasized this aspect of the manager's job (Mintzberg, 1973; Kotter, 1982). Even in bureaucracies, managers can often spend up to two-thirds of their time in interactions with other key people: "the manager does not leave meetings or hang up the telephone in order to get back to work. In large part, communication is his or her work," (Mintzberg, 1989). So this change is a matter of degree; we are intensifying and spreading the communication.

Setting up the Learning Subsystem

Creativity should come from everywhere in the organization; the feature that makes it possible to use creativity is the information system.

The Structural Skeleton

The learning subsystem is based on the communication process. The skeleton is already there in the form of the teams. The process of building the system is bottom-up, beginning with a few small teams capable of understanding that what they know, collectively and individually, is their most important contribution to the organization. They can be bound together by giving some members roles in other teams, or by creating teams that work across larger areas of the organization and deal with global issues. Ensuring the representative makeup of strategic or management teams is also integrative. The life-support system of organizational learning is partly these features and partly the information infrastructure.

Gouillart and Kelly (1995) offer three elements that could be incorporated into a model of the learning subsystem. They develop an argument that is familiar in the literature of change management—the idea that organizations are "living organisms":

> We have moved beyond the Industrial Age, but our business model is still

rooted there . . . . The communications revolution is merely the facilitator of a more fundamental social and business influence: an unstoppable trend towards *increased connectivity*. As more and more parts of the machine have learned to talk to each other, connectivity has become the dominant feature.

A simple example in the library world is the development of an attitude of mind and a system that would not only link all the internal and external physical and electronic resources, but it would also connect the specialism of the tyro librarian in a humanities team, who happens to be an expert in navigation history, with the maritime studies researcher in another part of the organization. In the public library, it would put the group library director, who is incidentally an expert on horticulture, in touch with the senior citizen with a specialized information need in that area—impossibly idealistic, and some directors would say "over my dead body," although this is true connectivity. To do it, the authors propose a knowledge architecture, a knowledge management process, and a technical infrastructure. Some additional elements will be added to this, but they form a useful basis for introducing some of the concepts of the learning organization.

Knowledge Architecture
This is interpreted as a conceptual framework that guides the development of the learning process. This conceptual framework has a number of components that have to be present if the approach is to work:

- Commitment to the individual
  In learning terms, this establishes individual development as a priority and dictates some of the tactical or operational moves in bolstering learning. It emphasises coaching and mentoring as means of developing individual talent and, therefore, the knowledge base. This is also related to enabling structures, empowerment, and devolved management. It confirms that effective libraries start with creating and sustaining the ability and knowledge to deliver the service. It also underscores the point that planning may start with, and run through, objective setting and policy, but implementation starts with skills, aptitudes, and prowess.
- Responsibility is taken by the individual
  The organization can provide support, but individuals have to share responsibility for what and how they learn.
- Team responsibility for development

This can be understood as learning from peers, supervisors, and group learning processes. It will again have resource implications and implications for the way learning is managed.
- A focus on learning from work
  This ties in with the observations about enabling structures, empowerment, and management styles, which will reflect the organizational commitment to the individual.
- A facilitation process
  Learning opportunities for individuals and groups must be provided, and staff must learn how to identify these opportunities for themselves, as they control their own learning. The technique of handling the opportunities must be absorbed and a learning cycle established (see chapters 5 and 6).
- Managed learning
  Both organizational and individual needs must be established. Individual and group learning must be supported by the formal development program, and based on matching the needs of the individual and the organization. The function of formal learning and the formal controls used by managers will not diminish, but will change. Although the argument of this book is that most of the learning in libraries takes place in an informal way and is not immediately visible to management, there has to be a symmetry between the formal and informal learning systems. This will depend on
  - The development of the learning subsystem;
  - The information system or technical infrastructure;
  - Changes in management styles (see chapters 7 and 8).
- Ensuring the fit (Gouillart and Kelly, 1995)
  There must be a permanent process of assessment. This will ensure that new skills and expertise will be developed and applied where they are of most value to individuals and to the library service. In team organizations, it may mean revising views on career progression. Job enrichment, job enlargement, and empowerment might mean that conventional ideas about a steady and planned climb up the bureaucratic ladder will no longer be relevant. There might be a need to accept that, instead of this, development might be seen as moving across an organization. Equally, salary improvements could be tied to specific learning outcomes. The idea of responsibility will be looked at in a different way. Personnel procedures in team-based organizations will reflect these ideas through techniques such as generic job descriptions and the formal measurement of team effec-

tiveness rather than individual effectiveness.

Knowledge Management

This is the foundation of organizational learning. Corrall (1998) contributed a reasoned overview of knowledge management. One of the definitions she offered was from Skyrme (1997): "Knowledge management is the explicit and systematic management of vital knowledge and its associated processes of creating, gathering, organizing, diffusion, use and exploitation." Its interest to us as far as learning is concerned is that it seeks to facilitate organizational improvement through developing the organizational knowledge base. Its major objective is "Converting informal personal contextualised knowledge to formal systematic organizational knowledge." This is the element in the model that makes the knowledge available so that, through processes of reflection, analysis, and action, it can be turned into learning.

Technical Infrastructure

This is the enabling mechanism that makes knowledge management possible. Information technology should provide the nervous system of the library. The information base would need to integrate:

- Management Information Systems (MIS)
- Human resources: skills, learning, experience, interests, goals
- Administrative business: budgets, meetings, decisions
- Performance information: measures, evaluations, feedback
- Professional and technical information, issues, and developments
- Documentation from the parent organization
- The inventory
- Special projects and change initiatives
- Good practice: professional and technical
- The results of individual and group learning
- Links with other systems

The Model

We can now construct a model of the learning subsystem, based on agreed individual, group, and organizational needs. It is influenced by, and, in turn, acts as an influence on, the organizational features described in this chapter. It is this subsystem that has to be created through:

- Making learning a strategic issue
- Designing process teams as a first step
- Designing jobs so that they can be expanded
- Creating inter-team links
- Bridging the gaps between operations and strategy
- Deploying a sharing style of management
- Setting up an information network
- Building a knowledge architecture
- Cultivating knowledge management

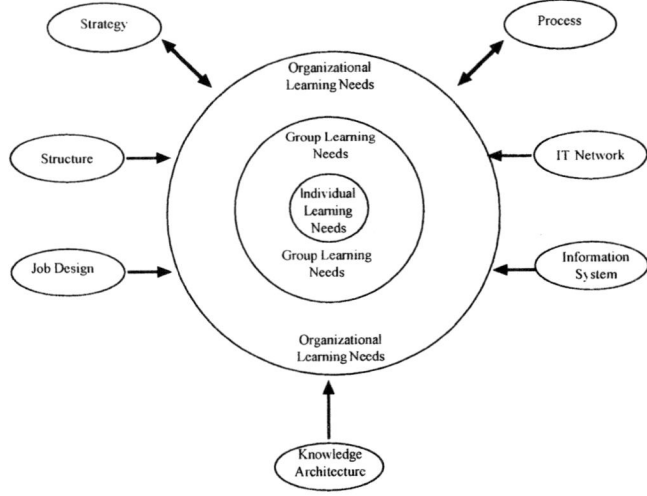

Figure 2.3 A Model of the Learning Library

The model describes a subsystem in which individual learning needs are the core. Onto the core is grafted group or team learning needs, which in turn are the foundation of organizational learning. The elements around the center are the organizational features that influence and nourish the character of learning. W.Edwards Deming once said that the one thing that influenced the way people performed in organizations was the system. The system is made up of all the elements arranged around the outside of the model. They all bear down on how people learn. This is why getting the system and its components right is essential.

Case Study 2
A LEARNING ORGANIZATION

The events in this case study took place in a small academic library.

The Situation

A multisite university, in a metropolitan area, had appointed a new library director to replace an incumbent who had held the position for almost twenty years. The process of appointment had been long drawn out and fraught. The institution had set high standards and found it extremely difficult to arrive at a shortlist. In the week before the interviews, advertisements were still being placed in the professional press. When the two-day appointment procedure began, there were twelve candidates who had been invited for interview. At the end of the first day, two candidates withdrew, and the others held a private meeting to decide whether or not they should withdraw en bloc and advise the university of their concerns about the position of the library in the institution. These worries had to do with what they saw as the negative attitude on the part of the university, and major operational and structural problems that they felt the university did not intend to solve. There being no agreement on a unanimous withdrawal, the procedure went ahead and eventually the post was accepted, with serious misgivings, by a young and ambitious library director. Until then, he had a very successful track record as a manager. His sense of foreboding was increased shortly afterward, when a very senior member of the profession who had acted as external assessor to the appointments board, and whom he knew, called to advise him not to accept the post. "Don't go there. The place hasn't changed in twenty years and won't in the next twenty, whatever you do," he said.

During the first few weeks of the new manager's tenure, the gloom did not lift. The library was traditionally organized and run as a typical bureaucracy. It was a multicampus operation with a massively centralized management structure and a central administrative unit that handled all the housekeeping routines for all service points. Policy and strategy had traditionally been laid down by the library director, who also established operational routines, managed the budget, approved all purchases, and appointed all staff. Some senior staff played a subdued consultative role. There were major backlogs in all technical areas and huge variations in professional standards. Most of the staff were not aware of their capacity for assuming more responsibility because they had never been encouraged to do anything other than follow the rules. There was little understanding of the need to improve service standards and, in general, the senior staff were resigned to their passive roles. They did not understand what they were really capable of achieving.

The director started to cast around for some unifying principles to which the staff could subscribe, and that would allow development to take place. He invited all the senior staff to contribute their views on what the problems were and their ideas on how to move forward. Only two of the eight responded.

The Solution

The one ray of light was the willingness of two people to make common cause with the director. These were the library managers for Art and Design and for Education and Humanities. Against them were ranged the Technical Services manager, the Science and Technology manager, the Nonbook Resources manager, and the Management and Social Services manager. The director set up a small think tank made up of himself and the two senior staff members who wanted to see changes. They worked through a program based first on the transformation of the Art and Design library. This was followed up with a series of seminars for senior library staff, other library staff, and library users. Particular emphasis was placed on the roles of the Art and Design library staff, who, led by their own manager, were eventually able to espouse the principles of a learning organization in the context of the university library service. The library management group was reconstituted, and there was a small change in their general attitude. The erstwhile opposition now assumed a position of passivity and neutrality in the face of the director's proposals. This was one occasion when their bureaucratic conditioning worked in favor of change: They would not oppose the director as long as their own positions were not disturbed. This was also the seed of their undoing.

The director proposed to create a team structure, but initially in the Art and Design library only. To the existing staff he added an experienced cataloger. A budget was devolved. Advantage was taken of a catchall phrase in the job descriptions, which allowed the director to vary duties at his discretion. With the agreement of the staff, and without the involvement of the university human resources managers, a more broadly based allocation of duties was decided upon. For example, for the first time, all staff were allocated duties in reader services, and all staff, including senior staff, joined the roster for circulation duties. Every staff member in the Art and Design library was interviewed by the steering group. Their skills, aptitudes, qualifications, experience, and ambitions were assessed in detail, and individual learning plans were agreed upon. These plans paid particular attention to individuals' views on what they felt they needed to learn in order to improve their performance and assume more responsibility in the work of the library. One staff member who did not wish to work in this way was transferred to another library. Under the leadership of the cataloger, two library assistants began to learn principles and procedures in this area. They coupled this with formal training to gain further relevant qualifications. A third library assistant with an academic qualification in art history undertook a distance learning master's degree in library science. All this was funded by the library service. Two or three experienced staff members were given responsibility for organizing specific areas. The service manager's own relaxed management style cemented everything together. Much of the work of managing the library was accomplished through informal discussions in the workplace. Team meetings were held on a regular basis, initially to implement a learning program on teamwork for all staff. As the team matured, the number of formal meetings fell.

The library had always maintained paper records of frequently asked questions, difficult reference queries, and other issues that arose during the course of the work. All of these, including the results of the skills and needs analyses, were added to the automated library system.

Within eighteen months, the team cataloger and the library assistant pursuing a higher degree had joined the reconstituted library management team. The new spirit engendered altered relationships with the teaching departments. A multimedia collection and an art history collection housed and managed inside the teaching faculty had been transferred to the library, together with their staff. Cross service links had presented the rest of the library with evidence of better job satisfaction and motivation. Over time, the other libraries introduced the same structure. The director was then able to move on to strengthen integrative mechanisms, build on the knowledge architecture, and develop knowledge management to bring all the teams within the orbit of the learning subsystem.

Comment

The literature indicates there are two ways of introducing learning organizations. There is a macro approach, that attempts to create active learners throughout an organization, and an approach that identifies a single area where the experiment can begin. Here the director chose the latter. He was able to select a reasonably self-contained unit that already possessed a degree of professional and subject expertise. Its boundaries were well-delineated, and within it there was the scope to devolve a real degree of power to the members of the team. Being the smallest of the library service points, it already relied on a degree of flexibility that the larger units did not display. The line manager responsible for the art and design library was psychologically inclined toward participative management, and the service was user-centered. The director had identified one of Mintzberg's simple organizations, and it served as an example to the other libraries.

The director also undertook his own learning journey. The process of introducing a learning organization should be participative, and the change should be faithful to the way in which the library would be managed. During the period when the appointment was made, the director had constructed his own reality about the situation into which he was going. His initial experiences appeared to bear this out. On reflection he would probably say that he failed to allow sufficient time to build a consensus. He also needed to engage himself in a process of self-development, beginning with a rigorous analysis of his own learning needs and the true nature of the working situation in which he found himself. However, at this point, he had not read chapters 5 and 6 of this book; indeed, he had not yet written them. On the positive side, within the service, compliance was ultimately won through a process of education. Through example, it was turned into wholehearted commitment. Outside the service, institutional management did not care. This may sometimes be a blessing in disguise.

Team building was started through changes in personnel. The redesign of jobs was painlessly accomplished, and it is significant that learning needs formed a large part of this exercise. Flexibility and interchangeability went into team roles to create learning opportunities. Individual learning was self-directed to some extent through the distance learning courses, and there was a change in the reward system to reflect, in part, the greater commitment to learning. This was seen not only in changes to salaries, but in the elevation of staff into the management team of the university library service. Both in this respect and in the way in which leadership opportunities were created inside the team, the organization was nonhierarchical.

The commitment to learning was made obvious at a process level. That is, it made an impact on the delivery of a broad-based service to the faculty. Some evidence of this was the transfer of two previously separate facilities into the library by the faculty. This was something that had always been resisted by the faculty, and would never have happened under the old regime.

The embryo information network set up to underpin learning and teamwork was available throughout the library service. It played a role in disseminating the principles and the practice to other units. The learning was therefore transferred into the workplace through the knowledge architecture and by example.

Most of the things that the director did reflected the principles of chapter 1 and those to be examined in chapter 4. There was work-based peer learning which was most clearly seen in the work done with the library assistants by the team cataloger. It was also possible to spot the application of experience, elements of self-managed learning, support for creativity, and a willingness to take part in thinking that went against the traditions and norms of the library.

Chapter 3

Managing Learning in Libraries

The ideas considered in the opening chapters will influence, if not actually dictate, the way in which learning is managed in libraries. The determination to consider learning as a strategic issue has obvious significance for the learning strategy itself, and for the relationship between that and overall organizational strategy. The adoption of particular structural forms, and other organizational features, has repercussions for how learning is managed, as do the promotion of certain learning styles. There is also the question of how the management of learning in the environment described here can be made to interlock with the major strategic and policy-making mechanisms at organizational level.

Strategies and Policies for Learning

1995 . . . when the hypothesis that organisations were basically measuring the wrong things gained some momentum. The light dawned that most of an organisation's value was in intangible assets. The major portion of the intangible assets portfolio concerns people—their capability, their knowledge and their wisdom, and how they are managed and utilised. [Strategy is] . . . the analysis and choice of options available, and . . . supporting the strategy through the use of resources. (Mayo, 1998)

Mayo is making the case already made in this book, which is that learning is a strategic issue. Because we are now more aware that people are the crucial resource, human resources and their development form the vital component for growth. Learning, now seen to make a major contribution to the character and efficiency of the library, is perceived as pivotal and, as Mayo intimates, is the key resource.

In the literature of training, there is recognition of some confusion between the terms "strategy" and "policy" (Diane Bailey Associates, 2001). For someone trying to work out a practical approach to organization development, this does not really matter at all. If strategy is accepted as being a broad-brush process, that sets a direction and indicates how things will be done, then policy can be seen as an overlapping feature that provides a set of guidelines, or rules, to turn the strategy into appropriate actions. Some trainers swap the two meanings around. What is important is that there is a document that sets the process in the organizational context. This relates learning to the overall library strategy, apportions responsibilities, and sets objectives. It offers a methodology and provides some practical rules, and a framework, within which decisions about development can be taken. The important thing is that both policy and strategy, for the library service and for organizational learning, are therefore the first steps in managing the process.

Training strategies are usually quite concrete and specific things. They deal with the amount and type of training to be provided, the responsibility for providing the training events, and how the training will be delivered. They are somewhat restrictive in that the process of devising strategy and policy, and delivering and evaluating training, is not seen as truly participative. It is usually based on a narrow definition of stakeholders. This includes senior management, heads of departments, and human resource specialists (Wills, 1998). Strategy and policy are therefore top-down. The result, even when a liberal interpretation of the term "training" is applied, is sometimes the opportunity to do no more than select from a menu proffered by a human resources manager and to join in reviews of development needs.

Learning has to be considered in a different way. It is much broader based; it has to do with changing people's capabilities, behavior, attitudes, or skills. It is not didactic. It is probably fair to say that it relies on a more varied set of delivery mechanisms than training. In the long term, it becomes development when the results of learning are put into practice through a variety, and range, of experiences (Mayo, 1998). Consequently, it is less tangible and less amenable to the kind of prescriptive approach that might be appropriate for the narrower training strategies. This is significant because our organizations have to meet the demands described in chapter 1. They can do so by boldly grasping ideas of behavior change, new relationships, questioning, creativity, learning based on insights, and challenging conventional wisdom, learning through the social interaction of equals, and the self-realization and strength of experience at the heart of adult learning. These responses cannot possibly be based on mechanistic strategies. This will reduce learning to a formula. The first step is to find the points where the learning strategy can be synchronized with the overall organizational strategy. This will be in the more elusive areas of mission statements, visions, and values.

The Mission, the Vision, and the Values

The mission is simply a general description of what the information service actually does. Couched in nonspecific terms, it will usually use words like "excellence," talk about the impact of the library on the users, and, in the United Kingdom at least, use phrases like "value for money." The vision could cover the general character of the service, and it could highlight the desired characteristics of the staff, the level of resources, the systems, and the internal and external relationships. As these ideas are translated into strategies they become more concrete. They are usually expressed in terms of physical changes, and success is often measured in a quantitative way. It is not all that common to find any reference to development. Nevertheless, there are values here that can be used to underpin imaginative and far-reaching learning and development programs. It is necessary to look for the links between what the library wants and what the learning function can be used to support.

Who Decides Strategy and Policy?

The questions of who owns the strategy, and by implication who takes part in framing it, have to be settled. Most strategies come from top management, give or take a degree of consultation. This book sets about the task of painting a picture of a different kind of organization. We can use the term "empowered" as shorthand for it. There is also a more specific argument for giving the indians a little more of the responsibility commonly retained by the chiefs and letting the chiefs see a little more of day-to-day life on the reservation. This should be incorporated into learning and development. Organizational learning has to match the objectives of all the parts of the service, and it has to resound with the interpretation of strategy and policy made by teams, work units, sections, or departments throughout the library. Creating the learning strategy is a whole organization task, and ownership of the development program is universal.

The other reason why strategy formulation has to be inclusive is that so many of the key players in the learning process are actually outside senior management. Chapter 6 (and other parts of the book) will propose that most people learn more from their line managers, and their peers, than from anybody else. As a result, work-based, self-managed learning is the most potent way to deliver learning experiences. Chapter 9 examines the powerful contribution of team learning. To leave these elements, and many of the players, outside the orbit of strategy and policy formulation introduces a radical weakness into the process. It also weakens motivation (see chapter 10). Learning strategy must, therefore, take an input from all levels of the organization. It is an exercise in gathering information.

Collecting Information

Linking development strategies to the organizational strategy and policy obviously ensures that aims and objectives are consistent with those of the organization. The strategy is the official viewpoint, and it puts learning into the organizational setting. It also has to be placed within the contexts of team, unit or departmental needs, and individual requirements. In modern information services, these will be varied and fluid. Opening up strategy formulation to a broad constituency is the first step in ensuring ownership and internal consistency. Putting flesh on the bones of the process then depends on a more detailed information-gathering exercise. Techniques like strengths, weaknesses, opportunities, threats (SWOT) analyses, focus groups, and surveys can be used. Nevertheless, the basis of the exercise will be training needs analyses (TNA), skills audits, and staff development and appraisal programs (SDAS). These are going to reflect the position concerning current knowledge and skills. From staff development and appraisal programs should come some additional information about attitudes to organizational issues and to learning. These in turn will indicate more development needs.

Unlike the narrower aims of training, it is axiomatic that learning strategies and policies go much further. The objectives are the renewal of the organization, and organization development, in ways that exploit talents to the fullest. This explicitly involves giving people capabilities that exceed the demands of their current jobs. It then involves locking them into personal development programs and career development, which create the opportunities to use these capabilities. This is aided by structures and job design, which increase responsibility. Supporting these things is a reaffirmation of the view that development can come through moving across an organization into a different team, or through not moving at all. This is because of empowerment, and because the distinctions between managers and managed are consequently blurred. This context, and the links between learning and other aspects of managing, should be made explicit in the strategy, meaning that strategy and policy have to:

- Make the case for learning in the library (see chapters 1 and 4)
- Set out the learning philosophy (see chapters 1 and 4)
- Establish where the responsibility for learning will lie:
  - For individuals
  - For teams or groups
  - For managers
  - For facilitators
- Locate the management of the process in the organization
- Indicate what the library will provide
- State the responsibilities of learners, facilitators, and managers
- Describe the general means of delivering learning
- Describe the learning and development subsystem
- Link the whole organization to progression and career development

Training Needs Analysis

The Training Needs Analysis (TNA) is used to establish organizational requirements. It is a proactive investigation of what is needed for development at all levels of the organization. It will gather information from individuals, it will look at needs within groups, and it will extend across the library. It will also consider needs emerging from changes in the environment in which libraries operate. It will monitor the ways in which user expectations are developing, and identify new skills and knowledge bases needed to match these requirements. Over a period of time, it will be a global activity. Of some significance for the learning model proposed here, it will consider the needs of particular processes such as the delivery of information to specific user groups. It will not confine itself to examining particular functions. A TNA will also form part of the management of projects, especially where major change is concerned. Basically it is a comparison of three elements:

- The skills, knowledge, attitudes, and capabilities needed to maintain the health of the library organization at the present moment
- The skills, knowledge, attitudes, capabilities, and aspirations of current personnel
- The potential skills, knowledge, attitudes, and capabilities required to meet
  - Changes in user requirements
  - Changes brought about by environmental conditions
  - Changes in operational, technical, and professional areas
  - Changes in the aspirations of individuals

As suggested earlier, this analysis is carried out at individual, group, and organizational levels. It demands a detailed awareness of library objectives and the service culture, a grasp of changing trends, particularly technological and professional, and an understanding of organizational learning. Carrying out the TNA calls for:

- An insight into the working situation
- The ability to spot potential developments and opportunities
- A critical skill in identifying gaps and weaknesses, and using this knowledge constructively
- Sufficient knowledge of organizational learning to propose development programs to rectify the weaknesses, fill the gaps, and exploit opportunities; this could also involve the ability to identify situations that might require action other than training or learning activities
- The ability to arrive at collaborative solutions for the issues identified
- Skill in implementing, perhaps delivering and evaluating, learning activities and programs

Staff Development and Appraisal Schemes

The TNA is management-driven, although it will not work without a sense of balance. Staff development and appraisal schemes (SDAS) approach the issue from two directions; the best schemes are also driven by the appraisee's assessment, and they have a longer term effect. Yet, both the TNA and the SDAS have the same objectives:

- Improving the quality of the library service
- Improving staff performance
- Supporting personal and professional growth
- Facilitating career development
- Agreeing where learning should take place
- Making a more specific commitment to learning
- Collaboratively matching personal and service needs

As well as an information-gathering exercise, the SDAS must be regarded as an integral part of the learning process. It offers:

- Communication
- Information for the knowledge base
- Support for personal and professional growth
- Proactive involvement in development
- The opportunity to influence the service
- The opportunity to express disagreement or dissatisfaction
- Recognition

The process of appraisal is based on the preparation of documentation to be used at preferably two meetings annually—the formal appraisal meeting and a subsequent review meeting, usually after six months. The format is as follows:

- Appraisees complete a career profile detailing up-to-date information on qualifications, experience, and responsibilities, which is accompanied by an objective assessment of strengths and weaknesses over the past year, and any organizational shortcomings that hinder performance.
- All of this is in the context of the agreed objectives of the area where the appraisee operates.
- The appraiser, who is the appropriate line manager or equivalent, also completes an assessment of performance, again identifying strengths as well as weaknesses.
- A meeting between both parties arrives at agreed objectives and a plan for achieving the objectives, which could involve training, learning experiences, or other steps to remove performance blockages.
- A six-month review assesses progress.

Apart from the benefits arising from the scheme itself, there are other benefits to learning:

- The exercise is work-based learning.
- It is learning from strengths as well as weaknesses.
- It offers an incentive in the recognition of achievement.
- It adds more information to the knowledge base.
- The outcome is a form of learning contract.

One final point should be made. The SDAS has two objectives. The obvious one is to improve performance. The other is the often less overt one of ensuring individual development, which is more than doing the same job better. The manager's approach to SDAS in libraries can be seen as one of the early stages of building a relationship. It involves developing a rapport. The sensitive use of techniques, such as listening skills, will draw information out of the appraisee, and begin to identify hopes, aspirations, and even worries. It can lead into better self-development on the part of the appraisee, as well as the use of approaches such as coaching and mentoring.

There are other methods of gathering the information that has to be fed into the learning system. Learning organizations are run by different kinds of managers. They are managers who rely on more open communication systems, and who are free to work outside the usual bureaucratic tramlines. This makes it easier for them to deploy the potent tactic of talking to people. Where appropriate, they can use techniques such as focus groups, surveys, self-surveys, and observation. They are also supported by information networks, formal and informal, which contain masses of information of potential value to learning and development.

The net result is a great deal of detail that can be formalized. Also documented are agreements on needs and rolling learning objectives. This formal process can be taken a stage further through the use of learning contracts.

Learning Contracts

Development of this kind places a great deal of responsibility on individuals. They have to take a role in controlling their own learning, deciding what will be learned and how, and in identifying and exploiting learning opportunities. There is also a responsibility for applying what is learned to work situations (see chapters 5 and 6).

There is an explicit learning contract in the SDAS and also in personal development plans (PDP). Learning contracts and PDPs can sometimes add other elements to whatever is agreed upon in the SDAS. Development objectives can be more precise. There can also be a sharper focus on how the learning will actually be achieved and how it will be transferred into the working situation. SDAS documents tend to specify concrete actions to be taken. If actual learning experiences are included, they are more likely to be linked to formal training events. Learning contracts should include a subtler recognition of wider possibilities. One example is the use of work-based learning, and how this will be managed and achieved, perhaps as a part of team-based learning, but also as self-learning. So a learning contract could be expected to include additional information:

- The methods of learning: these should be wider and less formal
- A statement of how the learning will be transferred

Learning, Development, and Structures—Again

Chapter 2 contains two examples of structures built around process teams. Learning and development is an organizational subsystem, and its tentacles should extend into all the process teams. The power of theoretical arguments (see chapter 1, and later chapter 4), is driving us inexorably toward work-based learning, self-learning, and learning from peers. The same reasoning emphasizes the social context of learning and the value of learning in groups. The arena in which the learning and development is fought out is inside the team, and this is where the activity has to be organized, managed, and delivered. Some of the world's massive library systems will have their own freestanding human resource, or staff development, functions; almost every library service will make use of the services of the parent organization. Some United Kingdom libraries have this responsibility fixed on one individual at a comparatively low level in the organization. In others, it is part of a portfolio of duties. In a bureaucracy this could be a problem, as the process will not be sponsored at the most powerful organizational level. It strengthens the tendency to regard learning and development as bolt-on extras, as suggested at the beginning of chapter 2. Putting the responsibility into empowered work units strengthens the learning process and the work of the teams. Key decisions will be taken at the right level, and another integrative feature will have been introduced. Figure 2.1 (page 43) depicted, as an example of an integrative structure, a two-layer organization with a strategic, or management, team. Figure 3.1 adds another element to this, because it shows the learning and development function as one that is within all teams and is improving communication, information flows, and integration between teams. Once again, the processes in the diagram represent the delivery of the total information and support package to a group of users, and are made up of a number of functions.

Figure 3.1 The Place of Learning and Development in the Structure

Roles and Responsibilities

A model of the management process for learning and development would take account of all of the elements described so far in this chapter. There are new roles for all the players. These will certainly differ in emphasis, and in style, from the conventional view of the behavior of managers and staff. It can be argued that the roles evolve naturally from the consideration of the organizational background, in chapter 1, and that the justification for them comes from the consideration of learning theories and their effect on libraries, in chapter 4. It is obviously true that the kind of organizational forms suggested in chapter 2 have a major influence on the ways in which people behave inside organizations. Chapter 2 also proposed that learning and development should form an organizational subsystem. Whichever organizational structure is seen to be appropriate for libraries that place learning and development at the top of their managerial agendas, and however flexible it is, the operation must be based on a clear and easily understandable process. The process shown in Figure 3.2 is based on the new roles proposed in this section, and also remains true to the principles advocated in this and the previous chapters. For the sake of convenience, the term "managers" in the diagram is taken to mean those who have responsibility for the overall management of the learning and development process.

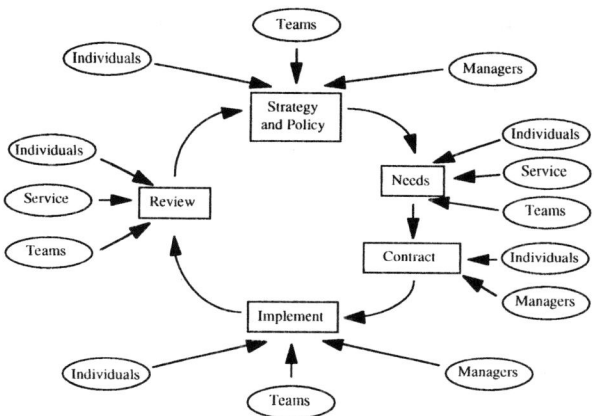

Figure 3.2 The Management Process for Learning and Development

The model shows a five-stage process in which the relevant contributions of all the groups in the library are shown at each stage. The process is one of a shared system of management in which ownership is spread throughout the library, amongst all of the interests identified. This is a vital point, not only for ensuring the correct fit between individual, team, and organizational needs, but also for motivation. Strategy and policy are formed through the interchange between managers, whose primary concern is strategy, and individuals and teams who also have a legitimate concern. Needs are established through collaboration. Managers identify both training and learning needs. Individuals and teams make their own input. The resulting learning contract is a compact between the individual and the service. All stages are global activities.

Strategy, Policy, and Managerial Roles

In the model, managerial roles can be discharged by line managers or their equivalents, team leaders, managers with hierarchical authority (albeit modified), coaches (again with modifications), and learning facilitators. These roles can obviously overlap. They share common concerns, deploy the same skills, and demonstrate similar behaviors.

They all need to be able to understand, and ideally have made an input into, the strategy and policy of the library service. They should also have been major players in forming learning strategy and making the connections between this, organizational strategy and concepts such as information strategies, if they exist. A requirement to subscribe to the philosophy behind the concept of learning organizations is important. So is an understanding of the way in which structures, jobs, functions, and processes are defined and connected. Simply subscribing to the ideas is not enough. Managers also have to create a vision of what learning will do for the library, and they must communicate it. They must demonstrate the virtues they proclaim by being learners themselves, which is perhaps the hardest part of all. The other skills they need are the skills of flexible management: an understanding of empowerment and a commitment to it, as well as the knowledge of how to do it and the will to make it work. They also need the attitudes and behavior that turn managers into coaches and facilitators (see chapter 7).

Assessing Needs

The second stage, assessing the needs, builds on some of the skills already mentioned. This is the information-gathering stage, where the first steps in matching all the needs of the system are taken. On one side, these come through the formal analysis of organizational requirements. On the other, they come from using communication techniques. Chapter 2 described an organization that was good at supporting learning. More than that, it adopted learning and development as one of its life-support systems. This entails using the information system and removing barriers to communication. The freedom that comes from loosening the grip of hierarchical communication and increasing the visibility of all parts of the library, is used to supplement formal methods of assessing individual needs. SDAS procedures, and the use of other interviews, will require close attention to the skills of questioning, listening, and collaborating in drawing up mutually beneficial learning contracts.

The other part of the process at this stage is setting objectives. Clear expressions of the desired outcomes must be agreed upon with the learners. When this has been done, the manager can move, once more in partnership with the learner, to decide on the means by which the outcomes will be achieved. Again, this is a collaborative process, with the learner assuming a significant share of responsibility, in line with views on the self-management of learning.

Providing resources, implementing agreed development programs, assessing their effectiveness, modifying programs, and providing feedback will add another layer of skills and behaviors. A knowledge of how people learn is important, together with the recognition that the members of the workforce will be at different levels as far as motivation is concerned (see chapter 10). Some learning facilitators and managers will be responsible for providing some of the learning experiences, and here a more practical knowledge will be required, with some administrative skills.

The Learners

More than anything, the learners will need to learn how to learn, in collaboration with trainers, learning facilitators, coaches, peers, and managers. They will have to adjust to the ways in which things are done in learning based organizations and adapt to new ideas about career development. This will mean taking advantage of flexible structures and different ways of designing jobs. It will mean taking on board the disciplines of self-learning, and of work-based learning, and embracing the systematic approaches that make these ideas work. Learners will need to understand how they themselves learn and what it is that drives them. Only when all these behaviors are cultivated will a genuine learning organization emerge.

This chapter tries to establish some principles that will offer a framework for managing learning in libraries. It does not deal with the topic in a functional way, nor does it deal with administration. For detailed accounts of these aspects, and some help with the practicalities of managing learning, the training handbook by Diane Bailey Associates (2001) is invaluable. This work has also influenced significantly the views expressed in this chapter. Wills (1998) also offers a comprehensive and detailed overview.

Case Study 3
THE LEARNING LIBRARY SERVICE

The Situation

A university library that provided an integrated information service combining conventional formats, multimedia services, a range of electronic formats, and networked information and computing facilities had for some time been working to develop information delivery through team-based services. Over a period of about eighteen months, the service had been restructured around seven broad groups of subject disciplines reflecting the faculty organization of the university. Appropriate traditional and nontraditional skills, and knowledge bases, were included in the teams so that information technologists, audiovisual technicians, and conventionally orientated librarians worked alongside each other. There was substantial empowerment, and team leaders, and other team members, had responded well to greater authority and responsibility. A reconstituted management team included carefully selected representation from grades of staff not normally represented. Below the management team, a coordinating team, made up of team leaders, provided cross functional links. This team was subject to rotating chairmanship. There was no deputy director of information services.

The gestation period for this structure had lasted over twelve months. During this time, team membership had been very carefully and systematically negotiated, and eventually all of the service staff had been placed in team roles that were satisfactory to them. There was a very small central core, under the service director's management. This dealt with service wide and institutional issues that were outside the remit of the teams. This central core included the mechanics of collection management, and also embraced electronic information. Professional and technical aspects of collection management, and the organization and exploitation of information, were vested in the teams, along with various collaborative schemes involving other institutions. There was a conventional staff development program.

Although there was some satisfaction with the development of the structure, which represented a considerable change from the old structure used by the library service for many years, there was some concern about what senior staff saw as a structure that was still subject to considerable division and demarcation. Staff from different traditions with different skills bases, different educational and training backgrounds, different cultures, and different ways of working all operated alongside each other. But the way in which they discharged their duties had not altered. Although they were in the same team, and serving the same group of users, there were still boundaries between librarians handling traditional information, librarians specializing in electronic information, technologists providing technical support, and audiovisual specialists providing technical advice and advice on the use of visual aids and media. The only area where cross functional activity took place was in collection management, which was distributed amongst the readers advisors in the teams, who provided support in the use of the library and its resources. Ironically, this had been a difficult change for some technical services staff to accept, as they became generalist readers advisors with similar roles. This continuing degree of separation was not what had been envisaged when the ideal of hybrid information workers, who could represent the "seamless web" of conventional and electronic information, as well as technical support, had been incorporated into the vision of the service. There were some additional difficulties caused by differential salary scales. These were historically justified on the basis of differing market forces acting on information technology specialists as opposed to librarians. There was a general perception that the possibilities of new ways of working were not being fully exploited.

The Solution

A fresh bout of institutional reorganization provided the first steps toward a solution. A rationalization of the multicampus organization, coupled with the sale of some of the university land, created the opportunity to build a single information center to serve the entire university. A user-friendly, open-plan building with very few, if any, barriers between users and staff, was created. Service management hoped this would be seen by the users as belonging to them. It was to be occupied by all of the information services, together with some other student and educational support services. A project team was set up to assess the current situation and consider the next steps.

The Assessment

The project team considered that the structure of the service had delivered some of the key features it had been intended to provide. The management of all aspects of information provision for the university was well integrated, and there was a growing sense of corporate responsibility. This was gradually becoming stronger, as the information service became increasingly technology-based. Some staff members, who would have been outside the strategic thinking loop in more traditional organizations, were also contributing well in their new roles as part of the management team. Multiskilled teams were a fact of life, and empowerment had been accepted. There were also some examples of new relationships with other institutions, sometimes across sectors, in the collection management area.

On the negative side, there was little evidence of a cultural shift. The old demarcation lines continued to exist within the teams, and job enrichment and job enlargement, based on the development of multitalented individuals (an elusive goal in any event), had not yet emerged. Job enrichment was a fact of life for some people; job enlargement was not happening. There was also little movement of personnel between teams. The examples of information technologists and librarians, who were successfully working across each other's specializations, were rare. It was felt that the main reasons for this were, first, that there was no system to support it. Second, the kind of learning necessary to make it possible was not understood within the service and had no focal point inside the teams. There were also university human resource policies that were not helpful, and the university staff development and appraisal program did not make provision for this type of learning on the part of support staff.

The Actions

The team concentrated initially on the infrastructure. Together with the professional associations and the university authorities, they created a single salary scale, which did not differentiate between information technologists, media specialists, or librarians. They then established four levels of staff, including senior management. At each level, working with specialist external support and advice, they agreed on a set of competencies that progressively built on skills acquisition and attitude change. At all levels, the competency statements covered the skills, attitudes, behavior, and knowledge necessary to do the job. Progressing through the levels, the competencies became more flexible, less tangible, and more demanding to achieve.

The team then turned its attention to job descriptions. All of these were rewritten to create more flexibility and allow for the possibilities of taking on more responsibility for particular tasks or functions, or for possibly combining one job with aspects of another. It was hoped that this would help spread, to other areas, the example of the collection management and technical services staff. They had become involved in much wider reader advisory work and project management.

The university staff development and appraisal scheme was formal, and the information service was tied to it. The team felt that on its own it did not meet the needs of the service, and introduced individual learning contracts to supplement it. The learning contracts were agreed upon annually, with a progress review after six months, and a formal assessment at the end of the year. This met the requirements of the SDAS, but went further. The learning program embedded in each learning contract was work-based, and gave the learner a significant say in what was to be learned and how it would be accomplished. It did not confine itself to the competencies required to discharge a function at a particular level. Due attention was paid to personal and career development, and to the need to equip staff for wider, or more responsible, roles within their present team, or in other teams. Progress up the salary scale depended on satisfying the competencies specified at each level of the scale. It also required staff to meet the terms of their learning contracts, which also detailed the support that would be given to individuals with agreed learning programs.

Inside the process teams delivering services, learning became a specific function. Learning facilitators were appointed to work with individuals, and a learning development team was created to ensure cross service integration. The agreed program addressed issues such as learning skills, the systematic process of learning from work, and the practical features required to support this activity. Job rotation, coaching, and team learning were included. Learners also had access to the formal provision of the program, through the university's own course structure, or funded attendance at other institutions and training events. A balanced learning program was created for all staff.

As staff were encouraged to develop in ways that might not have been immediately applicable to their existing posts, it was also agreed that meeting established criteria for posts in other teams would ensure eligibility for a transfer.

At a strategic level, learning became enshrined in the service development plan:

> the potential for development, and the right of all staff to develop and learn through doing their jobs is recognized . . . the absolute need for the service to ensure that learning and development opportunities are built into day-to-day working and are properly supported . . . is a fundamental requirement on management and staff alike . . . we will manage the service and the demands of change through our ability to transfer and apply new skills and knowledge bases into our working routines . . . all work tasks will be recognized as having a potential for learning and development.

The Results

After eighteen months in the new building, the missing components identified at the start of the review were beginning to emerge. The barriers between specialisms within teams were slowly dissolving. In some cases, significant cross functional and interteam movement was starting to occur. For example, an information technologist with a strong background in librarianship had moved to take responsibility for IT in another team; an audiovisual resources manager was managing the overall reader services in a second team; and another information technologist, with a library qualification, was successfully beginning to combine first line technological support with basic reader assistance. She was also working as an assessor for the continuing professional development scheme of the professional association. In the management team, the principle that any intervention in any part of the system had to be in a learning context had been adopted as one of the cornerstones of a change in attitude. To the already burgeoning skills of consensual management, they were adding the skills required to support and make possible learning in a nonthreatening environment.

Comment

This management team adopted learning and development as a unifying motif. By doing so they were able to take their development of an empowered organization to another level.

They dealt with the strategic issue by enshrining learning in the information services development plan, and by accepting responsibility for organizational learning and for their own learning as individuals. They also pinpointed the kind of learning that was preferred. This was done through statements in the development plan, and through the way in which the learning contracts were used to refine and direct the process.

Rationalizing the salary structure was important as a motivational and integrating force. Any friction that might stem from structural differentials was removed. Team development was aided by the fact that no specialism was seen to be more significant than any other. Tying increments to the successful acquisition of learning was also motivational, as was the willingness to encourage staff to stretch themselves and gain knowledge that was not always immediately relevant to current jobs. Career development was brought into play by this, and by the affirmation that people could make lateral moves across teams in order to broaden their horizons.

As the management team acknowledged, there was still much to do. The team organization was showing promise as far as delivering the service was concerned. Responsibility within the teams was intelligently distributed, and the roles of the participants were clearly becoming broader. The composition of the teams reflected two central planks of the theories in chapter 2: they were made up of diverse groups and yet they were showing signs of integration. On the other hand, the organization would need to take a more sophisticated view of how the team learning process, which is part of this, could actually be made to work. The emphasis on individual learning needed to be complemented by a greater attention to how learning skills developed in teams (see chapter 9).

Communication between teams was improved by the creation of a cross service learning and development team. Increasing the movement of staff across the service in this way was helpful, but the information network was underdeveloped and would warrant attention.

The system was capable of deploying a range of techniques dedicated to work-based learning. These included shadowing, attachments, job rotation. This would eventually involve considerable investment in coaching, and the establishment of self-help and support groups where needed.

Conclusion

This chapter brings together some ideas about organization development. It is about using the idea that people *want* to stretch themselves and manage their own performance by setting their own goals with management. These goals are based on a concordat and targets delivering a better service. People also share in deciding how they will learn. Mumford (2000) points to changes in attitudes to participation over the last thirty years. She advocates small, dynamic, technologically advanced organizations, which rely on self-motivated groups, working in empowered circumstances. Heller (2000) describes motivated groups and individuals working collaboratively. These circumstances can be created if learning and development are organizational bedrocks. Giving people control over their learning is essential. Learning must also be systemic in organizations. Glynn (2000) reported on dissatisfaction with internal career opportunities amongst managers in general. Challenge, achievement, recognition, and control are the aspects of organizational life that are valued. Other surveys have indicated that young people now tend to be less interested in promotion into management, so the idea of moving up an organization may be less important than some of the features listed above. This is where learning comes in.

Part 2
Self-Development

Chapter 4

How Librarians Learn

If the title of this chapter was to be posed as a question, the answer would of course be "much like anybody else." They learn in different ways, and they are involved in a range of different learning activities and experiences. Of these activities and experiences, there will be some that they believe are more effective for them, and that they prefer to use if possible. Learners will be different in terms of their attitudes to learning, their learning maturity, and their motivation. One common factor is that the learners and their organizations will profit from the creation of a particular learning environment, and from the management of the learning process in the ways described in chapters 2 and 3. This environment needs:

- Structurally flat organizations
- Technology based organizations
- Empowered staff and supportive managers
- Organizations that use teams
- Organizations that manage their knowledge
- Shared management of learning
- Organizations that change themselves through learning
- Problem solving organizations
- Double loop learning organizations
- Organizations that tie learning to performance improvement
- Organizations that treat learning as a strategic issue
- Learning and development as an organizational subsystem

- Learning as a basic component of organization design
- Learning that begins with individuals and spreads
- Inclusive learning—everyone is involved
- Learning that itself is always changing and developing
- Learning that is overt, deliberate, and planned
- Organizations that believe in learning
- A learning culture

Doyle (2000) commented on what he saw essentially as the failure to integrate development activities into the mainstream of organizational life, and a tendency to see development in terms of formal programs. Written in the context of management development, his views are also applicable to all development. Doyle has also, in an unpublished paper, made the criticism that development fails to embrace the principles of adult learning. The organizational environment described in this book is part of the key to the use of adult learning theories. This chapter looks at how these theories can be applied.

The Development of Learning Theories

Our reference point will be the emergence of theories about the distinctive nature of adult learning. These are the theories on that modern development is based, sometimes unconsciously. Even so, it is worth noting that some of the earlier themes of the "traditionalists" run through our ideas about the way that adults learn best. Not all of the authorities cited in the following sections are sheltering themselves under the adult learning umbrella. However, many of their ideas find parallels in the thinking behind modern learning theories.

This book argues that there is little that matters in modern libraries that cannot be learned through flexible, undidactic methods—even if, for some learning tasks, no new skills will be involved, no reasoning or problem-solving, and the learning experience will be limited to a small number of responses to two or three signals. Learning in these cases can involve a structured approach set in conventional psychology; training will be based on learning in small steps, the pacing of the material, and feedback. There are areas of automated library operations, for example, where this kind of training could be used. There are also some areas of problem solving, complex training, and even training where the trainer is concerned with assisting in changing attitudes, where this approach could be justified for a small part of the learning. Perhaps we should also remember that behaviorism is still with us in the management of modern training as well. What else are we relying on when we devise performance indicators, establish basic or core competencies, and introduce performance assessment? The question is whether it is the best approach. We can still argue that as our organizations change their nature, they will need to rely on theories of learning that fit with the new circumstances.

The Organizational Environment and Learning Theories

Hendry (1991) explored the links between cultures, structures, and training. Bureaucratic hierarchies had training structures and theories to match. The idea that priority should be given to the rounded development of workers as whole personalities was anathema. "To manage people effectively, Skinner would say, we should worry less about their illusions of freedom and dignity," (Myers, 1988). Argyris (1957), much earlier, had also identified bureaucracies and hierarchical organizations as features that hampered learning. Training in these organizations secured efficiency in processing work, through standardization, using workers who followed rules and workers who needed to apply only a minimum of thinking. Many traditionally organized libraries were examples of this kind of activity. Most of the management theories enthusiastically applied to libraries in the past actually worked against the promotion of learning—or knowledge-based—organizations. The kind of training would be mechanistic, producing competent but limited workers unprepared for anything but the restricted roles for which they had been trained. This approach succeeded in insulating learning and development in small cells. All learning was limited and contained within boundaries created by the bureaucratic forms (see also chapter 2).

While we need a little of the traditional theory, we also need to challenge ourselves with other ideas about how people could be managed and, consequently, how narrow views of training could be supplemented and, in some cases, replaced by a broad view of learning. These views will emphasize the intellectual and emotional development of individuals, and engage constructively with the issue of organizational effectiveness. They will include more sophisticated attention to the motivation of learners.

These ideas offer different perspectives on the need to develop the whole individual, and significantly provide ideas about the ways in that people learn to manage change. Modern views on this emphasize the rounded contribution of the individual. Modern learning theories, particularly those directly applied to adult learning, will be far more appropriate to our emerging organizations.

Adult Learning

Andragogy

This offers a good justification for approaches based on the ideas that training, as exemplified previously, must offer more than skills transmission, and that the approach to adult training depends on something different from the theories underlying school-based, or even some college-based instruction. Knowles (1984) characterizes adult learning in the following ways:

- The use of life experience as a learning resource
- The value of problem solving
- The usefulness of participative techniques
- The ability to relate and apply learning to job or life situations
- A continuing desire to improve performance
- An acceptance that it is never too late to learn
- A stronger motivation
- Learning as a social process, taking place in equal relationships
- Adult learning theories support the proposition that training is more than skills transmission; it is bound up with developing the whole individual and changing attitudes as well as behavior.

Central to this is the idea of "self-directedness, " (Kohn and Slomczynski, 1990). This refers to the contention that adults have learned how to exert direction over their lives, and that this should apply to their learning environments as much as to any other life aspect. Self-directedness is something that emerges as a necessary component in any strategy for coping with modern organizational life. It has been referred to in other contexts by a number of writers. The basic ideas about how modern organizations should be managed are sometimes seen as attempts to transfer the way in which we manage our personal and private lives to the way in that we manage our work (i.e, using techniques such as discussion, collaboration, applying our experience to decision making, involving everyone, deciding things for ourselves where we can, and deferring to the experience and knowledge of others where we cannot). Learning in organizations should also be like this. In the next few pages, we can look in a little more detail at some of the key issues in this approach.

Problem Solving

One of the key problem-solving techniques relevant to the way adults learn is by stepping back and viewing the problem or the issue as a whole. Looking at the total situation is followed by the making of connections and working out relationships. This depends on insight, that allows situations to be seen in new ways. It is from this that problem solving and learning springs. Self-understanding, and understanding the whole environment, will lead to learning and to behavior modification. The origin of this idea is in Gestalt psychology, and the approach has a huge significance for modern training. Developing insights, and taking a view of the issue as a whole, depends on information and knowledge—so does creating behavioral and attitude change. This underscores the need to create a supportive climate and an enabling structure. It is another justification for the openness and flexibility written about in part 1, for these things cannot be cultivated otherwise.

Gestalt philosophy is also significant for the formulation of strategies. In our context it is about understanding our particular world of work, and of developing fresh insights into it. This will direct training strategies toward the individual, to self-learning, and obviously to learning from work. This last facet is something that has to be managed as carefully as formal learning processes. It is also something that, more than most other forms of training, relies on the right kind of organization; that is, if people are going to develop through work-based learning.

Wertheimer (1959) is often regarded as the father of Gestalt philosophy. Leahey and Harris (1993), as we have already seen, also accepted the idea that learning came through insights, but argued that very often this was actually an incremental process (see case study 4). Child (1981) also stresses the importance of thinking and intuition. Whichever way it occurs, Gestalt psychology states that:

- Learning is a matter of acquiring insights
- It is long term
- Intuition is a contributory factor
- Learning depends on developing new ways of thinking
- It is essentially problem solving
- Learning from work is crucial
- Trial and error learning is also crucial

Other writers have also stressed the importance of basing learning on problem solving. Wood (1988) has pointed out that "Piaget's theory . . . places action and self-directed problem-solving at the heart of learning and development." Both action and self-directed problem solving are training techniques appropriate to the organizational characteristics described here, particularly to the kind of team-based organizations that are emerging.

Work-Based Learning

Our organizational environment, from which we take our experiences, could be described as "differentiated," (Piaget, 1997). It is made up of staff with different viewpoints, traditions, educational and professional backgrounds, learning needs, priorities, and cultures. It is also in a state of discontinuous change where double loop thinking (see chapter 1) is required. It deals with users whose expectations and viewpoints are now getting further away from those of the traditional library user. This is the cockpit in which most of our learning takes place. It contains the seeds of both professional and personal development; it has to be organized and used (see also chapters 5 and 6).

Work-based learning is also important because it not only strikes a chord with the diversity to be found in modern information services, but it also helps to teach how to deal with such diversity (Bruner, 1966). Bruner's view of perception also foreshadowed Hirshberg's concern with creativity, and O'Keeffe's espousal of "thinking outside the box," (see chapter 1). Bruner believed that perception was the ability to think ahead of the information available, and that problem solving implied the ability to explore alternatives, spurred on by uncertainty or curiosity. These are important skills for us today. The process also has to be maintained, directed, and systematized to keep it going. To Bruner, growth occurred in a number of different ways. It built an ability to handle diversity and deal with multiple issues, situations, and problems, which all surfaced at the same time. These are the demands and the conditions of contemporary information services.

A Desire for Performance Improvement

In this respect, we are looking for forms of learning that challenge and stretch our minds. Another key to this is Vygotsky's "Zone of Proximal Development." It refers to an activity, a skill, or any piece of learning, which is beyond the learner's present competence. This shortfall on expertise is the gap that has to be filled, and is the Zone. The Zone can be understood as the difference between present performance standards and the desired higher standards. (In coaching it has another meaning; see chapter 7.) The idea itself is one of the central planks of coaching. Crucially, new behavior, or new skills, can be acquired through learning from peers, pointing us not only to the informal learning process that goes on in many contexts, but specifically to workplace learning. Fixed in this is the idea of development: that this approach can be used to help learners acquire learning they would be unable to master alone. It confirms that even self-learning, and workplace learning, need to be logically and systematically planned for, and aims must be set. Learning is in fact a very complicated set of relationships between the learner, the working environment, and the learning facilitator, and it has to be managed. Together with the implications of work-based learning, we are directed toward techniques like coaching, mentoring, and group learning.

Learning Amongst Equals

Another of Vygotsky's contributions to our understanding of how learning should be prosecuted comes from his view of the relationship between the learner and the trainer. The Zone of Proximal Development, which is also explained as the potential the learner can realize with the aid of someone else, is not something that should be left to chance. Although this kind of learning experience can occur in a haphazard and informal way, to work fully it needs active intervention from a training agent (Daniels, 1996). This view of the exchange between trainer and learner is developed by other psychologists, who emphasize the idea of a relationship that is more equal than the traditional learner–teacher relationship. The point assumes more importance when adult learning theories are considered. Vygotsky (1997) and Bruner (1966) both emphasize communication between trainer and trainee. Again, implicit in this process is the equality of the relationship between the learner and the tutor. Structural and technical change in organizations, changes in power distribution, and educational change are among some of the developments in libraries that should have led to expectations of more equal relationships. They accentuate the significance of a social interaction to that the learner can bring experience, maturity, a will to learn, and his or her own insights. This exchange also contributes to the idea, examined later, that anyone who facilitates learning will be a learner themselves.

Vygotsky similarly stressed the importance of the environment as the source of abundant learning experiences. He put great emphasis on social interaction as a learning force. Although writing specifically of the education of children, Vygotsky (1978) quoted in Wertsch (1996) argued that learning comes from being completely immersed in the environment: "mental functioning in the individual can be understood only by examining the social and cultural processes from which it derives."

Self-Management

An important principle of adult learning is that learners are capable of taking responsibility for their own learning. The need for allowing workers a much bigger say in how work is done makes no sense if it is not extended to their learning. This has implications.

It means, first, that learning should take place in a nonbureaucratic situation: "It is essential that educators learning and learners educating make a conscious effort to refuse to be bureaucratized. Bureaucracy annihilates creativity." (Freire, 1983). Proper learning needs to be open to all, and can only have a real impact in organizations that are flexible and support empowerment. It means the use of participative techniques such as coaching and mentoring—techniques that also give responsibility to the learner, that imply a two-way learning process, and create a sense of ownership. Learning is not the exclusive possession of the teacher to be passed on to the learner. It is owned by everybody. Hirshberg (1998) said that creativity was to be found everywhere in an organization, and Freire believed that learning should be everywhere as well. This underscores the idea of an equal relationship in which everybody will always be learning: "Those who are called to teach must first learn how to continue learning when they begin to teach," (Freire, 1983). Elsewhere he says: "When the one who knows understands first that the process by which he learned is first social and, second, that in teaching something to another he is also learning something that he did not know already, then both are changed," (1983).

Last, this point justifies the behavioral change: It is further ammunition to support the move from trainer as pedagogue to trainer as facilitator. It can also be tied to the idea that coaching is an extension of the management role (see chapter 7): The leader as doer.

A Lifetime of Learning

Vygotsky also moved the argument forward by affirming that people can continue to develop intellectually, and still benefit from training, throughout their working lives. He discounted the idea that people's abilities and intellectual capacities are fixed, and that after a certain age they cannot be developed any further. The idea that it is possible to teach an old dog new tricks is something we need to keep in mind in the libraries of today. One of the interesting things about the last ten to fifteen years in librarianship is the way in which new skills are being learned, and careers are taking new turns, at points where people had either reached a plateau or started on a process of gentle decline. Perhaps the most encouraging thing about librarianship today is the way in which behavior is changing and new talents are being developed across the spectrum from neophyte professionals to seasoned skeptics, who might once have looked askance at some aspects of what is going on today.

Motivation

Motivation is also a key factor in adult learning. The argument is that individuals have a need to learn, and that this need is affected by self-esteem and self-perception (Brundage and Mackeracher, 1980). Gatfield (1996) reporting on the introduction of teamworking at McVities and Young's Seafood in the United Kingdom, indicated that even after a massive investment in communication, some sectors of the factory resisted the idea of learning new ways of working. They, particularly groups of engineers, were deliberately excluded and allowed time to consider their own attitudes in the light of the experience of the involved workers. Clear changes in self-esteem, self-perception, and a recognition of their need to learn led to their subsequent involvement.

Bruner (1966) also had some ideas about motivation. To him, it was an intrinsic thing, and he saw it in terms of a learning progression starting with the will to learn and moving on through harnessing curiosity and setting objectives that extend the learner: "study the possible rather than the achieved." Sustenance is drawn from actually becoming involved in learning itself and in progressing. Satisfaction can be derived from applying learning to the task of handling the complexity and uncertainty of organizational life. Engaging in joint enterprises (group learning and teamwork) is a motivator. The social character of learning was another energizer, as was the tutor-learner relationship. All of these factors lead us toward modern training theories and practice: creative thinking, double loop learning, and group learning. Bruner advocated a multifaceted approach, proposing that there was no one single way of reasoning or of solving problems.

To summarize, motivation is inside us. It can come from:

- Progressing along a path of development
- The satisfaction of applying learning to work situations

- The social element—engaging in learning with others
- The learner-trainer relationship itself

Team-Based Learning

Learning in groups is a theme that runs through the work of Piaget and Bruner. It is a prominent part of Freire's conception, and the cultural circles he describes are in fact learning groups by another term. He also sees working across specializations as an important way of helping specialists to learn how to immerse their expertise in the work of the group, without constantly defending their own narrower skills and knowledge bases. This has a sharp relevance to our present need to bring together different specialisms and integrate them in the interests of delivering a unified service to users.

Do These Ideas Work?

If you ever want to make an informed guess at the efficacy of any training theory or technique, the place to look is its application in extreme conditions. For example, a great deal can be learned about the strengths of coaching, team learning, and leadership by looking at the preparation, training, and execution of ocean yacht racing. All of the preceding theories are applied in this context, where it is a matter of life and death as well as success in racing terms. In World War II, bomber crews were organized on the basis of a very powerful form of teamwork. Apart from the team dynamics, there were elements of multiskilling—they learned at least the rudiments of each others' jobs, so that in a dire emergency they were to some degree interchangeable. If the application of these learning theories works in these circumstances, they can be made to work anywhere. Looking at any particular theory being put into practice in negative or hostile environments will give a strong indication of how much value the theory actually has.

Modern ideas about learning offer exciting perspectives on training. They enrich the learning experience of participants by emphasizing learning based on experience, problem solving, transferability of skills, and the participation of the learner. There is an insistence that work-related training can still have vitality, and can concern itself with individual development as much as skills development.

Emerging new-style organizations require workers who are multiskilled or multitalented, and who can work within group or team structures. They will need to make decisions about their everyday jobs and learn to manage themselves inside changing organizations. In a sense, the trainer is still concerned with the transmission of skills, but they are a range of skills of varying degrees of complexity. As such, they require a variety of responses, and can draw on a variety of theories to light the path that both the learner and the learning facilitator will follow.

Trainers will continue to adopt a catholic approach. Crucial issues of delivery, clarity, motivation, and retaining the interest in the topic can still benefit from the selective application of traditional theories. Training in some specific skills will be based on traditional theories, while training in complex skills will be based on modern theories—theories that emphasize participation, self-direction, experience, intrinsic motivation, and team learning. Trainers will choose their theoretical base to fit the training needs, and also select appropriate methods and techniques.

Across the spectrum of learning theories, there is much that can be brought together to provide a clear blueprint for training. In other ways, the ideas discussed in this chapter also provide targets to aim for and standards to achieve. The theoretical justification provided by the main tenets of learning psychology offer us some guidelines that we can use as the basis of a strategy and as a means of steering our practical training. They act as a template and as a set of targets. We can now sum up the main issues.

Inclusivity

The capacity for learning, and the ability to profit from it, can be found everywhere in the organization. It can also be found in *people* at every stage of their working lives.

Socialization

Effective learning in organizations has to do with sharing. Learning stimuli can come from peers, supervisors, managers, and group activities. As well as these relationships, it has to do with the relationship between trainer and trainee, which has to be different from the traditional teacher–pupil relationship.

Equality and Unity

Learning is also based on breaking down barriers. It may begin with learning from each other, and it may be founded on a new trainee–trainer relationship. It also has a function in bringing together the various groups of skills, attitudes, and professionalism found in information services.

More than that, it should dissipate the effects of hierarchical levels, and vertical divisions, in organizations. Many of us still work in organizations that can be described as "single loop,"(see chapter 2). These are the organizations where there is a demarcation between those who form strategy and policy, and those who put the results of this exercise of executive power into practice. Setting the learning process on the building blocks of inclusivity, equality, unity, and individual and group development wears away distinctions based on departments, sections, tasks, roles, and rigid distinctions between managers and staff. It permits a breadth of contribution to the delivery of the service.

Learning and Work

Learning comes from an interaction with the environment of work. The basis of this process can be an individual's view of the working environment, or his or her interpretation of the organizational situation. Equally, it can arise from engagement with other people. It can be an intuitive process. This instinctive awareness of what, why, and how things are happening can be incremental and it can also come from trial and error. It has significant elements of problem solving and action learning in it. We should also encourage learning that makes use of maturity, and supports the application of knowledge and experience. Learning experiences are within us and all around us.

New Thinking

Learning should offer a break with the traditional way of looking at organizational issues. There are a number of theories that emphasize the need to question accepted wisdom and develop new perspectives on how we should manage ourselves in work. This should involve the development of thinking that explores fresh options and seeks alternative ways of doing things. Equally important are the individual skills that should form part of this new thinking: self-criticism, analysis, reflection, and the application of the results to situations and to problems.

Strategy, Structure, and Culture

Under these circumstances, learning affects the direction of the service and the quality of what is delivered to users. It changes the character of the organization and invigorates the culture. It changes communication, it alters the way in which power is used, and it creates different relationships. Rewards are viewed in a different way, and people behave differently, so that value systems are altered. The organizational ethos changes.

Anything as powerful as this needs to be part of the planning process at the highest level. If learning is strategic, then it should be a factor in the structures that deliver the services. A library structure that is based on a learning system can be flatter, loose coupled, and team-based. Processes —the way in which services are delivered—can be controlled from much closer to the point where they are used. That is, where the users are, and their interests can be met by managing in a participative way.

Case Study 4
CIRCLES AND HOLES

This case study is based on events that took place over a few years in the life of one teacher-training college. In a small way, it shows the application of creative thinking, and also of "thinking outside the box," (O'Keeffe, 1998). It shows how insights can sometimes be attained.

The Situation

A specialist teacher-training institution had a new library built in honour of its first principal. The college image was one of quality and style, with programs based on high standards through a largely liberal arts-

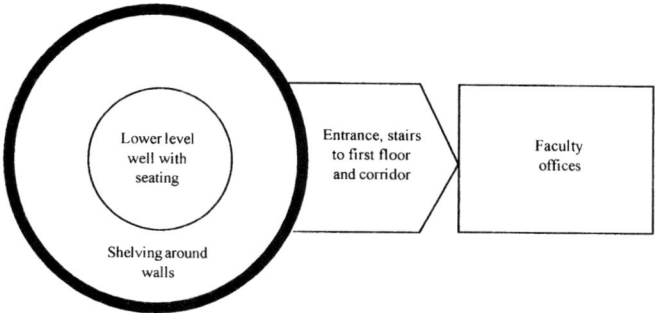

Figure 4.1 The Original Ground Floor Plan

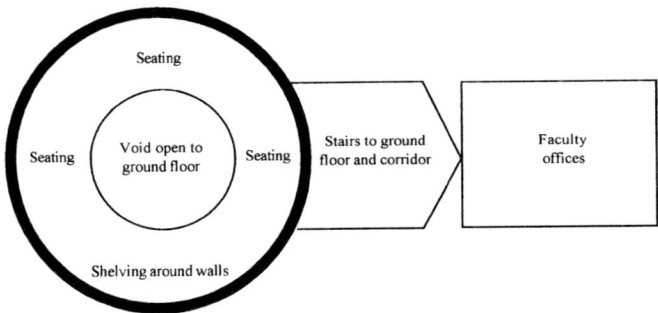

Figure 4.2 The Original First Floor Plan

based education. In the design of the new library building, the finer points of architectural aesthetics were of paramount importance. The completed building, on two stories in the shape of a circle, was externally attractive and won awards. It was a disaster as a library. Figure 4.1 and 4.2 show the floor plans.

The problems of the circular reading rooms are obvious—increased expense in obtaining shelving fitted to the walls and less storage space. All the library housekeeping routines and circulation services were on the ground floor. The open space in the middle of the first floor acted as a duct and transferred noise into the reading area above. The first floor was not a load-bearing structure. As the college expanded its student numbers, the library became increasingly inadequate.

The Solutions

Over the years, a number of solutions were attempted. The library occupied the faculty offices on the ground floor, allowing housekeeping and circulation to be transferred into this area. Space was therefore created in the ground floor reading room, and better study conditions were achieved by reducing the amount of disturbance in the reading area. This gave the layout shown in figure 4.3 on page 91. Soon, management was considering their next move. To create more space, their only option was to install shelving radiating outward from the ground floor well, like the spokes of a wheel. With study spaces between stacks, the area became crowded and

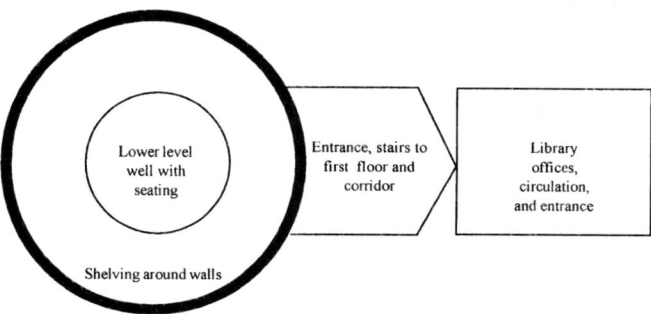

Figure 4.3 The Expansion Into the Faculty Office

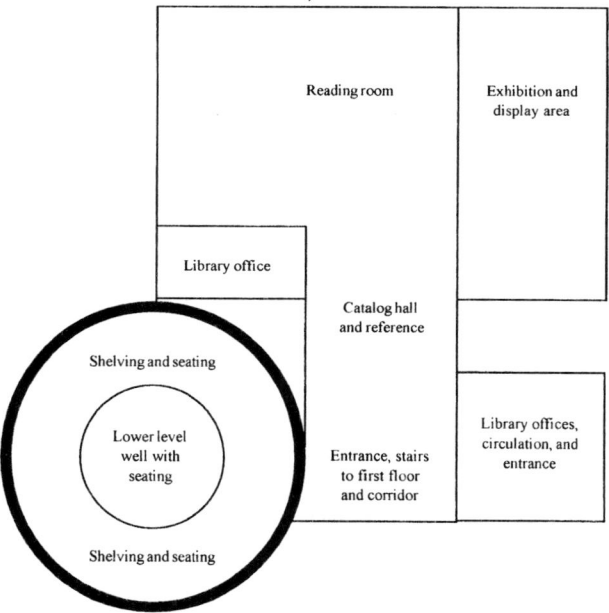

Figure 4.4 The Library Extension Mark One

cluttered, although the collections were now able to expand.

The next attack on the problem came with approval of funding for an extension, which is shown in figure 4.4 on page 91. But the piecemeal approach to development continued, and the earlier mistakes were repeated. There was obviously a failure of learning and an inability to understand either the problem or the kind of thinking that was needed to solve it. There were now resources available to provide a creative solution, but management had become locked into a way of thinking that they needed to unlearn. Their failure to do so led to a predictable compromise design.

It is relevant here to look at the process that led to this solution. It was a highly traditional piece of project management, in which strategy and policy were tightly controlled by senior management. Middle management became involved at a later stage, when implementation began, and at no stage was there any consideration of the views of the users or the people who would be working in the building. Ultimately, middle management faced the task of making it function.

Another problem was that the culture of the institution, based as it was on affirming the excellence of all things, meant that it was difficult to engage in a public debate about whether or not the extension to the building would actually meet the needs of the library. Library staff who had misgivings about the process, and the results, were reluctant to confront the prevailing orthodoxy. While some staff were willing to think the unthinkable, and privately opposed what was happening, there was an understandable unwillingness to go against the weight of opinion, that was that the extension met the library needs without damaging the aesthetics of the original building. So the scene was set for more serious problems in the future.

For several years this layout worked reasonably well, until the college found itself involved in a merger with three other local institutions in order to create a viable new university institution. As part of this it was considered necessary to upgrade library facilities and rationalize provision over what was now a four-campus operation.

When the library director began a preliminary review of the situation, he went back through the entire history of the building, by examining all the drawings and considering the whole process by which the changes had been introduced. He recognized that the net result achieved, by three attempts over a period of years, did not make the best use of the space or resources available, and did not make the layout intelligible to users. He also identified process failures. Finally, he produced a discussion document, which he placed before a meeting of all the library staff and user representatives. Following this, a working group was set up. There was a long process of consultation and communication, and a strong working alliance of staff and users saw the project through. Input came from all levels of the library, and the result of the redevelopment is shown in figures 4.5 and 4.6 (pages 93 and 94).

For the first time, the planners had been able to marry the functional needs of the library with the aesthetic considerations that were uppermost in the minds of the college management. As a result, they made the best use of the impossibly restrictive shape of the original circular building. In fact, they found a solution that was not inconsistent with the intention of the original architects, some twenty years earlier. Ironically, the final solution was acclaimed by the college when they eventually came to terms with what had been done.

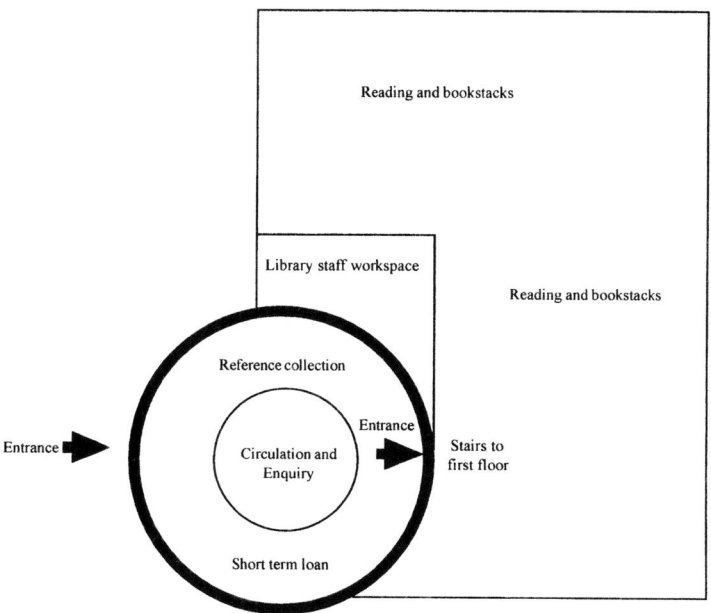

Figure 4.5 The Library Extension Mark Two: Ground Floor

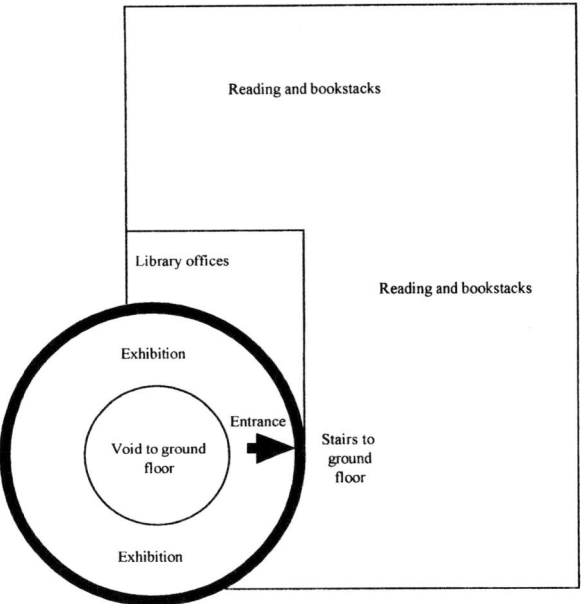

Figure 4.6 The Library Extension Mark Two: First Floor

This achievement may appear to be simplicity itself. In fact it represented the climax of a long, drawn out process that indicates, in a concrete way, the kind of thinking we need to develop. It also shows, in a simple fashion, the nature of workplace creativity.

Comment

The library director did a number of things that helped the creative process along. He first broadened the constituency of those involved in the problem-solving process. Ideas and inputs were taken from a broad range of staff and user opinion, and the final solution was crafted by a representative group that was inclusive, that constantly communicated, and took informed criticism from all directions. It was by no means a perfect example of team learning, but it was a beginning. Hirshberg (1998) insisted that creativity came from everywhere. This case study was an elementary lesson on what can come out of inclusivity.

Some learning theories were also demonstrated. Eventually, after a number of actions that turned out to be temporary palliatives, the director took an overall look at the situation. The scene was viewed as a whole, and then the problem become clear. Standing back, and considering the library building as an entity, enabled everything to be put in place. This was a move forward from the piecemeal solutions attempted before.

It led to some efficient problem solving. For the first time, the problem was properly analyzed, and the cause of the difficulty was pinpointed as the irregular nature of the library building. The next step was to break with the thinking that had led to temporary solutions, and in fact worsened the situation by increasing the irregularity of the physical layout. All of the efforts before the final one had attempted to work within the existing layout. They had resulted in the addition of small or irregular shaped rooms, and they had failed to make more appropriate use of the circular reading room. Once the real nature of the problem had been identified as the irregular shape, the solution also became clear: Turning the circular reading rooms, and the piecemeal extensions, into something as close as possible to a rectangle would create a functional library. The improved use of space would allow the circular reading rooms to be used for more appropriate purposes. Retaining part of the outside facade of the circular reading room maintained some of the aesthetic quality. This is the "double loop learning," that is advocated by Bateson (1972), Pearn, Roderick, and Mulrooney (1995), and many other writers: Breaking with convention, and thinking in different ways, led to what was an innovative solution in the context of the library. The shape of the building was regularized. The ground floor layout was duplicated on the first floor, and this completed the solution. It was much easier for users to exploit the collections; storage and display were more efficient; and the environment, which was less cluttered, and made of a few large open areas rather than a number of smaller rooms, was more conducive to study. The aesthetically attractive, but managerially unsound, circular reading rooms were turned into positive advantages. They were used for activities that could go on unhindered by the physical restrictions of the layout, and they also provided an attractive entrance to the library. On the first floor, they became effective exhibition areas comparatively unaffected by noise transmitted through the void in the center of the room. This was an imaginative solution, that would have found favor with Hirshberg (1998).

A learning cycle was also followed. The first stage in this was to consider the actual, concrete experience of using the library. This was a way into analyzing the problems in more detail than had been attempted previously. It was followed by detailed discussion, which led to some principles for the design of the new building. There was finally a further period of reflection and reconsideration before a design was agreed upon.

This was also group learning. For the first time, library staff from different levels worked together in a partnership. They learned from each other, and they learned from the cut and thrust of dealing with different opinions and personalities. Learning through social interaction was at work. Although it was only a small beginning, with a limited but very important project, it offered the participants the chance to alter their constructs through seeing several perspectives on the situation, and also through becoming involved with other people in a nonhierarchical environment. For some of them, their only involvement with each other before this would have been in a bureaucratic relationship.

There is one other interesting point about how this solution was achieved. When the director sat down and wrote his briefing paper, it contained the outline of a solution that had the appearance of an instinctive insight. In fact, it had arrived in stages, and through a trial and error process. What appeared to be a flash of insight was in fact incremental and based on a number of things that had happened over a period of time. It should also be remembered that the final piece in the jigsaw puzzle came through the interaction of a number of theories and ways of learning.

All of this took place in the working situation. All of the conditions for learning were found in the workplace. The case study emphasizes the importance of developing self-learning in the workplace. This is the main concern of the rest of part two.

Chapter 5

Thoughts on Self-Development

Some of the ideas on which this book is based are quite simple:

- Most learning in libraries is unseen, individual learning. It goes on under the surface. It is not susceptible to direct management influence.
- To make the maximum use of it, this learning has to be brought into the mainstream management of the library. There are management styles and organizational structures that make this easier. There are learning techniques, such as coaching, mentoring, and group learning, which strengthen and develop this individual learning.
- Libraries will in the future make more demands on the psychological, or mental, strengths of their staff. These could be as important as technical competence or acquiring more skills. Organizations will require from their staff a willingness to accept, and become involved in, change. This will call for flexible attitudes, and an acceptance that taking more responsibility at all levels in the organization is not a theoretical preoccupation, but an essential practicality.
- Libraries will be managed and operated by staff who need a strong sense of self-worth. They will be aware that their skills and attitudes make the difference in service standards. The approach to self-development will decide how far services improve.

Most writers who deal with the challenges of managing at the start of the third millennium argue that a primary requirement of all organizations will be the provision of education for everybody, at all levels, and without exception or hindrance. Libraries are as far away from this ideal as any other sector, but it is a worthy aim. If it is to be achieved, it will only be through the encouragement of self-development, and the underlying feelings of self-esteem and self-worth. The techniques and tactics advocated in the rest of this book make a contribution to creating this. They do so by "releasing the potential of others," by "taking the extra step," and empowering others—giving responsibility for learning to the learners (Atkinson, 2000). Much of it has also to do with how each individual staff member approaches the process of self-development.

A Definition of Self-Development

The standard definition of self-development is quoted in many training handbooks. Bailey (2001) offers it as a "learning or development activity in which learners themselves take the primary responsibility for choosing what, when and how to learn." Conventionally viewed as part of an organization's formal development program, many trainers and human resource professionals will include self-development as part of a wide portfolio of activities. There is an assumption that learners will:

- Make decisions concerning their professional and personal growth
- Plan their career development
- Be able to take a disciplined approach to self-learning
- Acquire the skills of self-learning and self-development

From the organizational point of view, there will be a requirement to:

- Provide support for the decisions learners will have to make
- Offer appropriate learning experiences based on, for example
  - Coaching
  - Mentoring
  - Shadowing, temporary attachments, job rotation
  - Group learning
- Ensure that the skills of learning to learn are imbued in learners
- Provide resource support in the form of
  - Resource collections
  - Self-learning materials
  - Where appropriate, distance learning schemes

- Increasingly, e-learning experiences
- Links with the learning subsystem of the organization

It is obvious that self-development has all of these formal elements within it. It is also obvious that it has to be managed, channeled, and supported in ways that make it efficient for the learner and the organization. Yet we need to add some new elements to the definition in order to make it fully understandable, and relevant, in modern libraries.

Self-Development and Self-Esteem

Self-development is more than making rational decisions about career development and turning them into learning plans that will ensure the achievement of lifetime objectives. At a number of points in this book, reference has been made to the fact that most learning takes place under the surface of organizations. Learning is not dependent on the tip of the iceberg represented by training events, but it is something that is embedded in the day-to-day work of staff at all levels. Learning of this kind begins with an internal engagement. Long before we get to planning a logical course of professional development, self-development is an attitude of mind that learners need if they are to take part in any form of development at all. Branden (1998) summarized this as the ability to think, to learn, and to make decisions with confidence. Increasingly, in libraries we will find ourselves working in situations where we do not have the skills and knowledge we need. One of the difficulties we face in dealing with many situations today is that there is little in our previous experience of managing that illuminates some of the problems we face, particularly those to do with technological change. Self-development is the creation of a mind-set that gives us the confidence to work with incomplete knowledge and to apply creative thinking in new situations. Branden (1998), called this the acquisition of self-esteem. So, long before we think about knowledge and skills acquisition, or attitude changes, there is an internal process that has to do with arriving at a realistic assessment of individual strengths and weaknesses, of the threats and opportunities of the working situation, and of the wider organization.

We can complete the definition we started on the previous page. Self-development, as well as taking to ourselves the responsibility for our own learning and all that entails should be a process that gives us the mental strength to deal with new and unfamiliar work situations. It should help us to propose confidently, and implement, novel courses of action. It depends on building our own self-esteem, and using this as the starting point for a process of personal and professional growth. It is naturally a technique that applies to work-based learning, and it is as much to do with how to deal with other people in work situations as anything else. The reason for this is the obvious one: our own self-concept and self-esteem colors the way we handle other people. Self-esteem is also affected by the way *they* handle *us*. Self-development involves a critical process of looking within and seeking what we can legitimately ask of ourselves before we begin to ask things of others. Managers, take heed.

The Origins of Self-Development

Erik Erikson: Psychosocial Development

Much of Erikson's work (1963, 1968) is concerned with the development of children, but he also identified some general principles that apply to adult learning. The first of these is that the potential for personal growth does not diminish. This is of course the foundation of some of the adult learning theories explored in chapter 4. Second, Erikson argued that the periods of young and middle adulthood are those in which psychological isolation and self-absorption can be replaced, if development takes place, by a willingness to interact with others and to consider bigger issues. This development depends on the provision of positive learning experiences. The argument underlines the obvious: The key targets for self-development in libraries are new entrants and younger staff.

Humanism and Carl Rogers

The humanists believed that there is a universal potential for development. They considered everyone to be able to:

- Manage their own self-development
- Set objectives
- Make decisions
- Act on their decisions

For the humanists, the success of individual development depends on:

- Honestly analyzing our own views of ourselves
- Honestly analyzing our own views of the workplace

- Turning these views into positive ones
- Working with others as part of the development process

Rogers further added that once an appropriate learning environment is provided, the drive for self-improvement is innate in everybody. He also argued that the vital self-actualization (how individuals view themselves) is a perception that may not fit with reality. If so, altering it is a vital step. Overall, Rogers (1969, 1983) put great weight on interactions with others, suggesting that everyone involved in this learning process would grow.

A. H. Maslow and Self-Esteem

Maslow's main conclusion on self-development was similar to that of Rogers: He saw the process as one of natural growth within a positive environment. Self-esteem was one of his higher-order needs, and ultimately this comes partly from self-actualization. It is a product of "self-confidence, worth, strength, capability and adequacy." (McInerney and McInerney, 1998).

These terms describe an individual's ability to cope with work situations and with other people in the workplace. Self-esteem influences:

- How well a job gets done
- The quality of social and professional interaction
- Whether or not an individual's potential is realized

Our own feelings about ourselves will control how well we work with, and manage, other people. In modern library services, it would seem that one of the main reasons for self-development is to build self-esteem in a situation where there may be less need for specific professional skills, and more need for verbal and social skills, together with the ability to work with complex and advanced technology in increasingly complex organizations.

The Process of Self-Development

We have tried to establish that self-development begins with changing the internal views held by an individual. Some writers have called this "getting rid of assumptions." Assumptions will be held about an individual's own ability, how he or she is seen by others and by management, and in what kind of organization he or she is working. The first stage in self-development is to face these views.

Confront Your Own Feelings

It may be quite unusual for individuals to have a balanced view of their own worth. Most people will either undersell, or oversell, themselves. The beginning of the process of self-development is a ruthless examination of where an individual stands. If the library is involved in exercises such as Training Needs Analyses, or Staff Development and Appraisal Schemes, then there will be formal opportunities for self-evaluation. Whether it is done in this way or not, there has to be an initial process of reasoned, and properly critical, analysis of strengths and weaknesses. A cold-blooded honesty about present performance is the only real basis for moving forward. Sometimes you will be uncovering, if you are truthful, a discordance between what you believe in and what you say on the one hand, and what you do on the other. This gap could be widened because of organizational attitudes or by your own weaknesses. Being realistic will certainly lead to an acknowledgment that some of the skills and techniques you use sometimes fall short. Looking at your successes and failures can illuminate tendencies to err on the side of caution, or to overreach and be too confident in one's own ability.

The procedure should then be extended to cover other people's perceptions of how well you are performing as an individual. Again, there should be input and feedback from a number of different sources. For example, 360° appraisal, which involves input and feedback on performance from peers, subordinates, managers, and clients, is one way of finding out how others see you. Taking on board other people's perceptions may well be the hardest part of the exercise.

The exercise is then taken into the final stage, where there has to be an analysis of how the organization feels about you. There is evidence to be gathered from many sources, and getting a feel for this is comparatively easy. There will be any number of indicators, such as comparative salary levels, the level of resource provision compared with the responsibilities to be discharged, the degree of involvement in decision making, the weight attached to your professional opinion, and the breadth of the contribution you are allowed to make to the organization as a whole.

Decide What Is Important

This exercise is about development. You now have a realistic assessment of where you are at the present time. The next step is to consider where you want to go, professionally and personally. Hopefully, you will have changed your perception of your self-worth. You will have revised your evaluation of strengths and weaknesses, sometimes upward, sometimes down. You will have a better grasp of how you are seen by the people with whom you work. There will be a disparity between where you are now and where you want to be. This disparity can only be made up in one way, and that is through learning.

Taking Action

Peter Senge (1990) makes the crucial point, once again, that self-development, or what he calls "personal mastery," is impossible in bureaucracies. A flourishing learning system in libraries depends on the kind of structural and managerial changes referred to earlier in the book. This is the supportive environment written about by Erikson and Rogers. If it is not there, self-development will not take place. With it, it is possible to offer positive learning experiences in an environment where learners will not feel threatened. Learning will be possible because there are structures that allow learners to take charge of their learning. They can set their own targets, based on the realization of the first part of the self-development

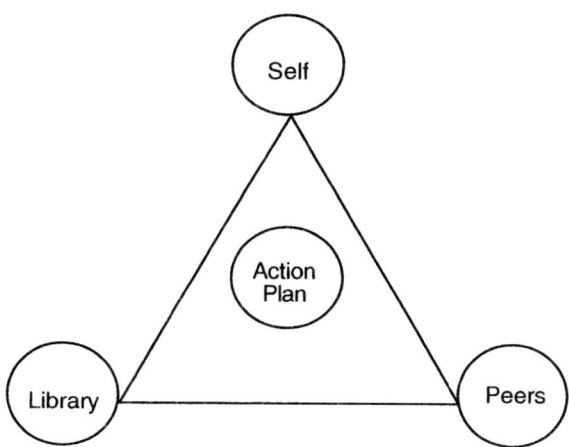

process. They can decide on their own preferred learning experiences, and
Figure 5.1 Preparing for Self-Development

they can be further helped by the use of group learning techniques, by coaching, and by mentoring. As figure 5.1 indicates, in a way, preparing for self-development is a process of clearing the ground by a simple exercise in triangulation. There is self-perception, peer perception, and organizational perception. There are times when the hardest difference to deal with is that between self-perception and organizational perception. There is also a difference between the intrinsic skills and abilities of the individual, and the skills and abilities of the same individual reflected in performance as a professional librarian or as a manager. This is usually because individuals will inevitably be hedged around by organizational imperatives or restrictions, and it is why so much emphasis is placed on establishing an environment that positively encourages learning. This helps to remove some of the impediments, structural and cultural, that I would suggest most organizations place in the way of improved performance.

Either way, the three legs of the triangle in figure 5.1 buttress an action plan, which will be based on learning. The most important part of this learning will come from work experiences, which are examined in the next chapter.

Chapter 6

Self-Development at Work

We have so far explored a number of arguments relating to the nature of learning in modern library services. We have also looked at the way in which structures, management styles, technology, and our knowledge of how people learn should influence our approach, as well as the kind of training that is ultimately delivered to library staff. In particular, it is clear that training is influenced by:

- The learning environment
- The complexity of tasks
- The different ways in which different individuals learn
- The need for forms of multiskilling allied to job enlargement and job enrichment
- The scope to develop and exercise problem-solving skills
- The ability to apply experience
- The capacity to learn from new experiences
- Learning from others

It is also true that the balance of most training programs is tilted toward an approach driven by the organization, and relies on learning events such as workshops and seminars, attendance at conferences, and other formal situations. By contrast, we are aware that in all library operations there is a process of informal learning taking place. This is based on the interrelated ideas of self-development and of learning from experience. This force is powerful, effective, and dangerous if it goes awry. It is often seen at its most obvious in training for routine tasks and in some aspects of the training of new entrants, but is apparent also in the use of procedures such as cascading techniques. Novel developments or ideas are introduced into organizations by staff who have already been formally trained, and who then transfer their learning to others. This has elements of self-learning and learning from experience within it, and embedding this approach in the learning system of the organization is a major task.

Learning from Work

Terms like "work-based learning," "informal learning," or "on-the-job learning," are often thrown into discussions about training with only a hazy idea of what is actually involved. Let us start with some indication of what learning from work means. In the context of this book, it is the learning of skills, changes in behavior, the development of attitudes, or the acquisition of knowledge through working situations. These situations, or experiences, are approached in a systematic way, and are linked with other learning or training experiences. The results are evident in the workplace, and become part of the organization's information base. The activities can be individual, or learning can occur in groups. Key roles can be played by peers, managers, or trainers, or the process can be controlled by the individual at the center of it.

This is very much more than learning the mechanics of a standardized or routine task from sitting alongside a more experienced colleague. The process is one of the places where the formal and informal systems of the library should meet—in an activity which pervades the whole organization. It can be seen in the actions of the director who knows how to manipulate personnel and financial regulations in the interests of the service. It is evident in the attitude of the technician who modifies bureaucratic controls to provide a better service to users. Sometimes, it is revealed at its constructive best by staff who devise simpler and better ways of operating routines. On the other hand, on-the-job learning, or whatever else it is called, can become a negative force. Most managers will have seen situations where work practices have been distorted to frustrate procedures that are already in place. They will have dealt with misguided initiatives that led to improper modifications of procedure.

Although more common on production lines, in libraries also this negative influence of uncontrolled on-the-job learning is sometimes seen in the shape of unbridled enthusiasm, which can result in the introduction of variations that might not be acceptable, and that might adversely affect the organization. This kind of learning can therefore exert both a positive and a malign influence on training.

The Contribution of Learning from Work to Training

Learning from work obviously takes place everywhere in all organizations. It is going to happen whether management likes it or not. It might not have much to do with staff who have a recognized training function. It will, at least in part, be less amenable to overt control. Given these characteristics, it is a matter of identifying how it takes place, creating the conditions in which it can have a positive effect, and integrating it with other learning initiatives. This effort is not helped by the fact that learning from work operates on a number of distinct levels. It can be direct, where the activity and the learner are supported by a number of regulated inputs from people working within an organizational staff development program. This is formal and trainer-driven. On another level it can be informal, on-the-job training, which involves peers, while it can also occur as part of the dynamics of group or team learning. Informal learning experiences are usually learner-driven, and will require the implanting of discipline, habits, skills, and the nurturing of self-learning. This is self-development based on the working situation, and should be followed as a consciously acquired technique. Learning from work must therefore be both controlled and developed.

Ashton and Maguire (1986) found that in a sample of young adults, over a range of skill levels right up to professional, managerial, or technical, major importance was attached to on-the-job training, except for the most unskilled level of worker. The techniques used were:

- Observation
- Receiving help while carrying out tasks
- Reading prepared documentation
- Brief lectures
- Visits to other relevant departments
- Learning through active participation

Work-based training in the higher-order skills was more likely to be delivered through a wider range of techniques than for the lower-order skills, and the most important facilitators or trainers were first line supervisors and colleagues. Again, it was in the higher-order skills that the influence of designated trainers was more likely to be seen. These findings have consequences for everybody concerned with organizational learning.

Learning from work has to be part of the conscious training approach of the library. It involves trainers as facilitators, coaches, or mentors, and it includes formal learning experiences. It is harder to measure the effect of this kind of learning, but it can be seen in the less tangible organizational effect of the transfer and sharing of the learning acquired. What happens under the surface of the library is the issue that should command the attention of managers and trainers first: It becomes a matter of controlling the negative effects of the informal learning that goes on, while accentuating the positive ones.

"Sitting Next to Nellie"

Partridge (1986) traces the origin and use of this famous phrase. I know that during what is now, unfortunately, over thirty five years in the business, I have heard the expression throughout that time in many different libraries on three different continents. I have not often heard it used in a pejorative sense, so I would hazard the guess that, if it has not been the only way in which learning from work occurred in libraries, then traditionally it has been the most widespread, the most favored, and the least analyzed. Known in mainstream educational theory as modeling, as a technique it presents a few problems for library trainers.

Modeling is what it says it is. Learners will imitate Nellie's actions and mimic her beliefs and attitudes. Within this process, there is first an inherent conservatism, as Nellie passes on no more than she herself knows.

The early chapters of this book tried to convey the sense of the rich backdrop of complexity and differentiation, which can be found in modern information services. This was linked to a view of learning as an elaborate process, influenced by a number of variables, including organizational and individual characteristics. If we are going to say that even the prosaic elements of running libraries can best be learned simply by picking up Nellie's habits, then we are needlessly removing from our learning activities some of the creativity and inventiveness demanded by today's libraries and their staff. We are also closing our minds to what we know about the multifaceted and intricate nature of learning, even for routine or repetitive tasks.

The "sitting next to Nellie" approach entails one other difficulty: the nature of what it is that we are actually modeling. As a role model, and as an operator at any level of the library, Nellie might leave something to be desired. Unless we can actually see what she is doing, then her influence might not always be a positive one, and could be damaging.

Learning from work, sometimes represented by Nellie on a good day and at her best, has an important part to play in library training. To maximize this, three things are required. The learning process has to be managed. It has to be theoretically valid, its operation visible, and its results assessable. Of equal importance, the individual approach of the learner must be based on an attitude, and a process, that will develop learning and problem-solving skills. Finally, what is learned must be shared.

Managing Learning from Work

When attempting to handle the process and consequences of informal learning, whether self-learning or from peers, there are two dilemmas. The organizational characteristics most appropriate for controlling what is learned are found in bureaucracies. The learning theories directed at control come from behaviorism and, at the extreme, with conditioning. These options should now be ruled out by the demands of our organizational environments, both internal and external. The expectations of our users, and the skills and abilities of our staff, also dictate a more flexible approach. If we remove the reliance on the bureaucracy and the hierarchy to control what people do in organizations, we need to find something else to do the job. We want to foster learning while ensuring the integrity of the informal processes of learning from peers and self-learning. In short, without the bureaucracy, we have a problem in controlling what goes on. There is no rule book that can be applied to informal learning. but we are fortunate that many of the organizational features championed in these pages are capable of being used to make the process more visible, and to promote accountability on the part of staff who are involved in it. The difficulty for managers is that we have to rely on processes that are much less tangible than the old ways of controlling what people learned.

In traditional organizations, control over the learning process can be exercised in a number of different ways:

- By autocratic managerial styles
- Through the bureaucracy

- By deploying trainer-centered methods
- Through the use of organizational structures that confine
- Through restrictive job design
- Through a negative, or at best neutral, learning culture

Most of these options are not open to trainers and managers operating in the kinds of organizations held up as examples of good practice in this book. The environment that we are trying to create will call for a much less didactic and much more learner-centered approach. The organizations are based on loose structures that support broad learning experiences, within an open and inclusive culture. Under these circumstances, ensuring the standards, and the appropriateness, of learning from work will depend on less prominent skills. We can control work-based learning by: encouraging self-management, using organizational culture, and linking the process to formal training structures. This means:

- Using the influence of role models
- Encouraging self-management of learning
- Using the influence of teams
- Using the influence of key people
- Tying the learning into the formal processes

The results give a greater degree of visibility to the informal learning that is going on and make it more accountable. The control may not be perfect for some managers, but it does give some degree of reassurance and certainty, in what is a crucial, but sometimes impenetrable, part of organizational learning.

Creating Role Models

This is done by building an environment in which self-directed individuals can take a lead. They can capitalize on the empowerment that comes from organizational flexibility, strengthen their own learning base, and demonstrate the virtues of self-development to others. They act as role models with a significant, if subtle, controlling function over behavior, and over the informal learning process.

Developing Self-Managing Learners

Related to the idea of using role models, this is part of the empowerment that has to take place if learning organizations are to be created. Kohn and Slomczynski (1990) work through the argument that self-direction—the ability, and the right, of workers to share the control of their own activities—is linked to "intellectual flexibility" and to general psychological well-being. It affects people's values and the way they think. Self-direction encourages a degree of nonconformity, which is needed for double loop learning (see chapter 1), but also sharpens awareness of the organizational environment and organizational needs. In other words it gives people a structure for their learning processes. It sets objectives, and it guides, without relying on the safeguards of formal controls. It will use internal mechanisms instead. It is akin to controlling the organization through cultural means rather than rule books.

To work in this way, the learning process has to be supported by the appropriate structure and managerial behavior. Self-direction thrives on:

- A reduction in the routine element in jobs
- Complexity and variety of work
- Minimal formal supervision

For the individual staff member, these conditions are significant. They depend on the existence of learning organizations with:

- Flexible structures, which support empowerment and offer wide responsibilities and rights
- Structures that allow boundaries to be crossed between parts of the organization and between jobs within specific areas
- Structures that allow job enlargement and job enrichment
- Flexible management
- Teams

The impact is considerable. The conditions described help to:

- Strengthen the individual's sense of self-worth
- Set high individual standards of work and conduct
- Increase awareness of the value of the job being done
- Influence the standards of others

Self-direction is therefore a crucial element in the make-up of role models. If it is encouraged, it not only gives workers a sense of direction in their learning, it also creates the positive role models that improve the quality of learning from work.

Team and Group Dynamics

Using self-direction as a means of self-control in the learning process, and controlling behavior through the development of responsibility, awareness, and intellectual flexibility in staff is fine, but alone it is insufficient. Individuals can moderate their own activities and behaviors, but the theory tells us there is also a further benefit to be gained from the positive influence of the group. Teams are another way of managing learning from work. Chapter 9 investigates, in more detail, the issue of how individuals belonging to groups or teams interact with each other, and how team learning processes actually work. It is sufficient here to make two points. The first is that individuals interacting can create norms and set standards, They can positively influence each other, so that the informal learning takes place in ways that meet both individual and organizational needs. The second point is that the internal workings of the team as a learning organism will also contribute to the effectiveness and quality of informal and formal learning (see chapter 9).

Using Key People: Supervisors, Line Managers, and Trainers

It is apparent from a number of studies, including Ashton and Maguire (1986), that the single most important figure in the informal learning process, apart from the learner, is the immediate supervisor. More of the informal, or self-directed, learning experiences come from the interaction between the learner and the line manager, team leader, or supervisor than from any other source. The case is therefore made for training the key people in these positions as trainers. This will give them the knowledge, skills, and attitudes to monitor, evaluate, and exercise some control over the direction and quality of the informal learning.

One of the salient features of the learning organization, considered in chapters 2, 3, and 4, was a change in behavior. This could be described as demanding:

- Staff who accept the need for continuous improvement
- Staff who embrace change
- Staff who wish to share decision making and are ready to take responsibility
- Managers who embrace the idea of learning as a comprehensive activity that is central to organizational success
- Managers who accept that they do not possess monopolies on knowledge or experience
- Managers who believe in teams

- Managers who empower
- Managers who encourage questioning

In total, it means having managers who are able to shift their behavior along the manager–coach continuum described in chapter 7, so that they work through developing a shared vision and embodying this vision in their own behavior. They support informal learning through leadership, facilitating learning, and being learners themselves. Managers are, therefore, visibly committed to a learning partnership and to a corresponding cultural change. Again, they also become role models who exercise influence over learning and embody a powerful learning culture.

Locking into the Formal Learning Process

It was said at the beginning of this chapter that learning from work brought together the formal and informal systems of the library. Control of the process can also be maintained through the connection between the informal learning that goes on everywhere and the mechanisms used to assess needs, as well as to monitor and evaluate learning at the organizational level. Information can come through the activities of learning groups, action learning sets, the staff development and appraisal scheme, the training needs analysis, team leader meetings, focus groups, user surveys, and through the information system, which is the memory of the learning organization proposed in chapter 2. Here will be found the records of problem-solving exercises, FAQs (frequently asked questions), successful and unsuccessful projects, innovative developments, and a range of documents, procedures, manuals, and informal hints and tips that help every library run properly. They all shed some light on the quality of informal learning, and on what is actually happening in the library.

Case Study 5
IMPROVING THE ROUTINES

The Situation

A number of years ago, Susannah, a young librarian in a new post as a library director, was faced with a dilemma. During her first term at a large teacher training establishment, she became aware that the basic library routines, particularly those that had to do with the circulation system, were not working properly. Library staff were dealing with a constant stream of complaints from users, who were being fined for overdue books that had already been returned. In addition, in those pre-automation days, a considerable amount of time was spent searching through the manual issue system to find the records of books borrowed. The system was based on slips of paper filled in by borrowers, and filed alphabetically in two sequences under author and borrower names. In any event this was time consuming, but it was doubly so because of the inaccurate filing.

The working conditions at the circulation desk were unsatisfactory. The area was physically cramped. While two members of staff dealt with the issue and return of books, a third was engaged in permanently checking the alphabetical sequences to rectify misfiling. This was known as "reading the issue," and was a shared responsibility of all staff. The physical difficulty was exacerbated by the fact that a large amount of floor space was taken up by an extensive and very heavily used short-term loan collection, with a separate issue record. This in itself was complicated by the fact that the material in this collection was only available by advance reservation, for periods ranging from two to twenty-four hours. There were two entrances to the library, both of which led directly to the circulation desk from different directions, which made a sensible queuing system impossible to sustain. The tea- and coffee-making facilities for the entire library staff, including an unsightly sink, were housed in one corner behind the desk, so this area was subjected to heavy staff traffic at break times. The area was generally untidy, with book processing and repair also taking place, as well as interlibrary loan requests being received, returned, and issued. Documentation and other items were regularly mislaid.

Susannah's predecessor had run the library in an autocratic way that brooked no disagreement. The senior assistant librarian responsible for the circulation desk was bureaucratic. Other than laying down rules, regulations and rotas, and dealing with the gross errors that occurred, he had no real involvement in the operation. He based himself in an office that was some distance away from the action at the desk, and also found it difficult to engage with his colleagues. There were no established staff development mechanisms that could be used.

The Problem

Susannah felt that the entire problem stemmed from the difficulty the library staff had in taking pride in their work, the fact that their line manager did not seem to be interested in what they were doing, and the poor working conditions, which led them to feel that they were generally undervalued. She also understood that the operation of the circulation system was too cumbersome, and that the burden of routine work on the circulation staff was excessive.

The group of people working at the circulation desk were quite tightly knit, and there was one strong personality who stood out amongst them. They mixed socially, and it was quite clear that Caroline, the strong personality, was an opinion former and a leader.

The Solution

Susannah's first task was to reduce the amount of routine in the circulation system to manageable proportions. In this she was lucky. Shortly before she took up her post, the institution had approved funding for the installation of a new automated library management system. If this option had not been available, Susannah would have introduced a more effective and economical paper-based system. Instead, she was able to arrange for the circulation staff to attend demonstrations of the automated systems under consideration, and their reactions and views were fed into the discussions of the small team of staff responsible for making the decision. At the same time, discussions were opened with the teaching departments, with a view to reducing the size of the short-term loan collections. The collections themselves became open access, and were relocated with the agreement of the teaching departments. In this process, Susannah was supported by two other members of the circulation desk staff. This group reported back to their colleagues. An interlibrary loans office was set up adjacent to the circulation desk, and book processing and repair were transferred to the acquisitions unit.

Simultaneously, Susannah redeployed Sheila, a senior assistant librarian, who took over supervisory responsibility for the circulation desk. This was a woman with considerable experience, adept at relations with users and library colleagues, and robust enough to counterbalance the presence and grip of the somewhat dominant Caroline, whose influence Susannah felt was not always positive.

Working with Sheila, the library director began to create an environment that would support all forms of team learning. Job descriptions were redrawn, and individuals were given responsibility for the oversight of specific areas within the circulation system. Rosters and duties were reorganized to allow people the opportunity to become involved in more varied work, and a learning group was set up for all the staff in the section. In its early stages, this group was managed by Susannah, but the agenda was both staff and management driven. It might be expected that this would change over time, or that the group could be replaced or supplemented by other things. Among the first issues to be explored were those of self-development and learning from experience. The learning group undertook a number of pieces of work in order to identify attitudes to these issues and to consider ways in which the concepts could be positively embraced. Formal staff development procedures were also introduced at the behest of this group.

Susannah established a process by which specific areas of activity were regularly reviewed with the group. Through this, she was able to identify weaknesses and features that could be improved, and, with the group, consider a range of possible measures they could implement themselves. Sheila began to attend a course on training skills, particularly coaching and learning from experience, and two other staff members began to attend one-day release courses. A staff library was also established.

The tea- and coffee-making facilities were disposed of, and all library staff began to use the college common room.

Comment

Susannah had demonstrated an immaculate approach to creating the conditions in which self-direction could be fostered. Putting a senior staff member into the situation as supervisor made it clear that management considered the area to be significant, as did the involvement of the group in the choice of the management system, as well as the discussions with the teaching staff about the management of the short-term loan collection. Increased responsibility stemmed from the implementation of empowerment for the group and from giving individuals responsibility for organizing specific areas of the work. This also introduced a degree of variety and complexity into hitherto straightforward situations. There were two other benefits. Susannah had an opportunity to show the staff that change could be a positive learning experience. They, in turn, realized that their burgeoning sense of self-worth would be matched by management's view of what they were capable of and what they could contribute in the future.

As far as possible, the routinization of jobs was restricted. The establishment of the learning group was another aid to self-direction, while Susannah's own involvement in it allowed management oversight. This could change as the group moved toward maturity.

Some aspects of Susannah's own behavior deserve comment. The practice of critically and constructively reviewing specific areas of work was beginning to model the behavior of the coach rather than the manager—a change she wished to institutionalize and a change which is central to self-direction. She was also introducing the concept, and process, of self-improvement and asserting its centrality to the operation of the library.

Susannah's work on attitude change was also good. She uncovered ignorance and indifference as far as self-development was concerned. This was not surprising, in view of the passive approach to work that the previous management had inculcated, but she needed to create a shift in opinion. She began to do this through formal sessions aimed at exploring and altering attitudes, through small group and one-to-one sessions on learning from experience, and by the use of a moderate degree of compulsion, when one or two hand-picked individuals were required to apply the techniques to a specific activity and report back to the entire group. Most important of all, she engaged herself in the process. She was aware that she had deliberately created a challenge through the moves toward empowerment and self-direction. She was able to show both her method, and the results, to the group, and this was instrumental in convincing them of the value of the approach. It also began to bind everyone together.

Finally, these activities were linked with the formal learning activities through the learning group and attendance at formal courses. The solutions to the problems at the circulation desk, where they were relevant, and especially the emphasis on the techniques of self-learning, became the property of the whole library.

This book advocates a holistic view of training, depending on a whole-library approach to organization development and cultural change. All this depends on how learning is tackled by individuals. The first part of this chapter looked at how learning from work takes place in all forms of organizations, and suggested that it can be less tangible and less tractable than other forms of training. To benefit fully from it, learning from work needs to be inculcated as self-development in the more precise sense of deliberately and methodically learning from experience.

# Systematic Learning from Experience

Self-direction is a key factor in organizational life. This should apply to an individual's learning environment as much as to any other life aspect. Sometimes called "self-directedness" (see also chapter 5), the idea that individuals can take control of their learning is central to self-development and to any form of learning from experience. In our everyday working situations, we have around us much of the learning material we need. This offers a base for constructing a scheme that will expand to embrace more formal and universal training theories, techniques, and events. It is also an approach that, to an extent, can operate independently of organizational structures, management styles, funding, and trainers. This is a good place to start training.

For proponents of self-development and learning from experience, the theoretical basis is found in a number of the more modern theories about how people learn as individuals. The vital ones are reprised below.

Theories of Learning from Experience

Basing learning on experience is a repeated motif in mid- to late-twentieth century learning theories. For example, Kolb (1985) in general assumed that learning began with a concrete experience, while others allow that things could begin with an abstract idea. The common view is that this beginning, concrete or abstract, is the first step in a cycle that involves analysis, self-criticism, exploration, evaluation, and behavioral change.

The Cycle of Learning

One of the difficulties in using the idea of self-development through learning from experience is the view that the process is instinctive and natural. There is no doubt that events, projects, and relationships, in everyone's working lives, produce lessons that are remembered the next time a similar situation arises. In that sense alone it is true to say that learning from experience is instinctive. But there is considerably more to it than that, and Honey (1993) goes some way to dispelling the myth and setting out a blueprint for successful self-development. No experience becomes effective learning until it is analyzed and reflected on. Equally important, it must be used as the basis for modifying behavior and for identifying lessons. These must then be put into practice, communicated to others, and transferred into the learning system of the organization.

Learning theories offer some help in making this point. The idea of the learning cycle, as an example, assists in imposing a pattern on learning from experience, and ensures that the sequence described above actually occurs in a way that helps the learner make sense of it.

There is a clear fit between the process outlined in figure 6.1 (page 123) and the work of Kolb (1985) and Vygotsky (1978), which stressed the value of experiential learning and the special gifts that mature adult learners bring to the learning process. Self-development and learning from experience, are, therefore, bolstered by the theories of andragogy and symbolic interactionism. Knowles (1984) isolated the main skills of andragogy as:

- The application of problem-solving techniques
- The use of experience as a learning tool
- The motivational force of the desire to improve

This is part of the "self-directedness" that colors learning from experience and self-development.

Symbolic interactionism approaches the issue from a more theoretical point of view, but offers us an additional perspective on "self-directedness." It proposes that self-esteem and self-perception must be part of the makeup of the learner. If learning from experience is to succeed, then this element of self-perception has to be present in the analysis of the learning experience, and it has to be ruthlessly honest, particularly in learning from mistakes. Self-esteem is part of a desire to improve and to extend horizons in a way that is not so easily achieved by other forms of training and development.

The Significance of Learning from Experience

Learning from experience is the cornerstone of personal development. Its advantages are:

- It is based on the raw material of the working situation, as seen in both concrete and abstract experiences.
- It is controlled by the learner.
- It invites the application of a range of learning techniques, including the use of experience, problem solving, learning from peers, and

in some circumstances group learning, as well as the use, by learner and trainer, of a range of practical tools that help tailor the learning experience to meet individual needs.
- Taking responsibility for learning supports empowerment.
- It opens the way for continuous improvement.
- It strengthens skills that can be applied in other contexts, particularly analysis, objectivity, and planning.
- It develops the whole person: Attitudes and emotions can be controlled and modified.
- It encourages self-reliance and improves self-esteem.
- It teaches learning from success, an exercise that is often neglected as a source of development.

The Process

There are a number of models of the process in the literature. Figure 6.1 (page 123) adds another element to the one proposed by Peter Honey (1993), which forms the basis of the ideas depicted. The stages of the model are discussed below.

Internalize

The initial step is *not* to begin by considering workplace experiences. There is first an internal process to be completed, during which the learner should examine his or her own attitudes to the ideas of self-development and learning from experience. We have already considered this first obstacle, which is the view that people come to learning from experience assuming that it happens naturally and does not need to be subjected to any process of analysis. This is true only to a very limited extent. This attitude breeds negativity on the part of the potential learner, as Susannah discovered in case study 5. So the learner's first task is to embark upon the self-analysis, which nourishes self-esteem and self-directedness. The attitude to be cultivated is one that accepts that self-development demands an honest recognition of the need to improve. This is a natural follow-on to the process of clearing the ground described in the previous chapter, but it goes a little further than honest self-analysis. It asserts the centrality of learning, and it acknowledges the fact that everyday working events are the stuff of learning. It is also based on an acceptance that learning of this type needs to be approached as a systematic and deliberate series of actions. As case study 5 demonstrated, the opening up of minds in this preliminary stage requires the intervention of the trainer.

Experience

Out of the miasma of workplace activities, which ones are the crucial learning episodes? The short answer is "all of them." They could be:

- The handling of meetings or negotiations
- Project management
- Change management
- Recruitment interviews
- Personnel matters
- Difficult information queries or other transactions with users
- Professional issues
- Routine modifications
- Both successes and failures

In all of this, it is possible to do more than react to events as they occur. With a methodical approach, the learner should also *seek out* new and different experiences. The purpose of empowerment and flexible structures, in this context, is partly to create opportunities that allow experience to be broadened. Team structures are also obvious places where it is possible to engage with more and different responsibilities, as well as new perspectives, which bring the promise of new experiences again.

Analyze

The analysis takes the form of an objective review of what has happened, and is a matter of asking some simple questions:

- What went right? Why?
- What went wrong? Why?
- Did anyone else contribute? What did they do?
- Is there anything you wish you had not done?
- Is there anything you are especially glad you did?
- What was the step-by-step sequence of events?
- Why was each step taken?
- What were the consequences of each step?

If the experience was a shared one, it is profitable to take into account the views of the other people involved.

Deduce

The information drawn out of the learning episode during the analysis is reviewed, in order to arrive at some conclusions. These need to be specific. They should also point to steps to be taken in a similar situation in the future. The learner is left with a plan of action, which can be implemented in broadly identical situations and, ideally, can be adapted to fit other circumstances and solve other problems.

If this part of the process is to work, it must not be left to chance. Participants in self-development need to set aside a definite time when reviewing experiences, setting targets, and planning actions can be undertaken. If this is not done, learning from experience reverts to being instinctive and haphazard. It leads to negative consequences, when what has been learned is not clearly identifiable. The result is that the experience cannot be used to set clear targets. The indirect effects are that the learning cannot be monitored and cannot be transferred.

Practice

In this stage, the lessons are put into practice. This process should consummate a learning experience of a different kind. The sought-after result is something that prompts new behavior and a different analysis, from which new lessons will be learned. This allows the learner to close the loop and begin the process again.

Transfer

The results find their way into the informal learning process as part of peer learning, and maybe team learning. This must be complemented by the final stage of the model, which is the transfer of the learning into the formal processes where it can be applied by other people in other sectors of the organization. This means that it is added to the information system and becomes part of the organizational memory (see chapters 2 and 3).

The Impact of Self-Development

When learning from experience becomes true self-development, in which experience is used constructively, the results are: there is clarity about what has been learned; the lessons have been implemented; performance has improved; a permanent process of self-learning has been engineered; there has been wide communication through the use of formal and informal processes. In cultural terms:

- Continuous improvement has become firmly established.
- Self-criticism is accepted as a positive organizational feature.
- Some of the skills necessary for modern flexible library services can emerge from self-development:
  - The way things are done is questioned.
  - Problem-solving techniques are learned.
- Staff are better able to manage themselves:
  - They identify their own needs.
  - They learn to set their own objectives.
  - They monitor their own results.
  - They become comfortable with organizational change.
  - Self-development is a way of changing oneself.
- Dealing with bigger and more complex problems in real working situations helps equip people to handle the complex working patterns and relationships in modern information services.

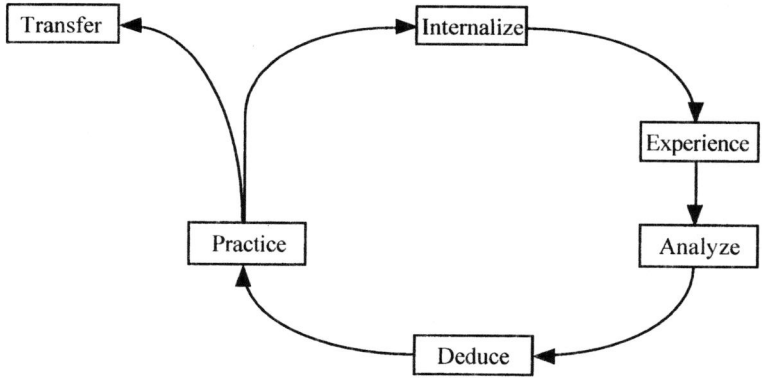

Figure 6.1 The Process of Learning from Work

The next case study looks at how self-development actually works.

Case Study 6

SELF-DEVELOPMENT FOR SUSANNAH

The Situation

The previous case study examined Susannah's way of dealing with a development problem in a particular part of the library. Concurrently, she faced some difficulties of her own.

At the time of the events related in case study 5, Susannah was in her early thirties, and had enjoyed smooth, and quite rapid, career development. After short stints in her first two professional posts, she became a research assistant in a department of information studies, and was then for three years a well-regarded lecturer in the same department. She returned to practical librarianship as the chief librarian of a small specialist college. Her four years in this post saw a rapid expansion in both the college and the library service. The first professionally qualified chief librarian to be appointed to the college, she inherited a library service that had been managed part-time by a lecturer in the English department, and on most counts the library failed to meet the needs of the college. Bolstered by large increases in staff and funding, and with a new resource center on the architect's drawing board, Susannah flourished. For the first time, the college management received the benefit of professional advice. Susannah's views on a range of issues were well received, and she was able to create one of the first integrated library and learning resource centers in the country. This quickly became a viable, effective, and imaginative service that had an impact on many areas of college life. With widespread support because of the massive improvement in the service, Susannah enjoyed an enviable degree of discretion in library matters.

A short distance away was a much larger, better known, and more powerful rival institution. For some of the things it did, the library of this institution enjoyed a national reputation. From a large field, Susannah was a natural choice as successor, when the library director of thirty years standing decided to retire.

The Problem

Susannah arrived with a good reputation to take up her new post. She also believed that she was coming to a library service of at least equal distinction, so she was disturbed by what she found in the first month. She realized that she had in fact joined a service with a reputation that was based on achievement in one or two more peripheral areas, while in terms of the actual resource collection, and all the key performance indicators, it was performing badly. She did not see this as a difficulty, but she was very disturbed by the complacency of library staff, teaching staff, and college management. Whenever she tentatively raised the issue of standards, the response was to extol the virtues of what the college had built up over the years. The passive and complacent attitude of the library staff concerned her in particular: She believed she could not count on their support for any changes that she felt the situation warranted, and she suspected that they sympathized with the views of the teaching staff.

Susannah felt that the college believed its own publicity about the library, and she realized that she would have difficulty in changing the perception of the service in the eyes of teaching staff, colleagues, and management. Although she showed no sign of it, her confidence began to suffer. She became very uncertain of how she should proceed, and in fact whether she should proceed at all in this particular institution.

Things came to a head during the first summer vacation, when Susannah tried to deal with two related problems. She was alarmed by the small acquisitions budget and by the fact that the library was effectively full. Susannah carried out a review of the book fund, and identified a reasonable sum of money that was being spent on a collection of contemporary fiction. When she examined this, she found that it comprised crime stories, westerns, romance, sports, and general light fiction. She could find no connection between this material and the teaching programs of the college. She was told by library staff that the material was used for recreational reading by students. She then offered the entire collection to the public library service, who accepted it. This created enough space for twelve months of acquisitions, and also freed an amount of money for purchases in other areas.

The consequences for Susannah were traumatic. She was confronted, in her office, by a senior staff member from the school of humanities and subjected to a verbal onslaught, to which she responded in kind. Both parties lost control, and the ensuing argument was heard by a number of library users in the vicinity. The episode ended with a vicious exchange about competence, subject expertise, and the right to manage the library. It concluded with slammed doors and red faces.

The Solution

That evening, Susannah sat down to analyze the problem. She realized that, in a general sense, she had completely misread the situation and had acted without taking heed of the prevailing political climate inside the college. While her own research had been meticulous, and her assessment of what could be done about the acquisitions problem was probably the only possible course of action in the circumstances, she had failed to share the ownership of the problem, or the solution, with a vital group of users.

She needed to look at the underlying reason for this behavior and understand that she faced two major difficulties. After years of building a quality library service from almost nothing, thereby winning the trust of her colleagues, and consequently their acquiescence to her forceful way of managing, she now faced a situation where people, rightly or wrongly, believed that their library already was a good one. She had to understand that building on something that was already there, and that reflected existing traditions and ways of working, needed a softer touch. Susannah knew she had to develop this for her own sake and for the service.

Her second difficulty was a crisis of confidence. This stemmed from the gulf between her own perception of the standard of the library service and the perception of her colleagues. She was daunted by the size of the task, unsure of her ability to convince her colleagues of what needed to be done, and for once was uncertain of a successful outcome. This provoked the classic authoritarian response: Information and decision making were confined to her personal fiefdom, and likely dissenters were cut out of the loop.

Susannah also realized that she had lost her temper in the discussion, not because of any direct personal animosity, but because she had been used to working in an environment where her view of library developments was unlikely to be challenged. Connected with this, she also came to see that she had failed to appreciate the more collegial approach that prevailed in her new institution and, therefore, had to rescue relations with the school of humanities before she could move on. As a result, she decided on a series of actions.

She set up a meeting with the deputy principal responsible for resources, the dean of the school of humanities, and the senior lecturer with whom she had the dispute. During this meeting, she apologized for her behavior and began to explain the reasoning behind her actions. From their side, the teaching staff set out their expectations of the library, gave their reasons for opposing the removal of the fiction collection, and contributed their view of how relationships with the library should work. Susannah agreed to put forward a coherent proposal for collection management, and to make full use of the college management and liaison mechanisms to deal with any issues that affected users. The meeting finally agreed to set up a working party to review library services and draw up a development plan.

The personal plan of action of the chief librarian centered on her now accepted need to understand and implement flexible management involving a partnership with users. She had already begun to create these conditions internally, and needed to carry the same general principles through into her relationships with teaching departments. To complement this, she knew she would need to totally share her approach with the library staff and win them over. Also, the idea of change had to be explored, so issues of change management, negotiation, and customer relations were taken into consideration for the formal staff training and development program.

Comment

Susannah had worked through most of the stages in the learning loop for self-development shown in figure 6.1. However unpleasant, she had used the experience constructively, and had been properly objective and analytical in assessing what had happened, and why. She had also drawn some honest conclusions about what she should do. Involving the deputy principal brought the imprimatur of legal authority to proceedings, and the agreement to use the existing management structure ensured accountability for putting proposals into practice. This would also ensure than the collection management ideas would be transferred to other relevant participants. The results of learning about other topics, such as partnership and change management, would also be disseminated widely through the staff development program and the appraisal and needs analyses mechanisms.

Susannah also had a problem with personal constructs. In her last post there had been a symmetry between her own assessment of her ability as a library manager, and the constructs of this formed by college management and library users. She now found herself in an uncertain position, and she knew that, in her own personal development, she had to recreate the attitudes that had illuminated her previous performance. The way she approached the question of learning from her first experience of handling a contentious issue, and the subsequent dissent, would be crucial. If she used the learning experience correctly, she could demonstrate the proper acceptance of criticism and questioning, as well as a willingness to acknowledge that management was not a self-contained and exclusive activity. In her response to the problem, she began to lay down the conditions for the cultural and behavioral changes essential for the kind of self-development that is the objective of learning from work.

Practicing, developing, and transferring the more internal learning, and the new personal behaviors this entailed, presented extra difficulties because they were part of a process which was novel for Susannah. Susannah's determination to learn about flexible management, and to develop ideas about partnership, would call for more support. The staff library, which Susannah had agreed to establish, would provide some assistance, but the mechanics of self-learning and learning from experience would also require additional measures.

Supporting Learning from Experience

Susannah would have benefited from some features that can only to be found in mature systems of learning. Knowledge-based organizations like libraries, where there has to be an emphasis on individual development and continuous improvement in skills, attitudes, and performance, need to bolster their general self-development program by using some of the key training techniques that are examined in chapters 7, 8, and 9. They also need to consider how they will develop supporting roles through the use of learning facilitators and other key figures. They finally need to make the connection between self-development through learning from experience and the set-piece training activities, which can be used in the formal program. As well as meeting the requirements set out above, these techniques have some other features in common:

- They are effective in clarifying existing attitudes to learning from experience and modifying them.
- They all have significant degrees of learner control built into the processes.

- They are based on equality between learners and facilitators.
- They draw practical lessons from work-based learning experience, and use them to improve skills, attitudes, and performance.
- They have great flexibility.

In many ways, learning from work is one of the cornerstones of modern training. It is the beginning of a process that leads to:

- Attitude changes by all involved
- Self-study and open learning
- Team-based learning
- Action learning
- Mentoring
- Coaching

Learning from work has major organizational implications. It influences the way organizations develop. It affects the ability to achieve the multiple objectives of modern information services. Learning from work is a training approach that is increasing in importance as the skills requirements of libraries alter. As information services work in increasingly unpredictable environments, greater emphasis will be placed on individual development. This can be supported through the techniques examined in chapters 7 through 9.

Part 3
Some Key Techniques And Issues

Chapter 7

Coaching

One of the propositions that this book tries to explore is that as libraries face the challenges of providing information in the twenty-first century, a new form of thinking is needed (see chapter 1). This is based on creativity, which is loosely defined as the ability to fashion new solutions to the organizational problems faced by libraries. Solving these problems depends on the energy that comes from the marriage of mutually supportive structures, systems, behavior, and appropriate learning techniques.

Coaching is the first of the key techniques that are most applicable in the organizational circumstances described in the first part of this book. It is also a technique that is related in some ways to mentoring. The coach, working over a shorter time scale or series of short-term projects, can be more directly and immediately influential than the mentor, who is dealing with a more diffuse form of development. Because the coach–learner relationship is more focused and more intense, it is a very powerful form of learning, and some of the issues discussed in the chapter on mentoring are equally relevant, if not more so. The argument about the difference between coaching and mentoring is complicated, and is touched on at the beginning of chapter 8. Both techniques are valid, and both techniques are important, but there are crucial differences in the nature, purpose, and process of these vital supports for learning.

A Definition of Coaching

"I don't like the word coaching, I prefer to call it coaxing," (Bowler, 1996). This conveys the sense of a learning process that brings something out of the learner—a potential which is already there. It gives us the first element of a definition: Coaching is a facilitating technique. Redshaw (2000) adds other elements to it. It is obviously one of the most learner-centered techniques, and it works in a one-to-one relationship or in a small group situation. More significantly, Redshaw (and many others) asserts that coaching is the behavior that a good manager exhibits in any case. It could be viewed as a technique that moves the balance of managerial behavior in order to tilt the emphasis toward the coaching end of the managing-coaching continuum (Pearn, Roderick, and Mulrooney, 1995) shown in figure 7.1 (from Redshaw, 2000).

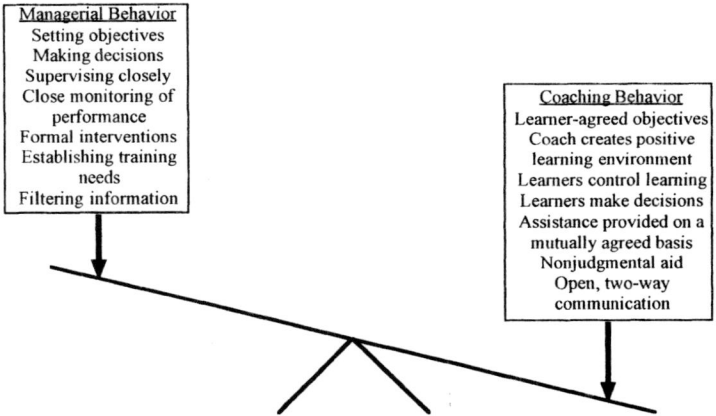

Figure 7.1 The Manager–Coach Shift

Sellars (1966) says that the impact of the coach is as much mental as anything else. In this sense, the coach is dealing with transferable skills —skills that can be applied in other work situations or in life outside work. The mental attributes encouraged by coaching are the things that create consistent performance in work. These will be examined in more detail later in the chapter.

create consistent performance in work. These will be examined in more detail later in the chapter.

The other noteworthy feature of coaching is that, if it is done properly, it should also make a contribution to learning how to learn. A good coach will have to model learning behavior, and will pass on a method for tackling work-based learning and development. This method will include some of the learning skills. It will also demonstrate a systematic approach to analyzing the elements of tasks or problems, breaking them down, and mastering key points.

Coaching is one of the areas where we can look to some highly developed models outside management and certainly well beyond library management. The natural analogy is with sports, and much is made of this. We need to be a little wary. There is an obvious, and huge, difference between a sporting competition and the day-to-day business of managing and working in libraries: The pressures are different, some of the coaching skills used in sports are not relevant, and others will have a different emphasis. Yet we can take two crucial elements from the coaching of high performance sportsmen and sportswomen. The first is the method, and the other is the importance of mental preparation, although even here this will not carry the same emphasis for us as it does for the Olympians.

Coaching strategy documents, from a number of sporting disciplines, refer to a process that helps achieve a quality of performance that would not have been possible without help. On the part of the coach, this implies a technical mastery of the task in hand (but *not* technical excellence). It needs a knowledge of how learning takes place, which is linked to the ability to create the right learning environment and the appropriate learning experiences. Dyson (1979) also emphasized the mental or psychological impact when he referred to the coach's responsibility to develop in learners "those capacities and habits of mind and body which will enrich and ennoble their later years." This is a broad responsibility, and it is clear that there are overlaps between coaching and many other developmental activities. As in the case of the overlap with mentoring, it is a question of emphasis. The very fact that some of these training activities can be seen as identical indicates how much work needs to be done to refine some of our ideas about how we can use the techniques in library management.

There is also an argument that coaching is instinctive. This may be so, but it is also a planned activity. If this systematic approach is taken out of it, it loses some of its potency.

Adapted from Redshaw (2000), the key points of the definition are that coaching is:

- Systematic
- Learner-centered
- Work-based
- Job-related
- Based on experience
- Planned
- A two-way process of communication
- Motivational
- Mental preparation
- It helps to create good learning conditions

> Systematically increasing the capability and work performance of someone by exposing him or her to work-based tasks or experiences which will provide relevant learning opportunities, and giving guidance and feedback to help him or her learn from them. (Redshaw, 2000)

The Theory of Coaching

Hudson (1999) traces the emergence of coaching down through a number of strands of mainstream developmental psychology. He identifies a Freudian influence behind some of the theory, and refers particularly to the importance of understanding symbolic actions, such as body language. This is taken to be a way of bringing to the surface those unconscious ideas that all individuals possess and can be harnessed in the coaching process. Make of this what you will. Adler, Jung, and Erikson carry the theory forward, through emphasizing the process of reeducation, which is a part of coaching, and the idea of development through social growth.

The psychosocial theories of adult development are another jumping off point for Hudson. He pays particular attention to the importance of major social change in people's lives, and he applies this to the role of coaching during periods of major change, when it is used as a life-enhancing technique.

The argument is that these theories help coaches gain insights into the states of mind of the learners with whom they are dealing. We can see the relevance of this to life coaching, although I might not agree that this is coaching as I prefer to define it. We would be fools if we could not see the value of understanding what was making a particular learner tick at a particular time. But, given the more finite timescale in which work-based coaching takes place, it might be more profitable to look to the adult learning theories of chapter 4 if we want a plausible theoretical justification for coaching.

Adult Learning Theories

The most powerful theoretical support for coaching comes from the adult learning theories. The salient points of the work of Freire, Bruner, and the advocates of andragogy (see chapter 4) offer the justification. Learning for adults is something that:

- Occurs in a social environment
- Involves using the experience of adult learners
- Is self-development, and cedes discretion to the learner
- Can be used to support elements of group or team learning
- Is built around open and equal relationships
- Develops the whole individual
- Is work-based
- Stresses the value of problem solving
- Emphasizes the usefulness of participative techniques
- Develops the ability to apply learning to job or life situations
- Encourages a continuing desire to improve performance
- Uses self-esteem as a vital motivator

Some of the key ideas of chapter 5, such as inculcating a sense of self-worth and the use of the learning cycle as the basis of a coaching process, are also important. The discretion given to the learner to decide on an appropriate approach, apply it, and evaluate the results will underpin this. The growth in confidence that leads to self-worth can also come from the process itself. This relies partly on a staged and planned approach to learning, through which feelings of security can be built as the mastery of discrete components of the skill is achieved.

Self-Worth

Another strength of coaching is that it satisfies personal construct theory. It is a way of improving skills and ensuring that the ability of the learner is at least equal to the demands of the job. In other words, it can be said that coaching is a means of matching the individual's view of his or her abilities with the demands of work as well as the boss's assessment of the worker. There is then a gain in job satisfaction and in motivation. There is a further impetus: to strive for a goal that is a little out of reach, and to attempt things that may be beyond the current grasp of the learner.

Safe Learning

Coaching is applied in an environment where it is in some ways safe to get things wrong. It involves trial and error, practicing and re-practicing. Failure is also a learning experience that offers the opportunity for further coaching intervention. In this way, a continuous process of learning and development is created.

Flexible Learning

Coaching draws strength from what we know about learning styles and learning preferences. It is a flexible technique. Depending on the nature of the learning task or the problem, the approach can vary from didactic to almost completely learner-driven. The choice of learning methods will be influenced not only by the nature of the task, but by the predilections of the learner. It may mean a piece of teaching, some behavior to be modeled, a group exercise, some theory, or individuals working on information provided by the coach.

Modeling Learning

For the coach it will be necessary to discreetly demonstrate the approach in a way that leads the learners to believe they have discovered it themselves. It has been said that a mark of great leadership is that, at the end of the project, the participants think they have done it alone. The same is true of coaching. At the end of the exercise, the learner should feel that they have been involved in self-discovery. More mature reflection will show the different coaching techniques in use and how behavior has been modeled. They will have absorbed another way of learning, which they can use in other situations.

Parsloe and Wray (2000) have written the best book yet on coaching and mentoring. They trace the influence of academics, sports coaches, psychotherapists, life coaches, professional trainers, and adherents to neuro linguistic programming (NLP). They make the following points:

- It is a key approach for complex and technological organizations.
- In many organizations we are feeling our way toward an understanding of what the technique actually is. Our understanding depends on awareness of where the ideas have come from.

The Application of Coaching to Libraries

The ground rules for running coaching schemes in libraries are similar in some ways to those for mentoring. There is one difference: Coaching should be seen as a development, or an extension, of management behavior. Coaching is a way of managing, and the skills of the coach turn managers into leaders. So it is an approach to be cultivated by line managers, supervisors, and others with staff responsibilities. There is a sense in which everybody is part of a coaching process. Randell (2000), summarizing the University of Bradford's research into the skills of leadership, pinpoints many of the similarities between the leader and the coach. He calls for leaders who possess:

- Cognitive skills: having values and a vision; able to think
- Perceptual skills: analyzing; diagnosing; responding
- Motor skills: verbal and nonverbal communication; interacting

Coaching is applicable to different organizational forms, although it works better in empowered organizations. It can also contain within it a number of different teaching and learning styles. Even in the kinds of organizations propounded in this book, there will be a place for small doses of pedagogy, and there may be circumstances where this is the only way to work. Other than the wide applicability of coaching, as a management as well as a learning technique, there are some ground rules that indicate particular circumstances where coaching can be used in libraries.

In a Skills Deficit

Conventionally, a skills deficit is considered to be a shortfall between the skills base of a post holder and the skills necessary to carry out the duties of the post. The question also needs to be put into the wider service context. For example, the move to electronic collections may create a requirement for technical staff to understand and apply the skills of metadata, in order to describe adequately the electronic artifacts. It may also create the need for readers' advisors to acquire an awareness of electronic databases, to develop the skills of Web searching, and to master the complexities of access rights to digital data. These are the skills deficits that have to be made up. The organizational objectives relating to these deficits would involve possible attitude changes and organizational change. All are skills deficits, and coaching could be part of the remedy for them all.

To Treat an Identifiable Problem

This could come from operational problems, or be picked up by appraisal schemes and assessments. For example, in case study 8, Hilda's difficulties in collaborating with colleagues, and in managing her section in a way that brought out the best in her staff, could equally have been dealt with by coaching in negotiating skills and empowerment. Carlos chose mentoring, in order to attack the underlying attitude problem. This could also have been treated as a long-term coaching aim, because the technique has advantages when remedial action has to be taken.

To Develop Mental Strength

Coaching is as much about mental attitudes as anything, and it is mental attitudes that influence things like concentration, attention, and accuracy. At the level of the new entrant into librarianship, these are attributes that need to be inculcated. As a young librarian, I shudder to remember my own powers of concentration, accuracy and consistency in routine but vital parts of the job. Coaching is as important for library assistants and clerical assistants as it is for new professionals, mature librarians, middle managers, and senior managers. The day-to-day work at all levels in libraries still calls for accuracy and consistency in what can be, for some of the time, not very exciting tasks.

Coaching, as a learner-friendly technique, not only builds these characteristics, it can open up the minds of non-learners. This will help them take the first steps to becoming proactive learners. Senge (1990) wrote about "mental models," which are the assumptions we all make about our working situations. In other words, it is our understanding of the environment in which we are working and of what is happening to us. It is also the view we hold of ourselves. Ideas about self-development, in chapters 5 and 6, depended on analyzing ourselves and taking the views of colleagues, and the organization, into our conception of what we were doing and how good we were at doing it. Figure 7.3 (page 149) shows the first stage of the coaching process as a time of assessment by both the coach and the learner. Together, in effect, they change the mental models and identify the developmental needs.

To Support Developmental Needs

This is particularly relevant in team-based organizations, where there is a need, and scope, for job enrichment and job enlargement. For example, a member of a subject team in a university will often share responsibility for training, or maybe take responsibility for some aspects of managing the library computer system. Serials librarians, and librarians with responsibility for electronic databases, will increasingly become copyright and permissions experts. The first involvement in project management could be another good example of both enrichment and enlargement. Any library service that is devolving management responsibilities, and giving its staff a greater say in how things are done, will deploy coaching as one of the appropriate techniques. The same kind of needs can also be met in the same way for new entrants, for staff who change jobs, or when the skills needs of existing jobs are altered.

As an Effective Instrument of Change

Coaching is particularly relevant to major change initiatives. It is a favored technique throughout the change process, but it has a particularly strong contribution to make during the implementation stage. As a way of dealing with the psychological aspects of change management, it is a powerful and reassuring tool. Any form of organizational change is an obvious area where coaching can be used. There is almost an umbilical connection between change management and coaching.

The Role of the Coach

As already suggested, coaching is managing and, if it is done successfully, it becomes leadership. It is analyzing skills, tasks, and processes. It is assessing, evaluating, and revising. In a team context, it extends into a concern for group dynamics and relationships. With the focus on the individual, it covers motivation, job satisfaction, and the well-being of the people it touches. It is influenced by and, in turn, exerts some power over organization development and change. Although it is comparatively short term when compared with mentoring, it can lay the groundwork for long-term attitude change.

It may be that many working situations offer the chance of spontaneous, or instinctive, coaching. In the long run, coaching is a much more formalized, logical, and planned activity. Coaches have a managerial role.

The Coach as a Manager of Learning

The general role of the coach is to develop learners to a point of maturity, where they will take over control of their own learning. This includes responsibility for performance improvement. The coach will model the desired behavior and demonstrate a staged learning process. There will also be encouragement of a systematic approach to the learning task. This approach is based on analysis, organization, practice, observation, assessment, review, and modification. In the process, the learner will also learn about:

- Decision making
- Problem solving
- Time management
- Setting priorities
- Working with others

The Coach as a Developer of Mental Skills

Most work tasks, as already suggested, require concentration, accuracy, attention to detail, and consistency. These are the mental skills that coaches can strengthen over time.

- The habit of concentration is built into the method. Coaching depends on breaking down the skill to be acquired, or the task to be learned, into small, understandable components. This is a way of reducing the complexity, by working all the time within finite boundaries. It is the basis of project management, change management, and other work-related skills and tasks. Concentration, therefore, becomes easier. In this part of the coach's approach, there can obviously be elements of conditioning and behaviorism, but learning to concentrate is also a long-term process and a long-term problem. Here the coach can look to some of the higher motivational forces described in chapter 10. Maslow's higher-order needs are met by setting testing objectives, and expectancy theory asserts that making the learning task a demanding one is important to most learners. Setting clear objectives, which stretch learners, is vital. If the task is made too easy, there is a tendency for the better learners to underperform as concentration wavers. Objective-setting should create a challenge that is a little out of reach of the learner, but is attainable with the support of the coach. This engages the commitment of the learner and sustains concentration over the longer term.

- Confidence has to do with the idea of "self-worth" introduced in chapter 5. As well as its general relevance in the context of learning from work, it is a particularly important by-product of coaching. Self-realization and the inner confidence of the learner again come partly from the setting and achievement of testing objectives. Self-esteem also comes from the shared and learner-controlled learning, which is the backbone of coaching. All these are cemented by the learning relationship between the coach and the learner, which is one of mutual respect and equality.
- Most of what has been said in this section is applicable to the librarian's need to master attention to detail. Breaking down tasks into smaller parts and maintaining concentration over periods of time are attributes that can be developed during the coaching process. Together with the habit of consistency, they also come from the regular periods of practice that are part of the coaching cycle.

The Coach as a Developer of Professional and Technical Skills

Coaching is probably more readily linked with the acquisition of better practical, professional, and technical skills than the mental skills, or attitudinal skills, referred to above. Coaching a new skill is obviously a more tangible use of the technique than developing the mental skills. However, acquiring the right mental approach is one of the preconditions for the coaching of all practical, professional, and technical skills.

The question to be answered first is how much knowledge of the technical and professional skills the coach needs in order to perform well in a work-based learning situation. High levels of expertise are a clear advantage, but in the modern library world it is becoming difficult to sustain the image of the old chief, usually a bookman, who could proudly boast that he never asked his staff to do anything he was not capable of doing just as well. The increasing specialization of modern librarianship is making this impossible, and it is likely to become more of a problem for coaches.

There is no ready answer to the question posed above. In other spheres, there is no clear correlation between the coach's level of achievement as a practitioner and his or her ability to actually coach the same skills to a high level. Some successful coaches obviously come from the "do as I say, not as I do" school. It is also fair to say that some teachers of management, and writers about management, are better in these roles than they were as practicing managers. In librarianship it is obviously going to be increasingly difficult for good coaches to be able to master the intricacies of electronic librarianship, although they are naturally in a more comfortable situation if they can point to a successful track record as practitioners. Management coaches may well find it easier to do this.

It is also quite likely that, in the libraries of the future, we will face problems that are new and areas of activity in which there are no ready-made experts. At the micro level inside some teams, this is already true. One of the difficulties we face now, in redesigning our library organizations to face contemporary change, is that we have few templates in past practice.

The issue is resolved by examining in more detail some of the aspects of this particular role of the coach.

The Coach as a Technical Advisor

Coaches should seek to help the learner identify the principles of a technique and develop best practice. It is not the coach's job to actually perform or work to the highest standard: that is for the learner, supported by the coach.

The Coach as a Diagnostic and Developmental Agent

The coach then needs to be able to recognize the degree of success or failure, diagnose the reasons for both, and point to remedial or developmental action. None of this has much to do with practical performance in working situations. Once again, it is the *process* of coaching that contains the seeds of success. It is only necessary to look at the achievement of many famous sports coaches who never enjoyed more than moderate success as performers, or to consider the predicament of great performers who failed as coaches, to understand that this is so, and that it is not a disadvantage or an obstacle to good coaching in any way.

Good coaches should not work alone, especially when they work with teams, but also when they work with individuals. A facilitator working with staff on a digital library project would not automatically be able to assist with the learning of metadata, knowing little of how to describe electronic data, but somebody in the coaching setup would. "The first essential was to build a formidable management team." (Henry, 1998). As Redshaw (2000) points out, coaches can work along a line from the subject expert at one end, to the facilitator, or process expert, at the other.

Subject Expert	Coaching Process Expert
Coach's attributes:	Coach's attributes:
Higher subject expertise	Lower subject expertise
Greater experience	Less experience
Formal authority	No formal authority
Coach's approach influenced by:	Coach's approach influenced by:
Need to maintain high process skills	Need to maintain high process skills
Competence and experience of the learner	Unavailability of subject expertise
	Stronger emphasis on trust in the relationship

Figure 7.2 The Roles of the Coach

The roles depend on the situation, and why should they all be found in one person? Coaches often work in teams. Figure 7.2 (adapted from Redshaw, 2000) illustrates this. When a learner experiences a new situation, or a problem where an innovative solution is needed, the process and the relationship carry the day, not performance skills.

The Coach as a Learning Model

The last part of the answer lies in the role of the coach as model. This can be divided into three elements:

- The modeling of the learning process: This is based on analysis, assessment, decision making, implementation, practice, evaluation,

review, and modification. Here lies the key to coaching. It is not magical, but it involves a great deal of planning and organization.
- The creation of a safe learning environment: Some of this is outside the power of the coach to deliver, depending as it does on structural change and management behavior. What the coach can do is support learning in a "no-blame" atmosphere. This does not mean avoiding responsibility for mistakes, nor does it excuse negligence or incompetence. Neither does it absolve anyone from the need to admit error. It allows learning to take place in a comparatively congenial environment, where the coach can act as a partial buffer between the learner and the organizational, and personal, consequences of what is done.
- The creation of an attitude of mind: Jobs are not done by coaches, and teams do not work well because they are made to by coaches. If learning takes place, it can only do so because people want to learn. The mental skills referred to above are part of the mind games that coaches must play, if they are to be successful. The willingness to learn has to be uncovered. Some of it depends on the learning environment and the mental rigor that the coach can help create.

The rest of it is inspirational and depends on:

- Creating a vision of where learning can take us
- Motivating
- Providing richness and variety in learning experiences
- Providing feedback and encouragement

To model these aspects of behavior, there are a number of talents that are indispensable for good coaching.

What Makes a Good Coach?

Some of the coaching skills are the skills of the developed and enlightened manager. First, there must be a cornerstone. This is an understanding of how people learn.

An Understanding of the Learning Process

The process involved in coaching is one of self-discovery. For most of the time, whatever the specific role of the coach, the process will be learner-controlled. Learning will be based on the learner's consideration of options, decision making, and implementation. Coaches need to understand, and commit themselves to, empowerment. They have to be able to give up power, but also continue to support the empowered learner. This takes place within a partnership embracing goal-setting, evaluation, assessment, and constructive criticism. The process can also be understood as a learning cycle similar to those described in chapter 5.

Knowing the Learning Styles

Honey and Mumford (1986) identified theorists, pragmatists, activists, and reflectors. Individuals also prefer to learn through becoming involved in various activities, sometimes alone, sometimes in groups, through reading, discussion, and other activities. Good coaches will find out which styles their learners prefer. They will not only attempt to provide learning experiences to match both the learner's needs and the characteristics of the task or skill to be learned, but they will also consider how to help learners achieve a balance of learning styles. Learning is supposed to be a broad process, and different learning tasks can be completed in different ways. The coach's own behavior will vary in the same way and for the same reasons. There will be the occasional foray into teaching, for example, when a piece of theory or a specific technique can best be demonstrated by this approach. This will be more than balanced by the learner-centered techniques.

Secure in this body of knowledge about how learning occurs, and sure of the ability to apply it, the coach will also need to demonstrate effective people-handling skills.

Being Able to Communicate

This is the skill not only of passing on information and providing feedback, but also of gathering intelligence about how learners prefer to learn and how they are performing. It is also about finding out how they are feeling. It is the skill of simply reflecting on what is going on in the coaching process, and of communicating this in a succinct and positive message. In the introduction to this book, it was said that there is a link between learning and leadership. Some of these characteristics are part of transformational leadership. In particular, these are:

- Listening, questioning, clarifying
- Planning: remember that coaching is a managed activity
- Assessing learning needs
- Setting agreed objectives
- Analyzing and criticizing
- Reviewing
- Facilitating: identifying and developing learning experiences
- Motivating: developing the right mental attitude

The Coaching Process

At the heart of the coaching process, shown in figure 7.3 on page 149, lies the quality of coach—learner relationships. One myth to dispel is that liking each other must come into it. Of an outstanding coach, it was once said by an elite performer: "As a coach, the best in the world. Yet I found it impossible to like him as a man." In another discussion, it was said, by another elite performer: "I've spent a long time wondering about the great differences between X as a player, X as a coach, and X as a man." There are examples of successful coaching partnerships that have been based on stormy relationships. Liking each other might help, respecting each other is better and more realistic. Relationships depend on mutual respect and the ability to inspire confidence. They also depend on efficiency. This comes from the process. Redshaw's definition of coaching emphasized its systematic and planned nature. This is reflected in a logical method for taking the relationship and the process forward.

Assessment

Coaching is an activity that focuses very sharply on the learning task. It begins with an assessment of present performance. Some models call this a "pre-testing" stage. This should jointly be carried out by the coach and the learner. The result will be an agreement on the areas where improvement is necessary.

Assessment is the beginning of two other features: building the learning climate and kick starting self-development.

Building the Learning Climate
Working together on this stage helps create the learning climate. It is the

partnership of learning, in which ownership is shared, allowing collaboration to develop. Agreeing on what is to be done is the first step on this path, and the precedent, once established, is carried through the rest of the process. This is the start of giving the learner control of the process, and of creating a learning partnership. It is the start of true empowerment.

Kick Starting Self-Development
The rigorous examination in this part of the model should lead to learners confronting themselves. The performance gap might be one the learner is unaware of: The analysis is the first step in creating awareness and then doing something about it. The process means something more than the coaching process. The analysis exposes the need to learn and starts the learning cycle.

Setting Objectives

This is another joint exercise, which builds on the previous stage. The traditional way of defining objectives is to say that the outcomes must be framed in a concrete way, which describes specific behavior. They should always be expressed in active verbs, and they should be measurable. The circumstances under which the behavior will be displayed can also be described, through the addition of conditions that will control the time taken to perform the task, or the things that will be used to aid the performance of the task. This is more memorably described in the literature as setting SMART, and sometimes SMARTER—**E**xciting and **R**ecorded as well (Sellars, 1966)—objectives:

- **s**pecific: a precise statement of the end result
- **m**easurable: setting the criteria to judge the success of the learning
- **a**ttainable: realistic while still being a test
- **r**elevant: appropriate to organizational and individual needs
- **t**imebound: achievable within a given period

Planning

The detailed assessment at the start of the process gives the participants a precise picture of where the development is to take place. Working together, the task to be learned or improved is broken down into its component parts. For each part, the possible ways in which it can be learned are discussed, and alternative ways of learning are considered. The exercise is carried out within the context of the learning objectives, and each stage is bound by the conditions of time and other restricting factors. The result is a stage-by-stage enactment of the complete coaching activity.

Other issues also need to be decided here, and there is again a need for documentation. There has to be a formal agreement that answers a few questions. We already know what development is to take place. We know who is to be involved. The agreement also needs to make clear:

- How the improvement will be achieved
- How long it will take
- Where the learning will occur
- When it will be done
- How it will be linked to the formal development process

The last point is important. Coaching exercises have a short time span. They also have a small number of precise objectives, often only one. The agreements underpinning this are not the same as the documents that form part of appraisal schemes, performance reviews, or personal development plans in the formal development processes. The information, therefore, has to go into the system, through line managers, team leaders, or designated facilitators or developers.

Practice

The results are put into practice. The learner carries out the plan, while the coach observes, analyzes, criticizes, and makes more suggestions until the process is considered to be complete. The manner in which the coach does this—the coaching style—is another critical area. The issues are outlined below.

Formal versus Informal

Informal coaching has its adherents. However, it is haphazard, and it cannot easily be assessed or evaluated. We might not know if objectives are being met. It is the same problem as treating self-development, or learning from work, as something that is instinctive.

Planned versus Unplanned

Again, as with self-development, unless a specific time is set aside for the activity, it probably will not happen. The purpose of setting objectives, deciding how the process is to work, and when it will finish, is to codify the activity and create a structure that strengthens the original purpose.

The other reason for adopting the planned approach is that coaches will be faced with a variety of issues. We found that learners in libraries would be in varying states of readiness and would have preferences for certain learning styles and experiences. We identified skills deficits, developmental needs, organizational changes, and other circumstances where a coach could be expected to get involved. If this involvement was with inexperienced staff, who might not be particularly confident learners, the coach's behavior would reflect almost a narrow training approach. The coach might also rely on subject expertise (see figure 7.2, page 143). If the involvement was with highly skilled and experienced staff, the approach would be closer to the process expert described in figure 7.2, and the skills would be the personal skills of observation, analysis, questioning, and feedback. There would be a corresponding move toward learner control of the process. What is important, as Parsloe and Wray

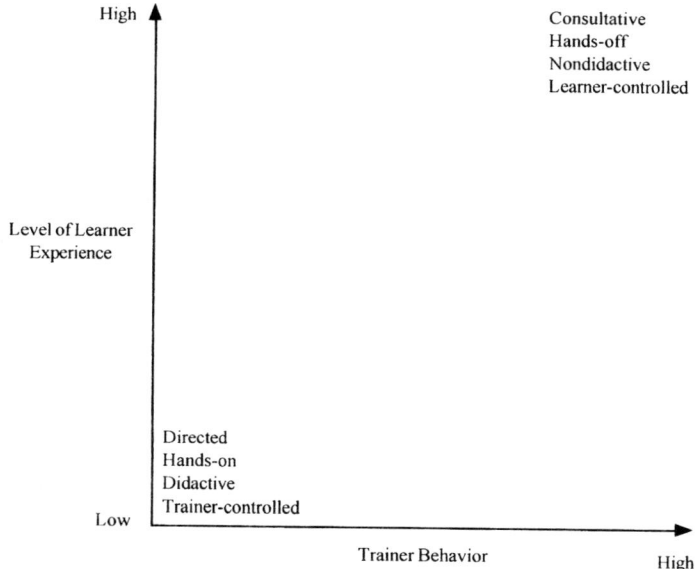

Figure 7.3 Coaching Behavior

(2000) assert, is that the balance shifts along toward the "hands-off" approach, because this makes for more effective learning. Figure 7.3 on page 149 illustrates this.

Reassessment

The entire process, from the initial assessment onward, is reviewed. The standards achieved are considered against the objectives set at the

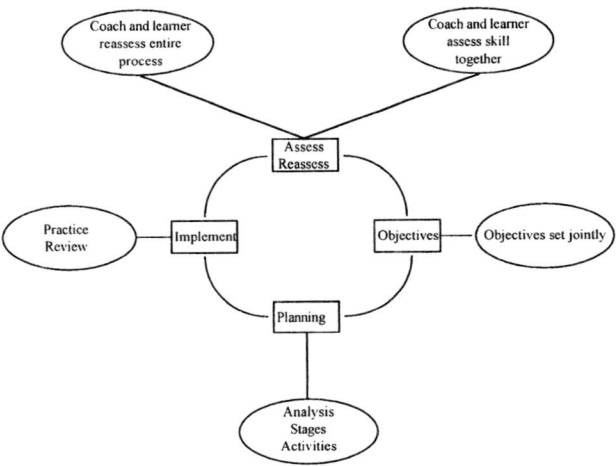

Figure 7.4 The Coaching Process

start of the exercise. This can sometimes be called the "post-testing" stage. The questions to be asked are whether the objectives were achieved, whether the performance has improved, and to what extent. Figure 7.4 sets out the process described in more detail in the text.

Coaching the Team

Team coaching relies basically on the same approach. One of the key differences is that teams are more likely to be coached by a coaching team. Let us take the hypothetical case of a coaching scheme being set up for a team of librarians in an area library of a public library service that is responsible for delivering services to a group of users. The environment is one of empowerment, where all the necessary functions and responsibilities will be devolved to the team. The process, as described on the previous page, could be worked through, with additional stages:

Analyze and Allocate the Areas of Responsibility

This particular team task could be broken down in a number of ways. For the sake of argument these could be:

- Acquisition and organization of information
- Dissemination of information
- Reference queries
- Circulation services

Team coaching has to work through intermediaries. The point was made earlier that one of the secrets of successful team coaching is the strength of the management (or coaching) team. What the coach is looking for, in each area identified on this page, is an experienced member of staff, who can take responsibility for organizing the effort and who is capable of supporting the overall effort of the coach.

Use the Process Again

When these two tasks are completed, the coaching process as described earlier can then be followed. There will be a concentration on creating the right environment, and instilling the proper technical and motivational or mental skills. Other elements will be added as outlined below.

Coaching the Coaches
Coaches will now be giving time and attention to coaching the coaches—those staff who have emerged as potential coaches themselves, and who can work as part of a coaching team in the areas identified.

Making Connections and Creating "The Zone"
The final component comes when the coach raises his or her sights. As each element in the team's area of responsibility is coached, so the focus has to embrace the links between the elements. The objective is to help

the team create what some coaches call "The Zone." This is where all the elements of the team mesh together. The skills and responsibilities complement each other, and the result is the provision of a seamless service to users. It has been described as a sense of well-being, which indicates that a successful team has been forged. It is where individuals are comfortable in using their own special talents as part of a more effective whole. The Zone cannot be created by the coach. It is created by the entire team, when they are making full use of the conditions and support provided by the coach. When this happens, the coach is close to the elusive and unattainable, if not undesirable, objective of creating a fully self-managing team. He or she has also passed the test of leadership.

Case Study 7
COACHING THE RESEARCHER

The Situation

Marian was newly promoted in the research and strategy department of a multinational conglomerate. She had previously worked as a general assistant in the same department, where she had gained some limited experience in contributing some fairly basic information to the vital work of teams engaged in large research projects. A psychology graduate, she was working for her first employer since leaving college.

The Problem

Marian's first project was an initial investigation into the viability of the telecommunications market in the former Soviet Union. The research and strategy group was considering recommending an investment in a company that had been set up in order to exploit this emerging market. There was a small amount of in-house knowledge on the topic, but not enough to offer much help to the researchers involved.

Ralph was Marian's section leader. He was generally aware that Marian needed support, and appreciated that, on her own, she would not deliver a report to the required standard. Marian had played a small role in some other projects in which Ralph had been involved, and the two already had a sound professional relationship. Ralph had supported her promotion to his group, and considered it to be thoroughly deserved. However, he had already given some thought to how he would deal with the question of her first solo piece of work. By temperament and belief, he was a flexible manager, with a relaxed and open but methodical style. He was successful in introducing empowerment for the staff who reported to him, and he intended to take the same attitude with Marian.

The Solution

Ralph reviewed a range of possibilities, including putting Marian into a team that would produce the report. Eventually, he discounted this and decided that, as Marian had already made a satisfactory input into several of his projects, he would work with her on the Eastern European report. He set up an initial meeting with her in order to establish some basic procedures and rules.

At this first meeting, they started by discussing Marian's level of skills relevant to the job in hand. She herself identified a lack of depth in her research skills. Although this was partly offset by a developing knowledge of electronic sources, it was clear that some work would need to be done in this area. Prompted and encouraged by Ralph, Marian began to talk about some of the problems she might encounter in preparing a report of this magnitude and significance. Ralph also suggested that, given the limitations of her experience in the field, her actual research strategy would have to be refined. By the end of the meeting, they had come to a realistic assessment of the skills level that Marian would need to reach in order to do the job.

A written record of all this was kept, and Ralph then sent Marian off to start the research. He gave her the two preliminary jobs of defining the scope of the research, and confirming how the information would be used by the recipients. He also gave her some tips to help with these early steps, before preparing a detailed analysis of the task Marian was about to begin.

Based on this analysis, at their next meeting Ralph offered Marian a work plan:

- Clarify the objectives, related to the needs of the recipients
- Set the boundaries of the research
- Decide what topics would be included in the research
- Define the search terms

- Plan the research strategy
- Decide the sources
- Establish criteria for verifying and validating information
- Plan the structure of the report
- Devise the order of the topics
- Draw up the process for writing the research
- Inject the skills of report writing into the project

Ralph also identified key points in the process, where problems were likely to occur. The meeting proceeded in the same collaborative atmosphere, while Marian and Ralph first reviewed the work she had done on the research preliminaries. They then went on to talk about Ralph's analysis of the task. At this stage, Ralph started to outline a simple learning plan, which they would be able to use throughout the project. The nature of the task obviously lent itself to one-to-one learning. By inclination, Ralph preferred, through discussion with Marian, to tease out the basic principles to be followed in each part of the task. They also began to use examples from other projects they had both worked on, as well as drawing from documentation and procedures already held within the research and strategy department. Sometimes, Ralph resorted to brief didactic sessions, when he set out, in simple terms, the principles to be followed or the tactics to be implemented in carrying out a certain task. For areas such as advanced Web searching, his intention was to use other expertise within the department. Marian concurred with this approach and they then turned to the next step, which was to decide the objectives for the research. They used SMART objectives to do this:

- *Specific.* The objective was to write an initial analysis of the potential of the telecommunications market in the former Soviet Union.
- *Measurable.* The success of the report would be judged on whether or not it helped the strategy team to decide if it was worth commissioning a detailed market analysis as the basis for an investment plan.
- *Attainable.* The targets were realistic, given the potential of Marian, her limited familiarity with the work, and the degree of support available. The targets would also extend Marian's skills and present her with a genuine test, and ultimately skills improvement and the development of new skills.
- *Relevant.* The relevance to organizational and individual needs was

made obvious from the beginning of the project.
- *Timebound.* The decision was to be made in two months, so this was the timescale for completing the coaching exercise and the report.

They moved on to consider what areas the report would need to cover. Ralph offered three or four methods of doing this, before working with Marian on two of them. He then left her to complete that stage.

The days passed in a mixture of practical work from Marian, and discussion, explanation, demonstration, analysis, and review. Along the way, some specific problems were dealt with. For example, Marian had some difficulty in changing her somewhat academic use of language into a style more appropriate for a business information report. Here Ralph took a piece of her prose and rewrote it, to show the value of a simpler style. He also related this to the requirements of the executives who would make the investment decision, reinforcing the point that they would appreciate a succinct and clear explanation of the options they faced.

Marian also made mistakes. One of these occurred early in the process. She made the basic error of the inexperienced researcher, and decided to leave the writing of the report until all the information had been collected and organized. Ralph returned to this issue after one or two meetings, when Marian had collected some more information. He was then able to draw out of the discussion an awareness of the difficulties she would face unless she changed her plan and wrote the report section by section. From this, Marian was able to move forward and devise a process of collecting information, writing, and reviewing what had previously been written. This brought her an additional benefit. Her knowledge of content obviously increased.

When the report was completed, Marian and Ralph reviewed the entire process, and set the result against the objectives they had agreed and the objectives they had taken from the people who were going to use the report. They looked back at the way the project had developed and at the degree to which Marian's knowledge and skills had grown. They concluded that the project had been completed. The report was submitted and accepted, with praise, by the directors.

Comment

The interaction between the protagonists is one of the keys to understanding coaching. We begin with Marian, who took a vital first step. At the first meeting, she acknowledged a deficit, in terms of her ability to complete the project unaided. Her crucial willingness to admit that she needed to learn can be contrasted with Hilda's response in case study 8, which follows. The need to learn has to be articulated before there can be any form of development. Here it was also a help in developing the embryo relationship, which was already there through Ralph's interest in Marian's career development. He had been willing to support her elevation to a post that would extend her. He was also aware that this would initially present her with some challenges, which she would not cope with alone.

Analyzing the task was important. This reduced the overall project to a series of manageable chunks, therefore lowering the stress levels. Marian was in effect given a series of staged objectives. They were less threatening than the overview of the entire task, but enough to maintain her commitment and concentration.

It should be noted that Marian made most of the initial decisions on courses of actions. Ralph's role was to spell out the options. It follows that she was also allowed to make her own mistakes, but these sins were committed in a forgiving atmosphere. The end result was enhanced learning.

Ralph's behavior was also noteworthy. He modeled the coaching process. A positive and non-threatening atmosphere was created. The learning was collaborative, although it could profitably have been driven a little more by Marian. Although she was not particularly experienced in the area on which they were working, as a learner she was mature. Ralph's choice of learning techniques, and his coaching style, were based on this, even if it was obvious that Marian's needs would be better met by individual learning. As a researcher, albeit an inexperienced one, she would also have been comfortable with the idea of working independently. Apart from this, Ralph used a balanced approach. Where necessary, some of his work was pedagogic. At other times, dealing with the critical stages of the process was a matter of problem solving. His overall approach was collaborative, and this was also shown in his willingness to deploy expert help.

By the end, both coach and learner were entitled to feel they had achieved something. Ralph had created and facilitated a learning process: he had "coaxed" Marian into attaining her objectives. Marian had directed her own learning. In doing so, she had taken important steps in learning her craft and learning how to learn.

The comment that coaching is managing has been made several times. This is obviously true in an administrative sense, but its significance also comes from deeper factors.

Coaching is part of structural change. It is a way of pushing forward empowerment, demanding, as it does, a change in the behavior of managers. First, it represents a different means of exercising control. Rather than relying on formal methods, the coach controls through persuasion and influence. He or she also controls through sharing responsibility and giving support to staff who share decisions about how they do their jobs.

Coaching behavior also contributes to the information system of the organization. Participation in the relationship exposes what is happening in organizations in ways that formal communication systems and formal structures cannot. Coaching increases the visibility of those parts of the organization where it is used. Communication should become more open.

Coaching is still setting objectives, and it still involves deploying and maximizing resources. The difference is that it concentrates on the most important resource area in the library—the talent and the potential of individuals.

Finally, coaching is directly concerned with the standards of the service to users. It is about performance, maintaining and raising standards, and quality. It is wholly to do with the development of the organization and its staff. As such, it represents a better way for managers to spend much of their time than working through bureaucracies and ossified hierarchies. All of these characteristics became apparent in the relationship between Ralph and Marian.

Chapter 8

Mentoring

This chapter looks at the issues and principles of mentoring within the context of development. It considers mentoring purely as a technique for supporting learning. For clear presentations of the practice of mentoring, and for a more detailed background of the topic, look at Norton and Tivey (1995), or at Nankivell and Shoolbred (1996), and best of all, again, Parsloe and Wray (2000).

Two of the important arguments in this book are that learning and development are personal issues, and that the processes of development described take place within a social and working framework. Some of the theoretical standpoints supporting this are examined (see chapter 4). In chapter 2 we looked at the ideas of introducing flexibility and openness into our organizations, in order to facilitate this kind of learning, while chapter 3 looked at management systems that would support development in this context. There followed, in chapters 4, 5, and 6, a review of the main principles and procedures that form the foundation of individual learning in the workplace. Chapter 7, on coaching, began to look at some of the most important techniques that will deliver this kind of learning and development. Mentoring is the next technique to be examined.

The appropriateness of both coaching and mentoring is seen in the way in which they depend on relationships. The essence of mentoring, like coaching, is to be found in the interplay between the two parties in the transaction. Success depends on the growth of confidence in each other, on a developing respect for each other's abilities, and a two-way learning process. The coaching relationship works in the same way, but to different ends and through different means, and is both individually and group-based. Within the learning process, both techniques are founded on a mainly nondidactic relationship of equals.

To avoid lulling anybody into a false sense of security, I would add that I have some difficulties with mentoring. It is related to coaching, but it is different. As I understand it, it is also essentially different from many of the other techniques now sheltering under its umbrella. I see not only theoretical differences but, in a minority view, quality differences. Nevertheless, mentoring is still a significant part of training, under the right circumstances, and I would not wish to deny its relevance.

A Definition of Mentoring

Looking at the literature of development across a wide swathe of professions, a striking feature is the massive explosion in writing about and using, in different applications, mentoring. Students in schools, colleges, and universities now have mentors, and so do their teachers. There are mentors who link education to the world of work, and there are mentors who work with businessmen exporting to the Third World and the re-emerging republics of Eastern Europe. There are mentors in golf clubs and yacht clubs, and in many other clubs, societies, and associations. We mentor colleagues through their induction periods, when they change organizational roles, when they are involved in change projects, and when they approach retirement.

Across this expanse of territory, all the mentors seem to be doing different things. They are coaches, facilitators, friends, buddies, counselors, guides, and coordinators. They are surely other things as well.

To say that this raises some difficulties is not an abstruse, Jesuitical argument over a meaningless distinction. It is a question of accuracy and of confidence in the intrinsic worth of some of the things we do. All of the activities described above are valid, credible, and important in their own right. The trouble is that they fall into several different categories of training interventions. They take place in different necks of the woods, and they also occupy different positions on the training-education-learning-development spectrum. Many of them are activities in which the individual subjected to the process has little influence over its nature or course. Lots of the activities are geared only to pass on basic information. Some of them have the characteristics of teaching; others are momentary episodes without any evaluation, feedback, or long-term commitment.

You can be sure also that the processes can sometimes have little real planning, and may occasionally be carried out by people who would be surprised to know that they are considered to be mentors.

Mentoring is a difficult, complicated, long-term activity. In its essentials, it has something that is missing from most of the examples used previously (except coaching); and between coaching and mentoring there are other kinds of differences. Some of the things that are now called mentoring could more properly be regarded as other activities, such as team learning or coaching, and vice versa. Hudson (1999), for example, in his manual of coaching, is actually writing about mentoring for much of the time. Even if we are clear on the difference between mentors and coaches, there are other areas of disagreement. Line managers, for example, can legitimately be buddies, guides, coordinators, and facilitators. There is a well-rehearsed argument for saying that they should never be mentors. In the United States, people will not agree with this; in Europe, they will. There are differences between the American and the European schools of thought. The American school allows that line managers can be mentors, while European thinking rules it out. We don't know who is right and who is wrong, and it might not matter: What is important is that ideas about the use of power are left outside the mentoring relationship. For some, being buddies and friends also rules out crucial elements in the mentor–mentee relationship, for we are told that the term means being an "experienced and trusted advisor."

It is necessary to acknowledge that there are elements of mentoring in most training activities. Coaches, facilitators, coordinators, buddies, friends, and guides can all be something approaching mentors of some kind, for some of the time. They may also enjoy a reasonable degree of success at it. The differences lie in the length of the process, the emphasis given to certain functions, and the end results.

I take the coward's way out by working with a narrow definition, while accepting that our thinking on this is developing. I apply the term to the relationship between a senior manager and a manager, or other colleague, at a lower level, so I am talking about mentoring solely in an organizational setting, and only in terms of career development from its beginning to its end. Parsloe and Wray (2000) are more inclusive. They justify this stance on grounds that are particularly appropriate for libraries. They correctly argue that, like coaching, mentoring is a new and evolving concept that we will refine as we get better at using it. Let us just acknowledge the differences of approach and concentrate on essentials.

The origin of the term is said to be from the Greek language, and the name of the advisor to Telemachus in the *Odyssey*. It describes a long-term relationship between two parties. These are, on the one hand, a mentor who contributes a breadth and depth of experience, political acumen, commitment, a belief in learning, and enjoys the esteem of colleagues. The mentor can also make use of a well-honed network, both inside and outside the organization, and will possess high quality management skills. He or she is a communicator, a good observer, and a good listener and questioner, with a still-insatiable curiosity about what is happening in other parts of the organization. This curiosity extends to professional matters in general. On the other hand, the mentee brings potential, ambition, and current functional knowledge of the organization. The two work together in a nonjudgmental atmosphere of trust and mutual respect. Their joint aims are to develop the broad potential of the mentee, through enhancing skills and increasing awareness of the organization and its way of doing things.

Mentoring in some forms was already a widely used training technique long before the current upsurge of interest. Clutterbuck (1991) traces it back to the development of the traditional craft apprenticeships, and the term aptly describes many informal relationships in all sorts of organizations.

There are two elements that make mentoring in organizations stand apart. One is learning and the other is development. The product of learning is a significant change in behavior and, later, attitudes. In our organizations this involves a large shift in perspectives on how we manage our libraries. Development is the long-term change that comes from the application of this learning to managing libraries. It is all of the subsequent changes in attitudes, behavior, management, and learning that arise from the evaluation and feedback from this continuing process. This is far more substantial and lasting than passing on information and ensuring that it is understood. So in this context, explaining procedures, rules, and systems to new entrants is not mentoring. Neither is showing people how to use a purchasing system, apply for leave, report a sick day, or requisition minor building repairs—all of which have sometimes been counted as mentoring. At another level, easing novice researchers into projects or research degrees is not mentoring. This is not to deny that there are elements of mentoring in some of these activities, but more of it is teaching or instructing, and mentors are not teachers; nor are they instructors. The emphasis in mentoring in a learning context is on creating a much more significant change. This is based on developing a mature and rounded attitude to organizational life. It is a process of powerful change in ways that "induction mentoring" or "new entrant mentoring," to take but two examples, can never be.

Some More Mentoring Issues

In the strict sense of the term as used here, the uncritical and unbridled enthusiasm for the technique, which is sometimes detected in the literature of librarianship, should be tempered with consideration of some of the problems that can arise in the use of mentoring. It is not an unequivocal panacea. Clutterbuck (1991) expresses some of the reservations:

- It requires a significant cultural change.
- It needs structural change in order to thrive.
- It can be too prescriptive.
- It could be open to accusations of unfairness.

We can look in more detail at some of these views.

Conservatism

Elsewhere in this book, subtle hints have been dropped about our overfondness for bureaucratic ways of doing things. The central argument is that we need to change our organizations in order to handle the present, and coming, realities of providing library services in the twenty-first century. Mentoring has always been a way of perpetuating an organizational culture. It passes on established norms, and these norms will include management styles and attitudes. This may not be what we or our organizations want. Chapters 1 and 4 argued for divergent thinking, and it is possible that mentoring arrangements will pass on conventional thinking instead.

It is one of my happiest conceits, which I have repeated elsewhere, that managers are clones of each other. Senior library managers in the late-twentieth century based their behaviors on the role models of the seventies and eighties. To get as far as they did, and we have all been guilty, they repeated the patterns that worked for their predecessors. Given half a chance, they will also pass on these features, and as far as we are all concerned, there is no flattery as attractive as imitation. One of the themes running through training and development literature is the need for managers, at all levels, to change. There are now a number of training organizations that have recognized the first problem with mentoring: to find mentors who are capable of passing on the habits and characteristics needed to prosecute organizational change and maintain the momentum of change. So it may not be possible to begin a mentoring program with the selection of mentors. We might first have to engineer and sustain an alteration in management approaches. The things we need to change are almost reflex actions by now, and they have been supported by traditional organizational cultures for a long time. The emphasis on learning, and the changes proposed in the first four chapters of this book, are where mentoring actually begins. If we cannot wait for this to come to fruition, then we need outside intervention in the shape of some change agents to alter behavior at the top of the organization. Attitude change starts here, and without it mentoring is not likely to promote dynamic change.

One of the themes of chapters 2 and 3 is the need for an approach to library organization that stresses the importance of learning as an organizational life-support system. If we accept the need for these kinds of change, the first question is where do our mentors come from? Of course, mentoring is a way of passing on an organizational culture, but in today's organizational environment there is little point in passing on a traditional view of management, if that tradition itself needs to change. When it comes to mentoring for management, today's managers may need to first revise their own views of what talent, and management potential, actually mean. We may well be unconsciously looking for what we were like earlier in our careers, rather than trying to connect with what the library will need in the future. There is an organizational challenge: recognize this problem and develop the ability to intervene where the mentoring process really begins. This will help senior managers to change themselves before they in turn begin the task of developing others.

Structural Rigidity

Mentoring can cut across the grain of hierarchical organizational forms. Introduced into a conventional hierarchy, it can cause uncertainty in the minds of line managers, and can become a source of discord if there are significant attitude differences between mentors and managers in the system. Even in flexible organizations, it can cause problems. It can be argued that the technique is useful for cross functional, or cross departmental, integration. Even so, it can still cause uncertainty and friction, because it may undermine the unified chain of command. Until I found myself managing a virtual team, with a dual leadership function, two chains of command, and, therefore, two lines of communication, I regarded this kind of ambiguity as a potential source of creative friction. I was totally wrong. It is in fact demoralizing, confusing and counterproductive. Mentoring can also be like that unless it is properly handled.

Selectivity

I think that one of the reasons why we have expanded the definition of mentoring and turned it into a "catch-all" term, including so many activities and initiatives, might be that we instinctively know that this is an inherently unfair system of development. If we are really trying to promote open organizations, we will move very carefully when handling a process which, because of logistics and organizational need, cannot reasonably be made widely available. It will inevitably exclude staff who would benefit from it. I can discover no other reason why, for example, there has been such a growth in what is called group mentoring. This may be an economical way of making the technique more widely available, but it is an oxymoron, and strikes a mortal blow straight to the heart of the concept.

One thing that is easier to understand is that there are not enough good mentors to go around. Mentoring requires special skills, which are not within the portfolio of all managers. There is no real reason why they should be, although there is a little of mentoring in most development activities, so the pool of quality mentors is likely to be small and certainly not big enough to meet the needs of an expansive scheme.

Even if we can jettison all of the baggage of the way we learned to be managers ourselves, and what we consider to be the traditional attributes of good management, spotting talent is a suspect and speculative activity. We can all think of the times when we have been wrong in our assessment of staff. There will also be examples of colleagues who, according to all the accepted canons and norms, should not make good managers, but they do. There are other staff, who creep stealthily through the organizational undergrowth, only to emerge unexpectedly in a position of authority and surprise everyone with their abilities. Others who arrive by the same path only confirm Parkinson's law that people can be promoted beyond their abilities.

People can be propelled into senior management by the oddest of forces, and via the strangest routes, making it all the more unpredictable. Yet others will show potential that will not be realized. A persuasive management consultant once argued that a surprisingly high percentage of staff in any organization will have, long before they reach their prime, in his word "turned": That is, they will have been good once, but no more. However well the criteria are set, there is no guarantee that mentoring, for managers at least, will succeed.

Favoritism

The one-to-one relationship at the heart of mentoring is an extremely sensitive one. Given that resource constraints and other factors will not allow wide participation, this relationship is open to misinterpretation. It can be seen as favoritism, and it is also possible for the mentee to become identified with a particular manager. Special relationships can cause suspicion and as much friction as mentors working alongside line managers, with all the potential clashes inherent in that situation.

Managing Mentoring

None of these difficulties are insurmountable. They can all be avoided, or minimized, by the way the scheme is devised and put into practice. There are a number of requirements that need to be built into the system, in order to avoid the pitfalls and make sure that the scheme works in a positive way. The following requirements are based on Nankivell and Shoolbred (1996).

Clear Qualifying Criteria

For all of those involved in mentoring, both as mentor and mentee, there must be a detailed and unambiguous statement of how entry to the scheme can be achieved. It is a fact that not everyone who would benefit from a mentoring scheme can join in one. Equally, other techniques, such as coaching, could also have a degree of prioritization. It is important that the criteria for entry must be in the public domain.

A Pool of Mentors

Some schemes allow mentees to select from a pool of mentors, others allow a choice from a shortlist of two or three, and some allocate mentors as a management exercise. The list of mentors has to be in public circulation. On balance, the allocation should then be made by management. This avoids any mentee selecting a mentor for the wrong reasons. Human nature being what it is, there can be a calculation of the relative power and influence of the mentors, and a choice on that basis.

Clear Objectives

These cover the objectives of both the mentor and the mentee, and relate closely to organizational needs.

The Resource Implications

There must be a precise statement of the resource implications. The commitment of both parties, and the support of the service, has to be quantified. This statement should detail the time input into the scheme. There is evidence that the regularity of contact, and the amount of time devoted to it, are important success factors. In a mentoring scheme for teachers in the United States, it was found that a minimum of twenty five hours at regular intervals throughout the school year was crucial (National Education Association, 2000).

Evaluation

Criteria for evaluating progress, determining success, and providing feedback will be written in at the outset of the relationship. This will be part of the objective-setting exercise.

Exit Strategies

A mechanism that allows the mentoring agreement to be terminated by either party, or by library service management, must also be included. This is a sensible precaution, in view of the uncertainty that will inevitably surround the selection of mentors and mentees, and the nature of the relationship that will develop between them.

The Establishment of Boundaries

If there are any areas not for discussion, such as personal problems, this should be documented. It is also better to draw a clear line between the role of the mentor and the line manager, although, as indicated, not everybody agrees with this. Issues such as performance appraisal and assessment, in general, are also taboo.

Openness

If the information that supports the scheme is then put into the public domain, it makes it open. The criteria for entry are known, as are the organizational justification, the evaluation criteria, and the means of exit. Explaining how and why mentors have been chosen, and not allowing mentees to chose their partners, removes another potential difficulty. Establishing responsibilities and expectations also helps to create transparency. In preparing the scheme, the overall aim is to maintain a generally professional tone and context. This will do much to reduce worries about unfairness, bias, subjectivity, and favoritism.

The Application of Mentoring to Libraries

Mentoring is the kind of learning experience that benefits all levels of the organization.

Junior Staff

For junior staff, mentoring can broaden the organizational perspective of the learner. It can begin to explore motivation, goalsetting, and how individuals prefer to learn, and help conceptualize organizational learning and its importance. For more mature learners, the emphasis can shift toward career progression and professional development.

Information Professionals

The group of people in all libraries who are mastering their craft, and consolidating their positions as increasingly competent professionals, are the key targets for mentoring. They are at the point where they will be making decisions that will influence the shape of their careers. The positive influence of a more senior figure, who has travelled the same road, would be valuable. In some ways the first move into middle management is more difficult than any subsequent move, and a guiding hand here is a valuable development tool. As learners, this group of staff may be well on the way to becoming proactive in their approaches to development, and they will be making key decisions about how they move forward.

Managers

Management mentoring can concentrate on preparation for senior management and the passing on of enhanced professional skills. It can do this without initially tying learning into appraisal and reward systems.

In the kind of loose-coupled, team-based organizations described ad infinitum in this book, management rightly becomes a dispersed function. Senior managers, working in mentoring roles, can bring a sharper focus to the thinking of mentees. In some ways, they can compensate for the diffused activity that is management in flexible organizations. They can play important roles as anchors, while still pointing to the skills needed for managing these kinds of organizations: communication, observation, listening, questioning, transactional leadership, and change management. They combine these behaviors with the more conventional management skills, such as demonstrating political awareness and networking.

Mentoring, Learning, and Development

Mentoring fits with the philosophy, principles, and practices of the sort of learning outlined earlier:

- Being outside power relationships, learning can take place in unpressurized situations.
- Mentors will not be judgmental.
- The learners have some influence over what and how they learn.
- Learning takes place in a partnership. Although it is not a partnership of equals, it is a reciprocal relationship. Mentees are engaged in a process of development, while mentors are honing their people skills. The latter also gain insights into parts of the organization with which they might have lost touch, and are contributing their experience and their views to the learning process.
- Learners are being introduced to a network of contacts, and should be exposed to a number of varied, and novel, learning experiences.
- Mentoring schemes are a part of empowerment. As well as giving mentees some control over their own learning, they also give a sense of direction and shape to career development.
- Mentoring is motivational: It improves job satisfaction, it sets targets, and it uses a role model who is acceptable to the organization.
- Mentoring improves the sense of self-worth and self-realization, through the fact that a more senior member of staff is taking an interest in the development of individuals.
- There can also be a huge boost to organization development. Applying mentoring to the problem of managing diversity can lead to attitude change, and to changes in policy, structure, and working conditions.

As well as its general relevance, there are specific situations in which mentoring can play a part in development. To begin with, it is a useful technique when things go wrong.

Remedial Action

There are times when things like attitude problems arise. These require a more subtle touch than merely improving a knowledge base. Mentoring has been used to change an individual's perception of the library–user relationship, to alter relationships between technical staff and reader services staff, and to improve relationships between a manager and external entities, even with comparatively senior managers. Once the need is mutually acknowledged, assignment to a mentor is again a less confrontational way of dealing with a development issue, and is better than unleashing the full power of official organizational responses and formal training events. It has its advantages in any situation where there is an issue of relationships in a sensitive professional or managerial context.

Diversity Training

In this context, the phrase is used to describe ways of aiding the development of individuals or groups of employees who might, for various reasons, be considered as having development problems. Some aspects, such as the importance of mentoring for women, have attracted considerable research interest. Within this category can also be included minority groups. Using mentoring in this context produces all the usual benefits, plus a few more:

- It may be considered to be positive discrimination. It reinforces the concept of fairness, because it indicates that management will recognize the difficulty faced by some employees, and be prepared to do something about it.
- It can put a positive value on diversity.

Change Situations

Most change projects require a full range of training and development techniques, such as coaching, group learning, action learning, facilitating, and counseling. Within the change process, there will be individuals who are at the fulcrum of the change effort. It is initially these individuals who will benefit from the support offered by a mentoring program. They will be working with uncertainty. It could be a project that may well challenge assumptions about how the organization is being run, alter relationships, change social groupings, and impose demands on communication within the library service. Change is one of the most fruitful learning experiences, and assigning a mentor who has already experienced the pressures and exigencies of change initiatives is a way of maximizing the learning. It can also be used to advise on the skills of change management.

The Skills of the Mentor

In considering the definition of mentoring, and its relationship with other initiatives like coaching, we have identified the skills, attributes, and characteristics that a mentor will need to bring to the relationship. They are:

- A broad range of experience at all levels of the organization
- A continuing interest in how the organization functions
- A detachment from the political aspects of organizational life
- A willingness to leave formal authority, and the customary use of power, outside the relationship
- The capacity to share the management of a mentoring relationship: to agree on objectives; to evaluate; to assess; to close the relationship
- A commitment to developing less experienced colleagues
- A nonjudgmental attitude
- The ability to empathize: to understand the way the mentee feels about organizational issues, and matters of personal development
- Understanding in general
- The ability to listen
- The skill of asking questions
- The skill of providing proper feedback

These last four points, the vital ones of communication, will drive the relationship. There is a full treatment of these aspects in Parsloe and Wray (2000).

The Mentoring Process

Most of the issues we have dealt with in this chapter can be summed up by describing the mentoring process from the first stage of setting the objectives of the scheme, to the final evaluation and closure. Figure 8.1 sets out this process. You will note that I begin by establishing the characteristics to be sought in mentors. To me, this is where mentoring begins.

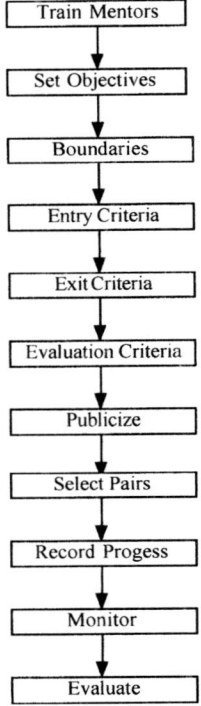

Figure 8.1 The Mentoring Process: Key Features

Case Study 8
A MENTORING DIFFICULTY

The Situation

A public library service, with a new library director, was engaged in the process of creating a team-based organization. One of the difficult areas that Carlos, the director, was grappling with was technical services. This comprised the acquisitions, cataloging, and interlibrary loan functions, together with the management of the library's automated system. Committed to team building, Carlos's first step was to broaden the responsibility for the management of the library system to include acquisitions, cataloging, and interlibrary loans. The position of technical services manager was vacant, and Carlos saw this as the fulcrum of the proposed changes. He had already looked at similar models in other libraries.

When he came to consider the appointment of a new technical services manager, he gave considerable thought to the new role he wished the appointee to perform. Eventually, he decided that he would seek a manager who would take a balanced view of the position of the library system in relation to other areas of the library. He particularly did not want to appoint someone who would consider the management of the system as the primary concern. What he wanted was a manager who would take a broad view, and would be able to play a wide-ranging part in the work of the section. It was also important that whoever was appointed would accept that the automated system was there to serve the rest of the library and its users, and would deploy his or her skills and talents across the service in general. He was looking for a staff member who would be involved in other things, and he saw the right kind of appointment as being essential to the development of the library. The ability to play a team role and to make a contribution at managerial, professional, and technical levels was essential. There was, therefore, a firm expectation that the new recruit would make a contribution to the management of the library service in general.

The information pack sent to all candidates contained a detailed exposition of the thinking behind the organizational developments and the intended role for the technical services manager. Stress was also given to the requirement for a positive contribution to the corporate management effort. During the selection procedure, all of the issues were probed with rigor, and eventually Hilda was appointed to the post.

For some time, everything seemed to go well. The new manager had qualifications in both computer science and librarianship, and she appeared to apply this combined knowledge expertly. Hilda and Carlos developed an open dialogue, and progress was made on a number of issues. Hilda also responded well to extra demands imposed by a staffing emergency in the library, and the positive nature of the professional relationship between the two was cemented when Carlos was able to recognise this contribution with a tangible reward. When Carlos looked back on the first year of Hilda's appointment, he was able to see that the amicability of the relationship stemmed from the fact that he had no reason to disagree with Hilda's views. This realization came later and gradually, over the first year, some discordant notes began to be sounded. At the time of the job interview, Carlos had some slight reservations about Hilda. This had its roots in the detection of a somewhat abrupt manner. It had been outweighed by the potential contribution that Carlos felt that Hilda could make. However, it slowly began to emerge that Hilda's way of dealing with other people was in fact quite destructive. Carlos's management style was very open, and he spent a lot of time talking to staff and users throughout the library service. His own observations, and some guarded comments by other people, led him to the conclusion that the management style inside the technical services department was at odds with the style in the rest of the library. He felt that Hilda's approach was authoritarian. It also emerged that Hilda was not developing her own role across the spectrum of activities within central services. She was working solely on the computer system, while other staff were continuing to work within their own limited areas. This was undermining attempts to develop the broad-based management of a pool of multiskilled individuals.

Carlos soon realized that he had other problems. The major change project to create a team-based organization had been under way before Hilda joined the service. One of the key features was the team-building exercise in technical services. Carlos felt that the area met many of the criteria that would allow a good team to be established. The main factors were its combination of specialist technical expertise, strong traditional librarianship, and the scope to devolve significant responsibilities to the team. Being reasonably self-contained, and hosting sufficient managerial, financial, professional, and technical responsibilities, it was considered to be an ideal starting point. There was also a groundswell of support from the section. Nevertheless, Carlos became aware that nothing was changing internally. Despite all the effort being made, Hilda's management style was not unfreezing, and the team ethos was not moving forward. Staff in any case chafed against the autocratic style of control, but were also becoming aware of the benefits enjoyed by other staff in areas of the library where change was taking place.

The library management committee was being reorganized to reflect the team ethos, and it was in this forum that things came to a head. The membership was becoming nonhierarchical and, for the first time, had representation from outside the management structure of the service. The changing character of this began to put Hilda under pressure. She did not agree with the new composition of the group, and she became increasingly entrenched. Matters came to a head during the discussion of a proposed replacement for the automated system. Carlos asked the senior staff to prepare papers setting out their requirements. Hilda was not initially asked to do so, and during the discussion she made it clear that she should be deciding on requirements, and it would be for the other staff to change their ways of working to fit with the requirements of the system she chose. The climax came with an angry response from Walter, the Business Information librarian: "After thirty years in the business I will not be told how I should be doing things by a technician with no understanding of the needs, or the importance, of users."

Because of the wider implications of the choice of system for the library, Carlos was working closely with the council's head of computing services. Sidney was a colleague and friend of long standing, and the cooperation between the two services was developing through a number of joint projects and voluntary links, which were improving the service to users. There was a joint services steering group handling the technical issues of the new system, and events at the next meeting of this body finally caused Carlos to act.

Sidney outlined a number of technical possibilities. Each one of these was summarily rejected by Hilda, with much headshaking and negative body language as Sidney spoke. She then put forward her own proposals. Some discussion ensued, before Carlos decided that he would meet with Sidney and Hilda to formulate a proposal for the technical specification. This could later be discussed more temperately by the steering group.

By now, Carlos knew he had to deal with what he saw as the bigger problem of Hilda's behavior.

The Solution

Carlos was lucky, in that Hilda's first appraisal was due, so he decided to use the SDAS in order to try and initiate the change he felt was needed. His first difficulty was in the documentation. Hilda had not indicated any areas where she felt she could improve her performance, but she had indicated some specific actions that she felt management should quickly undertake in order to remove things that hindered her. These included staffing increases in technical services and a salary regrading, which would pay her more than any other senior staff member.

The interview proceeded with equanimity. Carlos complimented Hilda on the efficient operation of the computer system, and went into some detail on her positive contribution. Together they reviewed the situation concerning acquisitions and cataloging. Hilda explained how things were organized in these areas, and did not attempt to hide her lack of interest in developing a team-based structure or in empowering her staff. In a neutral tone, Carlos explained his management philosophy and the general support it enjoyed in the library. Hilda did not respond.

When it came to setting objectives for the next year, the difficulties came to a head. Carlos talked about the agreed service objective of establishing empowered teams, and suggested that this might be a way of improving the staffing situation in technical services, without actually increasing the numbers. He suggested that they should jointly draw up a program of development, concentrating on Hilda's management style and her way of dealing with colleagues. She did not comment on his vision for the service, but simply said, "I don't need anybody to tell me how to manage, or how to deal with people." The meeting ended without an agreed set of objectives for the coming year.

Carlos was now in some difficulty. Hilda was not accepting the need for development, but he felt instinctively that she needed the close support of an individual with whom she could work. He had already expressed his satisfaction with Hilda's technical and professional skills. Indeed, he accepted that they were of a high order. As he saw the issue, it was a broad developmental one that was suited to mentoring. After some thought, he asked Hilda to meet him regularly in order to talk through issues as they arose. He also suggested they could look generally at how she was discharging her role in the library and how this could be extended.

Hilda agreed, and the first few meetings went well. She was pointed toward ways in which she could improve her time management and her setting of priorities. She was able to take options that she liked, and Carlos discussed the results with her. An agreed written record of each meeting was added to Hilda's file.

While this was happening, Carlos was receiving the results of the staff development and appraisal interviews Hilda was conducting with her staff. These interviews had been the source of a small disagreement between the two. Hilda was unable to see the need for the procedure, and was reluctant to carry out the interviews.

As the comments and issues were fed through the system to Carlos, his concerns about Hilda's approach to management began to grow. He started to direct their discussions back toward management philosophies and to the choice with which Hilda would increasingly be faced. He placed the discussion within the context of Hilda's future career, and pointed her to relevant issues and to principles aired in the professional press. He was careful not to be prescriptive, and the discussion was usually in the context of identifying general trends in management, and looking for ways in which the service, its staff, and the users could benefit from them. Over a period of months there was no movement.

Carlos was still left with the issue of Hilda's role in the department, and how this could be reconciled with his own view of how her role should be discharged. This topic was also a legitimate development issue for them both, and Carlos again tried to set their discussions in the context of Hilda's personal growth in the library service. During the course of one half-hour meeting, their relationship irrevocably changed, and Carlos found it impossible to maintain the mentoring relationship. Hilda openly acknowledged that she was developing her role in a way that did not fit with Carlos's view of service needs. She indicated that her priorities were not the same as his. She restated her opinion that the computer service was the most important thing in the library, and that everything else should be modified to fit the needs of the system. The meeting ended with Carlos's bald statement that she would discharge the obligations of her contract and job description, and that she would act in accordance with the development plan of the library.

Hilda, of course, did neither of these things. Around her, the introduction of teams into the library worked well, and the bulk of the responsibility for the technical services section was decentralized to these teams. The computer system was integrated with the council's computer service, and the staff running it on a day-to-day basis were transferred to the latter. Hilda remained in charge of the rump of the acquisitions process until she took another job elsewhere.

Comment

Carlos acted honorably and with the best of intentions. His failures were managerial, although even if this aspect had been thought through and properly constituted, it is unlikely that the outcome would have been any different. Without a formal mentoring scheme, Carlos's first serious action should have been to propose a service-wide management mentoring system. The introduction of teams had followed a textbook approach to implementing change. If the introduction of mentoring had followed the same process, it would have enjoyed wide support. Presenting it as a general development aid would have avoided the possibility that Hilda would have seen it as something aimed specifically at securing her compliance with Carlos's wishes.

Carlos never referred to the process as mentoring. If he had been more open, and if Hilda had known more about what he was attempting to do, there would have been at least a chance that she would have seen some of the potential benefits for herself. She was willful, determined, and direct almost to the point of rudeness. She was also talented, hard working, and intelligent. It is unlikely that she would have precipitated the denouement if she had been better informed of what Carlos was attempting. Ignorance caused insecurity and suspicion.

Attention to detail could also have avoided the terrible trap Carlos fell into, when he cast himself in the role of mentor. Even here, there were extenuating circumstances. The early relationship between Carlos and Hilda had been one of mutual respect. Hilda appreciated the freedom Carlos gave her, and benefited from their early discussions. For Carlos, Hilda demonstrated commitment, and a high degree of technical and professional competence. This changed because Hilda could not accept the ethos of the service, although she knew about this before she accepted the post. As a manager, she would brook no dissent in her own section, and carried this through into her relationship with her peers and her line manager. Deceived by the respect that initially existed between them, and aware of her deteriorating relationships with colleagues, Carlos felt he was the only choice as mentor. In a formal scheme, there would have been a pool of potential mentors, and this need not necessarily have restricted the choice to library managers. There was a good relationship between the library and the computer service, for example, and it might have been possible to exploit the common ground between Hilda and some of the senior staff there.

The fault did not lie in the fact that Carlos was Hilda's line manager as such. Line managers can apply influence in the cause of the development of the mentee, but Carlos failed to separate formal authority from his mentoring role. When he began to receive information from the assessment system, he inevitably brought it into the mentoring relationship. He was then trying to deal with the issue of underperformance in terms of Hilda's management of the section, while still struggling to put development on track. The one inevitably colored the attitude to the other. Once he reached the point where he could only use formal authority, the mentoring process was at an end.

Carlos also started from the wrong place when he decided on mentoring as an appropriate technique for Hilda. In spite of her professional qualifications, and her determined acquisition of IT qualifications, Hilda was basically a non-learner. She had no comprehension of the learning opportunities in her working environment, and could not recognize her own need to learn. Nor could she understand that there were many different ways of learning. Carlos's first step should have been to investigate this, gain an appreciation of why this was so, and apply some motivational techniques.

It is worth adding that there was, in any case, no procedure for terminating the relationship. There were no established criteria that would allow the parties to decide how to measure success, and there was no painless way out of the situation. The end came when Carlos began to use the information he received from the appraisal scheme. There are safeguards to this kind of questionable use, if the appraisal scheme is treated as a formal scheme and if it is used as an organizational learning experience.

Mentoring is part of the learning subsystem. It is also a learning experience for the parties involved. It is vital that the principles it is designed to uphold should be demonstrated throughout. This means introducing it in a way that will be consistent with its eventual operation. There is a need for openness, objectivity, ownership, and integrity. Debate, communication, and learning are therefore part of the model. This comes from ensuring that there is no link between mentoring and performance appraisal. Let us see how this should really work.

Case Study 9
A MENTORING SUCCESS

This case study is set in another library, in a university, a few years after the events described previously. The main protagonists this time are Francis, a younger librarian called Jack, and Carlos.

The Situation

Carlos eventually moved to a university, where he was able to develop his ideas about teams. The team structure he introduced was based on the faculty structure of the university. This included four faculties: Art and Design, Science and Technology, Social Sciences and Education, and Business and Management. The Art and Design library team was the smallest and, by far, the most successful in terms of performance. Relationships with teaching staff and students were good, and inside the team there was a strong coherence. Some of this was due to the influence of Francis, the Art and Design librarian, not only for his work in building a team, but in using his expertise as an art historian and art bibliographer to earn the respect of the faculty. As it was a small team, he was supported at a professional level by a young librarian in her first post. One other member of the team was working to acquire an academic qualification in the field.

One of the things causing some concern for Carlos was that Francis was within some six months of retirement. The team structure and the commitment to learning meant that Carlos wanted to find a successor to Francis from within. He was also anxious to perpetuate the conditions that, in his view, had led to their success: a committed team combining high professional skills with an appropriate depth of subject knowledge, good leadership, and a user-centered and innovative philosophy. Francis was also widely known and respected in the general field of art and design librarianship.

Francis and Carlos considered that two members of the team showed potential, but would need two or three years experience before they could be realistically considered as Francis's successor. The only other potential successor to Francis was Jack, the deputy librarian in the faculty of education. This was the largest of the faculty teams. Jack's previous experience included time spent as a film and photography librarian. He had a learning plan that was designed to equip him to take on a management post in the future, but Carlos was not sure that he was ready for the move to such a demanding environment as the art and design team.

Carlos and Francis discussed the matter at length before they decided to invite applications for a secondment to the post of librarian in the faculty of art and design. When Francis retired, Jack joined the art and design team as acting librarian. He also signed a formal mentoring agreement. The mentor chosen by Carlos was obviously Francis, who was retained to develop the mentoring relationship with Jack. The formal agreement between Jack and Francis stipulated that the mentoring arrangement would continue until Francis and Jack unanimously agreed that the objectives had been achieved. These objectives were: to equip Jack to continue, and further develop, the service laid down by Francis; to maintain the good relationships with the library users; to develop Jack's devolved management style. There was to be no involvement with performance appraisal or with specific skills. The purposes were attitude development and broadening experience.

Jack was acting librarian to the faculty for twelve months after Francis's retirement. During this period, the mentoring input went primarily into helping Jack to build a relationship with members of the faculty. Francis met with him weekly, discussed the issues that were arising from the work of the library, and offered a number of pointers to possible action. He listened to Jack's proposals, and was often able to offer him information about how people would react to issues, without dictating a particular course of action. From his thirty years as faculty librarian, he was able to provide background information, explaining why things were done as they were. He was also a fount of anecdotes and events about individuals. In this way he achieved the purposes of passing on the culture of both the library and the faculty, and extending and deepening Jack's knowledge of the people he was serving. There was always a safeguard: If the relationship stagnated or deteriorated, provision was made for its termination if either party felt it was not achieving the objectives.

As far as the internal operations of the library were concerned, Francis acted as a role model, without imposing his style on Jack. The latter was able to absorb the philosophy behind empowered teams, and gradually came to an understanding of the dynamics of the team he was leading. Some time after the arrangement was concluded, Jack was appointed librarian to the faculty.

Comment

Compared with his initial attempt, Carlos's approach to mentoring had been improved significantly. The scheme was documented and in the public domain. It was open for all staff to apply for entry, and the criteria for acceptance into a mentoring relationship were known. There was an appropriate mentor available. Appropriate in this case meant not only the ability and knowledge to contribute to the scheme, but to do so without the handicaps that dogged Carlos's relationship with Hilda. Francis met all the criteria for acting as a mentor: he had a reputation in his field; he was able to model the behavior Carlos wanted to encourage in Jack; he had a record of successful development of library services. At the point of retirement, in one way he was as disinterested as anyone could possibly be. In another way, he could be expected to commit himself to the task of perpetuating the culture he had helped create, and to ensuring that the library he had managed for many years continued to be an innovative, flexible, and developing organization. Bringing him back after his retirement was an opportunity that Carlos did well to take advantage of. By then, Francis was even further outside the politics and the day-to-day running of the service, while on the other hand he was still keen to see his final project through to completion.

The scheme was also well administered. There was a match between individual and organizational needs and expectations, and the resulting objectives were agreed upon by both parties. Meetings were held at regular intervals, and an agreed record was kept. Before the process started, the conditions for termination were also agreed upon. These were ultimately dependent on achieving the objectives, although there was also a mechanism for dealing with any failures in the relationship. Although the area of interest was wide ranging, the exclusions were carefully defined. No personal issues were to be dealt with, and there would be no attempt to deal with the more concrete management skills. Both parties found this latter restriction slightly artificial, because the focus on attitudes and relationships, which was the heart of the mentoring agreement, sometimes spilled over into more practical issues. Francis dealt with this by linking with the more general development programs of the library. One example was Jack's need to strengthen his bibliographic knowledge of the field. This was accomplished through the formal development program.

Finally, the success of the scheme was vital to the morale and motivation of the entire library. The staff had by and large subscribed to the vision of a learning organization, and most people had worked hard to turn the vision into reality. Anyone could have sought entry to the mentoring scheme and enjoyed the development opportunity afforded to Jack. While there were the usual grumbles when Jack was appointed as faculty librarian, even the complainers had to grudgingly agree that the process had been open and as fair as possible. This made a major contribution to organizational culture: It strengthened expectations. The next time a similar opportunity arose, those interested would remember how the previous instance had been dealt with, and would frame their expectations accordingly. In other words, their perception of how the organization behaved would increase their motivation. Having staked a great deal on preparing his own staff to assume greater responsibility, failing to recruit from within the organization, on the first occasion the system was put to the test, would have repudiated the doctrine of development and dealt a withering blow to Carlos's credibility.

In many people's minds, there was a link between Jack's success, Francis's continuing commitment on a part-time basis, and mentoring. This, of course, was true. The scheme fixed in the organizational culture the sentiment that mentoring was worthwhile. The success of mentoring as a development tool was assured.

Equally important, it set down a marker for senior management. Francis took on the mentoring role at a stage in his career when the end was in sight, and he was in danger of beginning to coast. It refocused his energies, and gave him a fresh challenge and an added interest. It was also a new incentive to other managers who might not have reached the career peak they thought was possible, but might benefit from a renewed sense of purpose in the latter part of their careers.

As always, the secret lies in the process.

Chapter 9

Learning in Teams

Learning in groups of one kind or another is an idea that has a very long pedigree in educational psychology. In some of its forms, such as Action Learning or other groups that are set up specifically to foster the learning process, it also brings together many characteristics that we see as being important in organizational learning. Team learning is the last link in the chain that creates the learning library organization described in chapter 2: the organization that will best meet the challenges of chapter 1, and will support learning at all levels. It is the mechanism that turns individual learning into genuine organizational learning. This is what leads to organizational change.

Coming to grips with team learning is not easy, mainly because of the extraordinary number of teams that now exist. The usual reasons for setting up teams are either to improve performance or to manage a specific project. It could be strongly suggested that achieving both these objectives depends on the quality of the learning process within a team. It is probably true to say also that in many libraries, and other not-for-profit organizations, the learning process is inevitably and understandably given much less attention than team dynamics in general, or the actual processes of team building and creating a successful working team. We probably come to it in much the same way as we do learning from work, or self-learning. The assumption is that it happens instinctively, and that it does not call for a systematic approach: If a group is formed for any reason, then we think learning will occur. This may be true to a limited extent. What the natural or instinctive approach will not do is support any kind of learning cycle. It will neither develop all of the characteristics that come from group learning, nor will it ensure anything like the full exploitation of the potential of group learning. Only if the idea of learning, and the learning system, are used as design features for the groups and their interrelationships, will this happen.

The success of team learning is once again partly dependent on organizational structures and on management styles. For example, a bureaucracy, or anything based on a strong hierarchy, is going to make use of formal status. It is also going to inevitably encourage confrontational or competitive behavior because, in these organizations, development is based on competition. Good teams rely on a different form of competition to some extent, but they also rely heavily on collaboration. Bureaucracies, with their clear demarcations, their way of investing authority, their way of separating the executive from the rest of the organization, and the weight of their tradition, make it impossible for collaborative learning conditions to be established. It is feasible to push responsibility down a bureaucracy and empower a part of it. The likelihood is that the characteristics of this part of the organization will resemble the nature of the parent. As we have seen in chapter 2, the other thing a bureaucracy, or a hierarchical system, does is make it easy to apportion blame when things go wrong, and this will not help learning. The barriers will still be there. This writer will take some convincing that real teams, that will stand up to scrutiny, can actually exist inside inflexible organizational structures. But if they do, they will not be learning teams, because the right learning conditions cannot flourish in that environment.

A Definition of Learning Teams

Something will have to be added to the standard definition of a team: "a number of people whose skills are complementary, who make common cause, who subscribe to agreed aims and a particular style of working while accepting accountability for their performance" (Pugh, 2000). We need to explore the kind of attitude to learning that must prevail before true learning teams happen:

> A team, before it is anything else, is about knowledge. How to get it, how to improve it, and how to pass it on. In the old days knowledge was a by-product of doing business; today it is a primary driver. The distinctions

between working and learning have never been blurrier . . . every dysfunction a team can slip into . . . [is] really a failure of learning. (Robbins and Finley, 1998)

To the standard definition, we can add that teams are organisms that will, with members acting collaboratively and in concert, consciously and systematically acquire and develop the skills of learning, within a working environment. Whether it is called a functional team, a work team, a project team, a process team, or a learning group of one kind or another, it will demonstrate the attributes described in the previous sentence. We can now put a little more flesh onto these elements.

Learning from Work

There is increased evidence, as mentioned earlier, both in the United Kingdom and the United States, that the formal learning systems of organizations are becoming less significant than the informal ones. The statement refers to work-based learning: Team learning plays a crucial part in this. If work-based learning is to have its maximum effect, it should take place in the right conditions. These are examined below.

The Scope to Learn

This means going back to the principles of part 1, and redesigning the organization so that jobs, and combinations of jobs, are amenable to expansion and self-direction. Along with this comes the empowerment of the members of the group. Teams achieve these things.

Equality in Learning

The internal workings of the team should be based on the equality of all learners. Teams call for a practical acknowledgment that the validity of everyone's experience does not depend on role, function, or position. Second, the team has to operate in a double loop organization. In short, there should be no impermeable barrier between the thinkers and the doers, or between the strategy formers and the implementers.

Collaborative Learning

The sharing of learning must be real. Learning, as we have seen, can be instinctive. It can sometimes occur in a group even when some members do not, and need not, contribute. It can also take place where the process is dominated by a few members to the exclusion of others. While there is learning, these characteristics do not make a learning team. Creating this team will need a set of rules to ensure everyone is equally involved.

Safe Learning

It follows that learning has to take place in a safe environment. There must not only be rules to ensure the process works for everyone, but the supportive function of the group has to be used to help create the circumstances in which things can be tried, and mistakes made, with comparatively little personal risk. The ground rules also ensure an even-handed treatment of all members.

A New Management Style

It also follows that there must be a change in management styles. Empowerment and the coach/facilitator/mentor roles are keys to creating the learning environment. What is more, there could be other changes in styles, such as the use of shared leadership or more than one facilitator.

Peer Learning

The presence of peer learning guarantees that a real team exists. One of the things we have learned from groupwork in schools is that students are often very capable of offering lucid explanations to their fellows. Aside from this, the coach, who could often be a team member, will spend much of his or her time on one-to-one relationships, that will help guide peer learning.

Learning from Diversity

Team learning is about learning from work, self-learning, self-development, and learning from each other. Modern librarianship is an ideal seedbed for exploring new perspectives and for the detached consideration of the standpoints of others. It is a place where it is necessary to appreciate the skills brought to work situations by people from traditional librarianship, information technology, and multimedia backgrounds. There are also, at some levels, even more diverse groupings.

Systematic Learning

Team learning is underpinned by self-learning, personal learning contracts, needs analyses, appraisal, and evaluation. It makes use of a method, and it adheres to the learning cycles of, for example, Kolb (1985) or Honey (1993).

If a group of people, who are brought together in a library for any purpose, whatever they are called, are displaying these characteristics, they are a learning team. They might be working as a short-term project team, or brought together as part of a longer-term change process. It could be an activity started by a manager, an Action Learning Group, or a fully formed, self-managing work team. If they do not work in an empowering environment, where they can realize the potential of learning, then they are not learning teams. If they do not learn systematically, and use the team learning skills as part of a learning systems approach, they are doing something else that is the subject of another book.

The Theoretical Justification

The emergence of learning theories that emphasize the value of learning in groups is a natural consequence of the movement of management theories, through behaviorism, constructivism, connectivism, and group dynamics, toward adult learning theories.

Chapter 4 dealt with the main theories that have led to the acceptance of the value of team learning. The educational psychology theories of Piaget, Vygotsky, Bruner, and Freire are discussed, and their main works are cited in the bibliography. The major ideas behind team learning are:

- Team learning draws its strength from all the differences to be found amongst the members of the group.
- The team is itself a very strong motivational force.
- The exchanges between the group members are the vital learning experiences. These exchanges must therefore be made systematic.
- Teams can be used to create an unthreatening atmosphere, in which participants will gradually learn that there is no need to constantly defend their own particular specialisms.
- There is an important link between structures and learning, with the argument by implication that bureaucratic structures impede learning. Teams are one way of creating flexible organizations.
- The leader must be a worker and a learner. By extension, this confirms the importance of equality within groups.

Eventually, most of these principles found their way into the beliefs of adult learning theorists. and have informed the writing of many experts who used and developed the idea of team learning. For example, they are part of the approach of the Organization Development movement, the Learning Organization proponents, and Knowledge Management adherents. Teams, in fact, figure in most of the proposals for new kinds of organizations.

The Nature of Learning Teams

Team learning is based on a clear process, or the set of rules that were referred to earlier. Without these features there is no structure, and the learning will become diffuse and unmeasurable. There are, therefore, ground rules to be put in place before learning begins:

Team Composition
Learning in teams needs diversity as much as anything else. The learning process demands that the team must contain a variety of backgrounds, roles, responsibilities, and functions, if it is to work.

Aims
Looking back over twenty years of practical work on introducing and developing teams into library operations, there is a particularly sharp and uncomfortable awareness that some of the obvious things were not done. One of these is clearly stating the aim and ensuring that this is understood by all the team. More than this, deciding on and clarifying objectives becomes part of the learning process. I can think of teams in libraries where this was taken as read. At the time, it may well have been felt that there was an implicit awareness of the destination and the route to be taken. With the benefit of hindsight this was not so, and outcomes would have been different if it had been.

Ownership
Developing from the previous point, there has to be a clear sense that the means and the ends belong to all of the team. This sense of ownership has to extend to the purpose and values of team learning. The learning objectives should be individual and group targets, and there is an obvious overlap. For most teams, the learning objective will be to provide a more efficient service to users. This will include subsets of both individual and group objectives. There should be a personal learning plan for all members. Collectively, the team objectives should be

- Learning how to learn in teams
- Learning how to work as a team.

Both of these elements will include issues such as motivation and conflict management. Conflict itself is an important part of teamwork and team learning. The creative synergy discussed in chapter 1 comes in part from conflict. The essential thing is that teams recognize it as a constructive factor in group dynamics—and learn to capitalize on it.

- Problem solving as a team
- Job enlargement, job enrichment, and how to deal with empowerment will be key issues at both the personal and team level

Organization

There are elements of systems thinking, and organizational learning theory, in team learning. At the start of this chapter, the point was made that effective team learning does not happen instinctively. For many people, it is not a natural process, and it needs to be managed so that there is a systematic approach that creates common ground out of the visions of individuals and overall team needs. It is also a process that should be subject to the same rigor as other forms of learning, in that it has to be assessable and transferable.

Coaching

Do teams need a coach or facilitator? There are lots of examples of self-managing teams in the literature as well as reports of teams who manage their own learning processes without intervention. There is certainly an argument for excluding anybody who cannot dispose of formal authority or legal power, as case study 10 demonstrates. There is, on the other hand, a clear role for one or more team members who can extend the process of individual coaching and take it forward on a group basis, as case study 10 again indicates. There may or may not be a need for a formal trainer, but the learning has to be managed in a broad and subtle way, and everybody should be aware of it. It is a process that runs silently on the learning dynamics of the team, the sharing of responsibility for facilitating, and on the skills of team learning.

Learning Resources

Another key factor that is often ignored is that team learning requires the same support as any other form of learning, in the shape of access to resources and specialized assistance when required. Here the more conventional role of the coach as assessor, analyser, prompter, and motivator can be deployed when it is called for.

Complexity
The learning should involve complex areas. There is increasing evidence to support the efficacy of teams for dealing with complex ideas, or for working in complex situations where creativity and innovation are needed (Slavin, 1995).

Team Learning Skills

Peter Senge's seminal work on the learning organization (1990) is the jumping off point for much of the thought on the skills that need to be nurtured in teams, if learning is to occur. Senge's long list of team learning skills include:

- Dialogue
- Discussion
- Collective thinking
- Inclusive thinking
- Listening
- Systems thinking
- Reflection
- Inquiry
- Practice

Out of these we can pick the key skills for further discussion.

Dialogue
To Senge, this is understanding what other people mean. It is a form of exploration of ideas and positions, and it is not confrontational. More than a statement of a position, it is an unthreatening beginning to a process of identifying common ground. Dialogue must accommodate all the team members and create a larger, shared insight than that enjoyed by one person. It disposes of half-formed, uncritical, or prejudiced judgments, and shows individuals that there can be such a thing as "collective thought." Everyone becomes stronger because they begin to see the weaknesses of their own positions and viewpoints, and a common meaning and purpose starts to emerge. Senge believes this depends on

- A preparedness to set aside assumptions
- A willingness to dispense with ideas of formal authority and status
- A facilitator who can keep the rules, prompt, and support

Another key issue is that, in the dialogue stage, there is no ban on the wide expression of views. The dialogue is non-judgmental and not intended to defend a position. It is holding things up to scrutiny.

One of the conditions for team learning outlined earlier was that it can only take place where there is equality. There has to be almost a collegial situation and a set of relationships based on what Senge calls "seeing each other as colleagues"—not necessarily agreeing or deferring to other views, but accepting differences as a learning point. This is also where the facilitator is important, in order to keep the dialogue on track, ensure that it remains open, and maintain balance.

Within this broad skills area, there are other skills that contribute to the overall learning process:

- Listening. This involves taking in the information being offered, analyzing it, rephrasing what is being said, and repeating it to confirm and enhance understanding. This process also assists in maintaining the objectivity of dialogue. Productive listening demands a clear mind. The natural tendency, when listening, is to prepare a response on a point-by-point basis as the statement is being made. This is because both the speaker and the listener are not automatically in a dialogue mode; they are ready to defend positions and argue cases, so they are already at the discussion and decision-making stages. Learning to listen is, therefore, one of the first steps in learning how to conduct a dialogue.
- Developing the right body language to show that proper listening is taking place. This involves facing the speaker, maintaining eye contact, or taking a small step toward the speaker to confirm the focus of attention.
- Understanding the body language of others in order to appreciate the emotional message of what they say
- The skills of the facilitator or coach (see chapter 7). If the coaching role is being carried out in a larger team, it might be useful to break down the team's activities into smaller, more specialized parts, and give coaching and organizational responsibilities to other team members, or enlist help, as part of the learning process.
- Negotiating skills

- Conflict-management skills
- Problem-solving skills. The skills of problem solving are the skills needed for most learning tasks. It is no accident that trainers presenting team learning usually illustrate the topic with a problem. Defining the problem, analysis of cause and effect, establishing a range of solutions, selecting the optimum solution, planning and implementation, and finally evaluation are the required skills.

Discussion

The purpose of dialogue is to understand. Discussion is the decision-making stage, when a conclusion, based on the results of the dialogue, has to be reached. This is not a linear progression: the learning of the team will move backward and forward between dialogue and discussion. However, the quality of the discussion, and hence the decision that is made, will be improved by the richness of the dialogue.

The key skills, that have to be learned in order to make use of the process of dialogue and discussion, are those of reflection and inquiry. Two critical points identified by Senge are:

- Take nothing for granted; test all the thinking.
- Never make unsubstantiated generalizations.

Failing to behave in this way might lead to incorrect assumptions about other people's behavior and character. This would put obstacles in the way of the learning process. This is part of Senge's process of developing the correct mental model, which is one of reflection, exposure, and investigation.

Practice

This is the final stage of the model. It involves setting up situations where the skills of dialogue can be jointly developed. It requires:

- An understanding of the ground rules
- Correct use of the difference between dialogue and discussion.

Applying these skills to the day-to-day business of the teams leads to collective decision making and to decisions that all the members of the team can own. The same can be said of the actions that stem from these decisions. Figure 9.1 (on page 195) shows the process. It is a process that can turn back on itself, and can move around the circuit in either direction.

Figure 9.1 shows the process of learning about ideas in teams: team dynamics, managing the team, task organization, decision making, problem solving, and so on. We should also remember that much of team learning has to be practical. The model, and the principles behind it, can also be applied to learning about each others' jobs, learning new skills, and the practicalities of learning to take more responsibility.

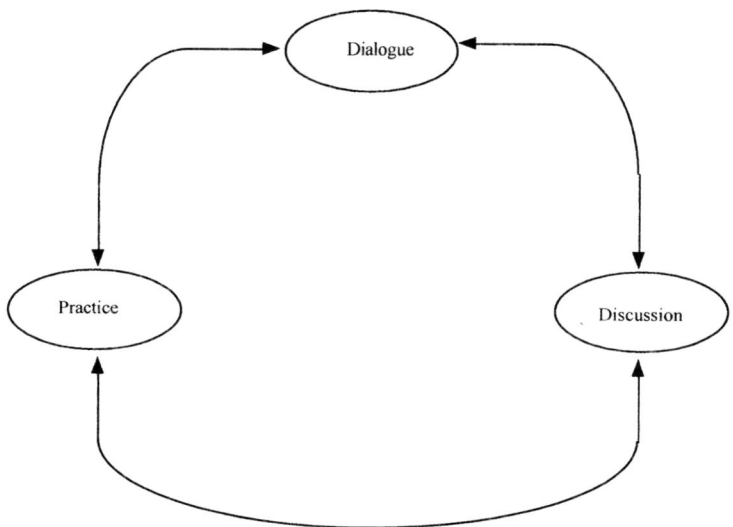

Figure 9.1 The Team Learning Process

The Value of Team Learning

We have already touched on the point that team learning is the final step in a long process of turning individual learning and personal development into organizational learning. It is the key layer in the organizational structure proposed in chapter 2, but it is more than a structural feature. It has a crucial influence on motivation, self-esteem, improved service delivery, and better team building in general. It is in fact a crucial part of developing a learning-based library organization.

Building the Working Team

The process of team learning described above makes a contribution to team dynamics. It reflects the need to understand other viewpoints. It is based on acknowledging the validity of other skills, opinions, and specialisms. It is a feature divorced from formal or role authority: Team status comes from the quality and nature of the contribution made.

Performance Improvement

Team learning improves performance, particularly in decision making and problem solving. The improvement comes from the wide-ranging dialogue stage, where all viewpoints are objectively considered, so that the discussion stage takes place in a much more informed atmosphere.

Innovation

Team learning is a contribution to innovation. It presents the opportunity for comparatively risk-free experimentation. In a culture of equality, where there is respect for the talents of others and, it has to be said, a competitive atmosphere that is different from that in hierarchies, there is a greater incentive to try things out. If success is earned with the assistance of others, then responsibility and rewards are also shared.

Equality and Self-Worth

Team learning takes place in a hierarchy-free zone. Any staff member can speak with the same authority as anyone else. The appreciation of each other's worth is crucial to the success of the process, and when this sense of equality and value is understood, it has a corresponding effect on the individual's self-esteem. It is therefore a positive motivator.

Motivation in General

Let us also say emphatically that team learning makes learning more fun, and this is important for motivation and for self-esteem. Team learning still uses a facilitator to maintain the pace of the learning, to answer questions, and generally keep up the impetus of the process. From time to time, this will involve lightening the burden and introducing an element of relief. This happens in any training event and in the working situations that form the meat of team learning. But team learning is a learning experience with a difference. The team has the extra benefit of the interplay between the different personalities, which interact in conditions of mutual respect and equality. This again possesses the potential to inject some humor into the process and sustain the appetite for learning.

Learning from Work
Finally, but vitally, team learning is work-based. It is a very important component of work teams, or project teams, where it is a central part of team building. Teams also help disseminate the results of learning. The membership of teams can be drawn from wide areas of the library, and will spend the rest of their time in distributed locations. Team learning offers a means of ensuring that the learning is widely spread and applied in the workplace. Issues dealt with at weekly team meetings can be taken back into the workplace, and the results can be discussed at future team meetings. Some trainers call this overcoming the problem of "fade," when what is learned loses its immediacy because of lack of application.

Case Study 10
LEARNING TO SOLVE PROBLEMS

The Situation

The events in this case study occurred in the library service of a higher education institution. The college itself was undergoing a period of considerable change, with substantial implications for the library. As a consequence of major academic developments, that had taken place over years, the institution was seeking formal recognition of its status as a university. It was putting in place a number of changes designed to consolidate its position. This process involved a rationalization of the academic programs and the academic support services, including the library. A number of library staff had expressed concern over the implications of the changes. As part of the library response to what was happening, the director of library services had introduced what he called a learning group. This group met once a week and covered an agenda set by the library management. Attendance was open to all, and the ensuing debate on the various implications of the change process was wide-ranging and, as far as the director could see, unhampered by the fact that the group, reflecting the hierarchical structure of the library, was a mix of all staff levels, including clerical assistants, professional staff, middle managers, and senior managers. The director also introduced one other development, in order to help the dissemination of information and to further explain the nature and consequences of the changes. In the seminar room in which the group met, he employed what he called the "brown paper" approach. Glass (1996) has also referred to this trick. Along the walls of the room, long strips of brown paper were pinned. Using a felt tipped pen the director began to develop a flow chart of the progress towards university status. Everyone who attended the group was able to add his or her own comments, queries, and suggestions at every stage. The process chart soon began to show a number of branches as people started to put up alternatives, and dissect the proposals of senior management.

The Problem

Gradually, the director began to build up a picture of the staff concerns about the change process. He also started to see another pattern that surprised him. Staff attending from one faculty library were raising underlying concerns about communication, management attitudes, job satisfaction, and degrees of professional responsibility. While these issues might not all have been immediately relevant to the project in hand, they were an indication of other problems that might interfere with the library's capacity to play a full part in the new developments.

The director's first move was to talk to his secretary. He did this because she occupied a pivotal position in his informal information system. Discreet and trustworthy, she was approachable and communicated widely with staff throughout the library service, and with users. Aware of her role, she had, on several occasions, acted as a willing conduit when there was a need for the director to know about something. To his surprise, in this instance she readily related a tale of tough management and dismissive and disrespectful personal treatment of the staff. She also talked of friction between professional staff, and the frustration of other staff who felt that they were not being allowed the trust and responsibility their capabilities merited. The secretary further confided that some of the staff had already asked her to talk to the director, but she had been waiting for the right time to do so.

The director went away to think. He was disappointed, but not entirely surprised by the story he had heard. The library service to the faculty had been problematic for some time. The faculty itself was an ill-fitting mixture, and its academic management was at odds with university management over a number of resource issues. Some senior faculty staff had indulged in vigorous criticism of management, and the need to provide better library facilities had been used as a political issue by people who had no genuine concern for improved resources. The same group of lecturers had also fomented student unrest over the question of service standards in the library. Winston, the library manager, naturally inclined to old-fashioned command-and-control management, had become confused and uncertain. He drew more power and responsibility back into his personal domain, and managed by rote and rule book. The small group of staff for whom he was responsible became dispirited, nervous of Winston's mood, and negative themselves. The matter finally came to a head when a comparatively junior member of staff, who had maintained generally good relationships during a deteriorating situation, failed to return to work after a long weekend. Instead, she sent a long letter to the director of human resources, detailing her worries about the aggressive, blunt, and dictatorial management style.

The director now acted. Before talking to Winston, he held detailed discussions with the pro-vice chancellor in charge of academic resources and the director of human resources. They considered the outlines of a course of action before the director started discussions with Winston.

Dealing with the issue proved to be difficult. Winston acknowledged the breakdown in relationships with his staff and the faculty, but was not able to accept responsibility for any of the problems. He was unwilling to see the difficulty of his position, but, after a series of rigorous discussions, agreed to draw up a learning plan with the library director. This plan was a combination of attendance at short courses, other formal training, a period of secondment to a neighboring university library service, and the one-to-one support of an industrial psychologist.

At the same time, with the full involvement of Winston, the faculty library staff were completely reorganized. The lady who had written the formal complaint did not return. The remaining staff were redistributed around the other faculty libraries, and an experienced senior librarian was transferred into Winston's team to strengthen it. At a lower level, four staff members were also redeployed from elsewhere in the service. Finally, two recently qualified assistant librarians were appointed to Winston's staff in their first professional posts. This last action had taken place only two weeks before the matter came to a head again.

The Solution

The other measures had failed. It seemed that once again every member of Winston's staff had a problem, as indeed did Winston. The director and Winston discussed the situation once more, and agreed to a suggestion that the library staff would meet on a weekly basis to work through the issues arising from the management of the library. Because the faculty was small, and there were only eight people including Winston, the director felt that the creation of a learning group was a possible way forward. At the first meeting, the director sat in as an observer. What he saw and heard caused some concern. Winston opened the meeting:

> I want to make my position perfectly clear. I am always available for people to talk to me, and I am approachable. I think you can all feel that I have everybody's best interests at heart, and I am here to give you all the support and guidance you need to do your jobs. I also have to say that I have not been happy with the way the staff have contributed to running this library in the past, so when you are wrong, it is going to be pointed out to you. When all is said and done, I am the manager of this library, and my job is to actively manage it according to the way I think is best.

Margaret, the senior librarian who had been transferred from another faculty, responded:

> I've worked in a few libraries in my time, and there are different ways of doing things. If you want to get the best out of us, it's a question of sharing responsibility and asking us what we think, and how we would deal with things. As it stands, you tell us what to do, we don't always understand it all, you don't offer us any clarification, and then you tear us off a strip when we get it wrong. You also do this in front of other staff. Sometimes we have to ask your permission to do the simplest thing, then the next day we're thrown in at the deep end when you should actually be there alongside us.

Winston's response was to the point: "I'm a manager, not an air hostess." The director was also surprised when the two new assistant librarians, who had only been in their posts for two weeks, also spoke in support of Margaret.

The meeting continued in the same vein, until it was drawn to a close when the agreed hour was up. The director went away to think about things again. He eventually decided to seek the help of an external facilitator from outside the university. The choice was Mary, a freelance trainer. The two met, and Mary was given a detailed description of the problem and what had been done until then. She accepted the role of facilitator for the group set up by the director.

At the first meeting, Mary began by asking them all to try and accept the notion of a learning group that was not based on the formal hierarchy of the library. Moving around the table and asking questions, she was able to establish that everybody in the room had a degree of uncertainty and worry about the situation. She also saw that there was, in fact, a genuine desire on everybody's part to resolve the problem without spilling blood. They also agreed on the general nature of the issue.

At the second meeting, Mary asked the group how they thought the business should be conducted. Eventually, they agreed that there would be no personal criticism, there would be no attempts at justification for past actions or attitudes, and that there would be no hierarchy within the group. It was also agreed that whenever other people's ideas or actions were discussed, there would be a requirement to acknowledge positive aspects before criticizing. Mary also stated the learning objectives in a way that commanded general agreement.

Mary opened the third meeting by asking Winston to talk about management. He began to defend himself and was politely stopped. Patiently, after a few false starts and regressions, Mary succeeded in getting him to talk in a more abstract way about his notions of management in general. Other people began to ask questions and, over time, began to offer their own perspectives on what it was like to manage and to be managed.

Progress was slow. The early exchanges confirmed that everybody had shared problems and worries. This commonality was strengthened as they all became contributors to the group, and the idea of equality within the group became accepted.

The next sign of progress was when the group moved on to consider ideas on how the faculty library service could be best managed in practice. It was still not easy, particularly for Winston, to move on from the old entrenched positions or to dispose of adversarial approaches. Some time was spent in exploring the causes of the conflict amongst the library staff, and while the team was not immediately able to solve this, they drew up a set of rules for handling it. The group dynamics were beginning to shape an approach that was based on allowing everybody to express themselves. Mary consistently reminded them that they were to deal with concrete issues and facts, and they were all beginning to question and listen in an analytical fashion. There gradually emerged a consensus on things such as communication, consistency, and the need for balanced and open exchanges over the running of the library. At the end of each meeting, they took back into the library the principles they had established.

Each member of the team also had a personal target to aim for. In the meetings that followed, they were able to look at how things had changed in practice and how far forward they were in meeting their targets.

In practical terms, the learning that was agonizingly developing in the group showed itself in mutual support. This enbraced all the members of the team. On the one side, there was a greater willingness to ask questions, and on the other, a readiness to give answers and to work alongside colleagues. It was clear that friendship was never going to be a strength of the relationship between Winston and his colleagues, but respect. goodwill, and self-interested collaboration were emerging. The ultimate proof of the improvement came when Winston felt confident enough to use the same teamwork, which had hesitantly flowered in the group, in a project to physically remodel the library. Eighteen months earlier, he would have handled this exclusively.

Comment

Winston was of course the main problem. Yet he deserves sympathy. He was doing nothing except behaving in the way he had been taught and the way his instincts told him he should. When the changes began, he was at first flung into a program of self-development, but it had been imposed by management. He had never owned it. He also had an industrial psychologist imposed on him. At a deeper level, it was impossible for him to feel ownership because he had failed to recognize his own need. Chapter 5 proposed that self-development should start with an honest examination of one's own position and the work situation. He was unable to take the critical step of acknowledging his own need to learn.

The value of the director's other actions was also mixed. He correctly diagnosed Winston's need, and then proceeded to impose a solution. Arguably, he also had no choice, because Winston would not have entered into the process with any enthusiasm, whatever the director's approach had been. The result was that none of the learning acquired in the formal training courses was transferred into the working situation. It might also be supposed that Winston's lack of enthusiasm would have ensured that only a limited amount of learning was acquired in any case.

Laying down the rules was also significant. By doing so, Mary ensured that there would be no personal attacks. Compelling the group to look for the positive aspects in everything depersonalized issues. It undercut the natural tendency to find fault with other people's ideas, and supported the "no-blame" culture. "No-blame" excludes avoiding responsibility or accountability: In fact, the examination of actions and attitudes, and the acceptance of responsibility, was central to the task of improvement.

Action Learning

Things changed when the director sent for Mary. She introduced what is often called the most important team learning technique available. For detailed accounts of this, on which this section of the book draws, two of the most significant texts are Revans (1998) and Pedler (1997).

Revans himself has argued that Action Learning is indefinable, and if you can describe it, you are not doing it. This argument must be tongue-in-cheek. In any case, I will go out on a limb and say that this case study describes some of the principles of Action Learning. It is one interpretation of many. Nevertheless, Mary's approach, outlined below, suggested a possible template.

Admitting the Weakness
The process started with an admission of weakness. It was necessary that everyone involved admitted their need to learn. One reason for the initial failure of learning, as suggested on page 204, was that Winston refused to acknowledge his own shortcomings. This is also part of the first stage of the self-development process considered in chapters 5 and 6.

Jettisoning Some Assumptions
There was a related need to dispose of preconceptions. The best example of this was the behavior of the two new librarians. They had worked at the university for only two weeks, yet were willing to subscribe to the generally held view of Winston's behavior as a manager. They may have been right, but on the evidence of their own experience, their assumption was unjustified: "to appreciate your own ignorance, however high and mighty you are, is the first rule of good teaching and training." (Levy and Delahoussaye, 2000). Out of this exercise, the team drew collective and individual learning objectives.

Using Dialogue
From this standpoint, the team developed its own way of finding out the facts. They allowed everybody to express their views on what was hap-

pening in the library in a neutral tone, and they asked the simple questions of What? How? and Why? This is the first stage in Senge's process of team learning—the use of dialogue.

Setting the Rules

They drew up rules that controlled team operations and ensured objectivity. One of the principles was that of equality. By the time they reached the discussion stage, they were able to develop arguments objectively, and in the context of team ownership of the process, irrespective of position.

Analysis

The learning task was analyzed. The team members defined the parameters of the problem, in breaking it down into its component parts, and in drawing objectives for their own learning out of this exercise. They also proposed the range of solutions.

Practicing, Transferring Learning, Reflecting, Practising

Meeting on a weekly basis was important. It gave the team the opportunity to practice (Senge, 1990). The learning was transferred into the workplace, to be followed by reflection, further team discussion, more practice, and hopefully behavior modification.

Self-Learning

The team learned about themselves. They began admitting to their own weaknesses, and they followed this by considering the situation they had helped to create in the library. They also sought solutions by changing their ways of looking at the work situation.

Changing Their Mental Models

Each one of the team sought solutions to their problems by trying to change their own ways of looking at working situations and altering their conceptions of what was actually going on.

This case study is also an example of how team learning could work in a general sense. Another thing to be emphasized is that there are, paradoxically, very strong elements of self-development or individual learning at the heart of team learning. The final point is perhaps the most important. Learning was the basis of personal development and performance improvement. Managing the learning process equaled managing the library.

Chapter 10

Motivation

In a way, this entire book has been about motivation. There is a case to be made for saying that we should have started from this position, and that everything else followed. This chapter does in fact pull together many strands that are woven into earlier chapters, because almost everything that has been written influences attitudes to learning in one way or another. As ever, there is a theoretical justification for the behaviors and actions described.

Theories of Motivation

Some of the theories about how and why people learn can be quite turgid to read. Many educationalists will admit that it can be a difficult area in which to work. Practicing librarians, and interested observers and trainers like this writer, who are setting about the job of improving the organizational learning of their library services, need only understand the basic principles. In this area, I have always worked on the assumption that the complications of the arguments, and fine distinctions of theory, are not really going to make a lot of difference on the ground. It is in no way intended as an insult to McInerney and McInerney (1998) to say that they have written one of the most readable, perceptive, and usable accounts of learning theories. Equally, Peter Honey in his work, and Honey and Mumford (1986), have been criticized for what appears to some writers to be a lack of awareness of the nuances in some areas (Buckley and

Caple, 1995). Even so, the practical applications that trainers have been able to draw from their ideas have arguably contributed as much to the development of learning in organizations as anything else has. This chapter draws on the works referred to above.

The theoretical basis for ideas on why most people are interested in learning, and conversely why some people do not want to learn and have to be led to it, are very similar to the development of learning theory set out in chapter 4. The progression starts from ideas that matched behaviorism and the principles of scientific and classical management. It goes through a variety of standpoints, which emphasize more positive views of human resources in organizations, to the point where the crucial importance of human talents is recognized. A parallel stream emphasizes the development of our understanding of the different ways in which people learn, the differing positions from which they approach the activity of learning, and a flexible attitude to the activities to be used in practical learning.

Incentive Theory

There cannot be many people who would seriously question the view that the idea of rewards is a significant factor in motivating learners. Universities would be at least half empty without it. In libraries, it has been more difficult to apply this. Because of the strength of our bureaucratic heritage, our salary scales, benefits, and reward systems have been tied to rigid organizational features. In the last ten years, we have begun to see this alter as salary progression became more overtly linked, in some systems, to development. The acquisition of skills and knowledge, and the cultivation of new attitudes, are ways in which it is now possible to acquire material rewards. Case study 3 showed the benefit of a formal link between development and salary levels. It also showed the value of a link between development and the opportunity to qualify for larger and more expansive roles in other parts of the organization. Material incentives will work: To work at their best, they need to be seen as one element of a bigger idea. If incentive theory is to work, then it will have to move a long way from its beginnings in industry, and its application to work study and production lines. In the flexible organizations that libraries are becoming, team-based activities, particularly team learning, will further obscure the issue. It is also possible, in the future, to foresee a much smaller workforce, with very highly skilled individuals providing highly differentiated services tailored to the needs of individual users, while they rely on massive technology and a limited number of support staff. They could be working with what almost amounts to a series of personal contracts with clients, and ideas about rewards and incentives could change again. We may well live to see more and more changes in the skills bases of library staff, and matching rewards to development in this context could be more difficult.

Hierarchies of Needs

Incentive theory is part of a basic view of what it is that actually drives people to achieve new goals. Hill (1997) points to a broader and subtler interpretation of drives and reinforcement. She documents motivational factors such as the seeking of new experiences, curiosity, actively doing things, and companionship. She also considers the idea that motivation increases as the learning experiences presented become more complex, more intense, and novel. To the nonpsychologist (like this author), her arguments may well be difficult to follow and quite arcane. Put simply, they convey the message that the way we approach learning, and the way we provide the events and activities from which people learn, must stretch them mentally, maintain their interest, involve them in active learning, and take place within a social context. The activities must also be work-based.

A. H. Maslow

Incentives and rewards are connected with the needs of learners—the things that people want and are prepared to work for. Maslow's (1943) hierarchy of individual needs showed five levels in a pyramid, with the higher-order needs such as status, esteem, and self-development at the apex. It is these higher-order needs, such as the realization of one's full potential, and being valued and respected because of roles and contributions, that are powerful motivators when it comes to learning. Creating these conditions, in which learning can flourish, is the best way in which learners can be motivated. This has as much to do with eliminating negative characteristics as it is with accentuating the positive ones. These ideas are related to those of Hill and Herzberg's views on hygiene factors; "satisfiers" and "dissatisfiers" are also apposite.

Chapter 10

Hygiene Factors

The work of Herzberg (1959), on a very broad canvas, categorized the influences on workers into two subdivisions. The first group was made up of things that were likely to encourage workers, and the second group was composed of things that were more likely to produce negative responses. This latter group included the hygiene factors in the immediate organizational environment. This book has spent some time dealing with the hygiene factors: making strategy and policy, structures, decision making, empowerment, leadership, coaching, mentoring, group work, reward systems, and learning support. If they are not right, then motivation is likely to be a problem. On the other side, Herzberg uncovered a tendency to regard the actual work itself as a positive feature, so this is something to be used. It leads us back to learning from work—making deliberate use of those things that learners tend to view as attractive.

Expectancy Theory

If learners with a certain level of ability are faced with a task that they think is below their capability, then they display a tendency to under perform at it. Expectancy theory indicates that the amount of effort that goes into a learning task must be considered to be worth the potential result. An individual considering training, or becoming involved in any learning activity, will see a relationship between the effort he or she puts into the training and an improvement in performance, which will offer increased rewards and meet the higher needs of the individual. If it is possible to persuade learners that the degree of effort they will be asked to put into any task is going to lead to a worthwhile improvement in performance, they will be motivated. This process of motivation can become complete if a performance improvement then leads to increased rewards. These need not be material rewards, as long as they meet the learner's requirements. Therefore, what a learner expects from a learning experience or training event is crucial (McInerney and McInerney, 1998). What they expect from work experiences is equally crucial: Make it boring, or fail to challenge them, and they will become demotivated.

Personal Construct Theory

Coming from Piaget, people have a view of training, as everything else, based on their previous experiences with education, learning, or training, and their expectations are based on this view. The trainer's first task might be to modify these views by offering new experiences, ideas, and information. If people can create new constructs, and look at their relationship with learning and with the world of work in a different way, then their interest in learning will be engaged, and their enthusiasm will be kindled.

Self-Worth

When our staff gets to the point where they need to engage with the idea of learning, we are not dealing with blank sheets of paper on which it is possible to inscribe whatever we will. Everybody comes to learning with some preconceptions. They might have some half-formed sense of what they might be able to achieve and what lies outside their capabilities. Some of this sense of self-worth might be negative and, if so, it needs to be turned around. There are examples in industry (Pugh, 2000) of unskilled, unqualified staff with basic levels of education who have been transformed through empowerment and who came to believe in themselves. For the first time in their lives, they were actually helped to acquire new skills that were recognized by their organizations. The first objective of any motivational technique is to create this sense of self-worth. In every organization, there will be a group of people who think that anything to do with learning is outside their capabilities and has no useful purpose. They will need to be presented with information that shows this is not so. This is related to the idea of self-realization discussed in chapter 5.

Different Kinds of Learners, Different Styles, Different Experiences

What learners come to expect from a learning experience is going to be colored by their past experiences, that might not have actually helped their self-worth or their appreciation of learning. The literature of organizational learning identifies a number of basic learning types, and it is likely that every library service will have examples of each one of these types. Low self-worth is likely to be one of the reasons why the first group of learners, the "non-learners," take a negative attitude. Without assistance, they would never consider taking part in any kind of learning or training. If their expectations are to be altered, and their sights raised, there has to be a sustained effort to change the way they think about learning. They have to be convinced that learning is a way of:

- Ensuring personal development
- Improving performance
- Providing better job prospects
- Producing rewards commensurate with effort
- Boosting confidence and the sense of personal worth

Combining this effort with effective development programs will move learners through several stages of increasing maturity until they become "proactive learners." They will then have their own personal development plans, and are committed to a managing their own learning in the workplace.

Honey and Mumford (1986) also worked on the related idea of learning styles. The four learning styles they identify—Activists, Reflectors, Theorists, and Pragmatists—all involve learning in different ways. Learners also have learning activities that they tend to prefer. In the practical delivery of training, these factors must be accounted for, in order to maintain interest, and therefore motivation, once people are actually involved in learning and development.

Summary

Motivating learners depends on

- Linking learning to incentives, that need not be material
- Creating positive organizational conditions
- Changing, strengthening, and heightening expectations
- Instilling self-worth
- Fitting the experiences to various learning styles
- Providing supportive management

Motivation in Practice

Creating a thirst for learning, and the drive to satisfy it, is a large part of personal and professional development in libraries. I believe that motivation can be managed as systematically as any other aspect of organizational life. As always, there is a process. or more than one process, and it can be broken down into three basic stages, as suggested by the literature:

- Making the case for learning
- Providing the support for learning
- Maintaining learning

Making the Case for Learning

The rationale for learning is taken from the theory we examined earlier in this chapter. From senior management right through to team members who share a responsibility for delivering and supporting learning, there is a mantra that has to be repeated over and over again: learning–development–performance improvement–rewards–career development–self-esteem–peer approval–status. Another strand of this has to do with the formal process used to sustain learning organizations (see chapter 3). The justification for learning has to be written in to SDAS, PDP, performance reviews, and learning contracts. At another level, it has to be enshrined in strategy and policy. In the workplace itself, the motifs will have to do with self-learning, work-based learning, peer learning, group learning, and self-managed learning. The objective is to make learning an automatic assumption in organizational life.

Making the case for learning is a tolerably good start. Getting the message across at all levels of the organization then has to be backed up. One of the techniques referred to in chapter 5 was that of modeling. It is also applicable to motivation.

Modeling

If managers and others are going to be advocates for learning, they should try and demonstrate the desired behavior themselves. This may be one of the most difficult things about the entire idea. It may be a contentious position to take, but some managers tend toward conservatism, and it may be that when we talk about the need to change behaviors, it is managers who might be the last people to do this. Elsewhere in this book, it has been implied that, despite the enthusiasm for flexible structures and teamworking, there has been little real change in the way we organize our libraries. If this is so, then the general concept of managerial behavior will be to the left of the manager–coach continuum presented in chapter 7.

One of the best ways of encouraging learners is for managers to model the behavior they desire in others. This demands that managers show a commitment to learning. It also means demonstrating the skills of learning and the practicalities of the self-management of learning. It means playing a part in the delivery of some of the learning experiences. It means sharing the development of learning objectives and being involved in answering the question of how these objectives will be achieved. Essentially, some of the coaching skills must be acquired and used, and in some circumstances perhaps an aptitude for mentoring would also be appropriate. If this vital function as a role model is to emerge, it needs visible managers who communicate in a number of ways, and who set up supportive organizations.

Providing the Support for Learning

To support learning properly in modern information services, a certain amount of organizational engineering is required. This is an issue of cultural change, and a start has already been made by opting for a change in management style. Buttrick (1997), and Glass (1996) define culture almost identically as "the way we do things around here." We are going to do things through learning, and this is a neat phrase for almost everything that goes into making up the character of an organization. Hannabus (1988), writing of library cultures, included in his definition the things people believed in and the relationships between individuals and groups. We might also include the things the organization itself believes in, and the whole range of ways in which people are dealt with. Culture is also made up of stories and interpretations that color recollections of events, and almost assume a mythical status as indicators of the nature of the service. These are the features that offer people support, comfort, and opportunity. They create something that people feel they can belong to.

The culture is an important force for motivation. If it is to nurture a learning environment, then it must assume a certain character:

- It has to be open. Communication must flow naturally around the organization, not just up and down it. It must make information freely available, and it must have mechanisms that allow everyone to contribute to the information bank.
- It has to be flexible. This means allowing people to delve deeper into the jobs they do, test the possibility of extending their jobs to embrace other responsibilities, and test the possibility of movement into other areas of work.
- It has to be supportive. Not only will it be necessary to provide resources and facilities, but it must allow the freedom to try things, to learn from success, and sometimes to learn from getting things wrong; and this is without fear, in a "no-blame" culture. We know that emotional intelligence is an important factor in learning. Learning is likely to be less effective, or will not occur at all, if learners are afraid or angry. Learning situations must first be nonthreatening.

Then it must be possible to work and learn in a cooperative atmosphere, where support can be drawn from colleagues.
- There must be role models all over the library system.
- Learning has to be owned by all the learners.
- Learning has to be managed in a way that demonstrates its importance as a strategic issue. This idea is explored in chapter 2.

A cultural change is achieved by a number of actions:

- Structural change
- Teams
- New management styles
- Proactively managing learning
- Job redesign
- Implementing a learning and development subsystem
- Implementing an information system
- Linking learning and development to rewards

This is not a culture that is prescriptive or that overtly compels participation in learning. To do so would be counterproductive. What it will do is establish pockets of learners. These pockets will act as examples and motivators for those parts of the organization that might be less enthusiastic initially.

Maintaining Learning

As well as maintaining the essentials for supporting all forms of learning and development—budgets, resources, appraisal procedures. reviews and evaluations, administrative systems, and the like—it is a matter of the selection and use of appropriate practical techniques. Placing a justifiable emphasis on learning from work not only means finding the raw material of learning in the day-to-day activities, it is also continuously creating opportunities for putting the benefits of learning back into the work environment. The structural changes suggested in chapter 2, and the behavioral changes recommended in various places throughout the book, are some of the things that make the transfer of learning possible. This constant application of new knowledge, and the impetus for development from this process, are key factors in showing the benefits of learning and development, and thus maintaining motivation.

Even before this, when we begin the task of turning non-learners into proactive learners, the newly awakened interest is fragile and likely to wane, unless it is properly supported. There is also a need for help in focusing on the process. To the novice, learning from experience, which is what work-based learning amounts to, is something instinctive, which happens without any kind of stimulus. As indicated earler, this assumption is wrong, so not only is it necessary to teach people how to learn from work (see chapter 6), they also need to learn how to learn in a more abstract way. Without the tools, they will dissipate their energies, underachieve, and lose heart.

If there are tools and techniques for learners, the same can be said of trainers, learning facilitators, coaches, or anyone else who supports the learning process. They also are learners, and they need to be given the skills to ensure that the learning experiences they provide will strengthen the will to learn. They have to continue to provide challenging and relevant experiences, without which the determination to carry on will be dissipated. Chapter 4 described the approaches that are felt to be appropriate for the learning needs of modern library services. These are the bases of the techniques and skills to be acquired by trainers. At the level of practical delivery, we are charged with the responsibility of providing interesting, and increasingly complex, learning experiences, that will make the learner reach constantly for higher targets. It is important to remember the organizational context, in which facilitating learning becomes the responsibility of many more people in the library than a designated training officer or a staff development officer. If team leaders, supervisors, peers, line and other managers have this responsibility, then they have to learn to be learning facilitators. Otherwise, the learning is not presented efficiently. It will lose its currency, and it will atrophy.

To sum up, the learning program is maintained by:

- Sustaining all the administrative and logistical support systems
- Keeping a focus on the need for role models
- Teaching learners how to learn
- Teaching trainers how to train *and* learn
- Using organizational flexibility to enhance the transfer of learning
- Drenching the learning process in vitality and relevance

Case Study 11
HELPING MANAGERS TO LEARN

Case study 11 explores a not uncommon, but tricky, situation, where managers are faced with an irresistible force for change. Change is not only a most potent learning experience, it is also a phenomenon that tests to the utmost the capacity to learn.

The Situation

Arthur was the director of a small public library service in a largely rural area. Changes to the pattern of local government led to the forced merger of the library service he ran with an adjacent, much bigger, and better, metropolitan service. At a point in his career when Arthur was still a comparatively young man, with some years of service ahead of him, he found himself applying, against his will, for the post of director of the new system. Largely devoid of ambition in the conventional sense, his motive for doing this was self-preservation. He wished to retain his authority and avoid what he understandably saw as the indignity of working under a new manager. Minimally qualified, and up to that point with no interest in continuing professional or academic education, his home and family circumstances precluded any attempt to continue his career elsewhere.

Mildred became the new library director. She was well qualified, with research degrees in both library science and modern history, and her curriculum vitae was impressive.

Settling into her new job, Mildred was forcibly struck by the difference in standards between the part of the service formerly run by Arthur and the rest of the now larger service. She naturally decided that one of her prime objectives would be to raise standards uniformly.

Her first step was to create a streamlined structure for the new service. She did not feel that she could move immediately into the structure she wanted, and that she felt was most appropriate, but she began to take the first steps toward this. She decided to divide the new service into four geographical areas, one of which was made up of the formerly independent library service managed by Arthur. It was this area that presented her with the greatest difficulty. Very little had changed during the time of Arthur's stewardship. Service levels were basic, and the lack of leadership was reflected in a passive staff. More disturbing, Mildred felt there was a tacit collusion, between Arthur and the majority of his staff, to ensure that the quiet and undemanding tenor of the library was not threatened. They all worked hard, but Arthur's horizons were limited. Users felt that the service offered some positives, but it could be improved, and it had not been a priority in the eyes of the local government. Buildings were also inadequate. Mildred felt that if the culture of negativity was to be broken, the key to the problem lay in how Arthur was handled.

The Solution

The first move was to appoint three new area librarians to join Arthur. Two of these came from within the library, and one was a new appointment. Salary levels for these posts were higher than that enjoyed by Arthur. In the short run, Mildred intended to maintain this differential. With the exception of Arthur, who represented a totally different problem, salary progression was tied to the achievement of objectives with very strong learning components. These, in turn, were linked to a staged transfer of power from central management to the area services. In this way, empowerment became a reality and, as people learned how to handle it, they were rewarded. They also enjoyed a commensurate increase in job satisfaction as their influence grew. There was a commitment to extend this system over a period of time.

A new senior management team made up of Mildred and the four area librarians was set up. This team had a fixed term of office of three years, after which the membership would be reviewed. The strategy of basing development on the maximum exploitation of the talents of all staff, and of encouraging and supporting long-term development, was adopted and clearly communicated.

Arthur's participation in these early discussions was minimal, and he actively opposed the next step. The team decided to carry out a comprehensive redeployment of all staff below area librarian level. A massive staff assessment, carried out in a fully consultative manner, resulted in a collaborative exercise that eventually placed every staff member in a position that both they and management agreed was right. This new deployment was to form the basis of a team-based organization to be introduced in the latter part of the life of the management team. A staff development and appraisal scheme was introduced at the same time.

By the end of the first year, several things had happened. The empowerment process had moved forward, and the three new area librarians had demonstrably achieved their learning objectives. This was through a combination of work-based learning programs, internal and external training events, and academic study. Their learning objectives were largely concerned with creating a change in their management styles. In some parts of the service, teams were being set up, and learning contracts were agreed upon with team members. Other areas remained conventionally organized.

Initially, Arthur decided to do nothing. Mildred then spent some time discreetly observing the situation in his area library, as well as talking to other staff and some users. When she was certain that Arthur was not subscribing to the agreed approach, she asked for a meeting with him.

During a long and delicate exchange, she gave Arthur her assessment of his modus operandi, and probed his attitude as neutrally and carefully as she could. To her surprise, Arthur did not demur, but he expressed his own fears about the situation and revealed a feeling of inadequacy. Eventually, he indicated that he was considering resigning. Objectively, Mildred felt this might be the cleanest solution, because of her private worry that Arthur might not be capable of working under the new conditions. Professionally, she considered this possible action to be a failure of human resource management on her part, and she spent some time in persuading Arthur not to go through with it, against her better judgment.

Over the next few weeks, the two met regularly. They identified decision making, time management, and leadership as the areas where Arthur needed to start. For the entire area staff, learning to work together was to be the priority. An external consultant was engaged to work with small groups on a regular basis. At Mildred's suggestion, the staff of the four service points in Arthur's area met with him each week. Here they were able to discuss any issue that worried them, and a number of practical problems were resolved amicably and quickly. Also at Mildred's suggestion, Arthur installed a large whiteboard in each of the four staff work areas. This was used to note problems as they arose. Other people, including Arthur, contributed ideas and suggestions. Arthur also noted his progress in dealing with issues brought to him. In a few weeks, Arthur was beginning to spend more time talking, thinking, collaboratively solving problems. and making decisions, instead of sitting in his office immersed in the routine tasks he used as a barrier. As Arthur's behavior slowly began to change, people around him began to feel more comfortable. They started to sense opportunities to do a little more, and the thawing out of Arthur's management style encouraged them to try.

Arthur also entered into a learning contract, based on the issues he had identified with Mildred. His program was a combination of self-learning (in the skills of which he received some tuition), involvement in formal events in-house, and attendance at external events he had identified, with Mildred, as useful. There were two other features of note.

The first concerns Arthur's relationship with Mildred. She became Arthur's coach (see chapter 7). She reviewed the work Arthur was doing with his staff, analyzed his actions, considered alternatives, and guided him toward solutions.

The second development was also an initiative of Mildred's. She set up an action learning group (see chapter 9). This group was initially the province of the area librarians, plus another external facilitator. It later included some other senior staff, but not Mildred. When the group first began to meet, they undertook a project that was not relevant to the difficulties being experienced by Arthur, but he gradually began to contribute to the cooperative learning effort. Eventually, the group began to work on one of his problems.

Slowly, the situation began to change. Arthur never became a highflier, but he did learn how to run an efficient, if stodgy, library service. He started to achieve some of the targets set in his learning contract, and he became a contributor to the corporate management effort in the library.

His staff showed the most dramatic improvement. As the communication got better, the influence of the new staff who had moved into the area as part of the redeployment process became apparent. They all improved significantly, and some of them excelled. When the appraisal schemes and learning contracts were extended to all staff, they performed as well as the staff in other areas of the service. Two of them eventually served on the senior management team and made a valuable contribution.

Comment

Not all of Mildred's ploys worked. At first, the quality and behavior of the other area librarians had no effect on Arthur, except to increase his insecurity. They therefore failed as role models. The reason for this was that role models have to be in a position to influence. This need not be dependent on formal authority, although it can be. If Arthur had believed in what his colleagues were doing, then he might have seen them as role models. It is not certain that he ever came to believe in them: He changed his behavior, which realistically is the best to be hoped for in the short term, but maybe not his attitude.

Redeploying the entire staff was an attempt to create role models in all parts of the service. It did not work in Arthur's area because the culture he had created was negative; it was cronyism and favoritism, and it was based on low achievement.

He was also totally indifferent to material rewards. Because of this, Mildred's decision to leave Arthur on a lower salary grade than his colleagues, and then tie financial gain to his development, was dubious.

Motivation came from an unexpected source, and was an example of the way in which hierarchies of needs, personal constructs, self-realization, and self-worth can operate in unforeseen ways.

The first impetus for change came from Arthur's insecurity. He was perturbed and confused by developments that clearly challenged the basis of his entire professional career. He sensed the changes could cost him his job, and he was not ready for this. His basic need for security prompted him to change.

The catalyst was the arrival of the new staff. They had a view of their own value and abilities that did not match the way in which Arthur's library service operated. Their constructs were different, and their refusal to accept this was a force for change and the key motivating impulse.

Hygiene factors, incentives, and expectancy theory all began to play a part. Mildred set about changing the way in which Arthur conducted his business, and she introduced different ways of dealing with people. This had the simple but important effect of making people feel more comfortable. Basically, she altered the way in which the staff perceived the service, and also sought a better fit between what the staff felt they were capable of doing and what management was prepared to allow them to try. Once they had subscribed to the basic principles, the targets set for them ensured that they were stretched. They were also able to see that the effort they put in would be matched by the rewards, in terms of self-worth and professional self-respect. Eventually, there might also be material rewards. Resolving the hygiene factors—the things that annoyed people—then left her free to start appealing to the higher-order impulses and bring into play motivating factors such as self-esteem and the appreciation of fellow workers. Open communication, involvement, and sharing decision making dealt with the hygiene factors.

A genuine dialogue was commenced, and this led to collaborative learning. As empowerment increased, everybody faced more demanding tasks that required greater effort. Eventually, the formal devices of appraisal and development were introduced, and motivation through other rewards became a possibility. In this way, the motivational forces were sustained.

Arthur was still the key to solving the problem, and here it might have been felt that motivation was an impossibility. Mildred might have been wiser to cut her losses at the outset and let Arthur go. Fortunately, she was strongly motivated by the same feelings she was eventually able to awaken in others. She therefore began from the position that she was a good role model, and was clearly able to model the behavior she desired to see in her colleagues. She built this into her coaching.

If learning is to take place it has to do so in an unthreatening way. The fear of getting it wrong is a major demotivator (see chapters 2, 4, and 9). Arthur's mistakes were legion, and his sins manifest to all. Mildred conducted the discussions with Arthur in a non-accusatory way, that gave him the opportunity to unburden himself. Her refusal of the proffered resignation was similarly designed to allow everyone to move on, and offer hope for the future.

Choosing the learning techniques was equally important in creating an atmosphere that would support learning, and was motivational in itself. Coaching was an appropriate choice. It allowed Mildred to create a relationship of equals with Arthur. Within the relationship, learning could flourish, and Arthur's sense of self-worth would be bolstered.

The same comments could be made about the action learning groups. In a nonthreatening environment, and working with a small group of people, Arthur was able to contribute to solving the problems of others. This process helped him to grow in confidence, and playing a proper role in the work of the group gave him the encouragement he needed to persevere with his own learning plan. It also gave him the strength to develop a more proactive role outside the group.

In her general approach, Mildred had identified what we know is unarguably one of the most important aspects of motivation. Job satisfaction is crucially influenced by relationships. From experience in a similar situation, I would say that Mildred was absolutely right to break up the existing staff groups through the redeployment exercise. The initial effect of this was destructive. Arthur lost some of his support base and felt more threatened. Equally, those staff who had felt comfortable with his flaccid management style were discomfited by the presence of new colleagues with a different approach. These consequences were counterbalanced by the learning groups and open communications. This led first to a stabilization of relationships, and then to the growth of learning in an atmosphere of increasing trust and mutual self-interest. The introduction of group working within the area library service for Arthur and his fellow area library managers was a key factor in creating motivated learners.

There is one other lesson to be drawn from this case study. It is related to one of the possible boundaries of learning, although to describe it as such might be excessive. Attitudes will only change over the long term, but people's behaviors can be turned around very quickly, whether they initially believe in what they are doing or not. There was no certainty that Arthur ever truly accepted the new philosophy he had been shown, yet he was able to accomodate it. Pragmatism is essential in practical learning, and anyone starting the task of changing an organization through learning could, in the early stages, temporarily jettison any worries about whether or not attitudes are changing. Long term development, where belief is needed, is a very different situation (see also chapter 11).

Chapter 11

Epilogue: Some Issues for Learning

We began with creativity. Over the last two or three years in the United Kingdom alone, we have seen strenuous, government-sponsored attempts to foster creativity in public sector organizations. We have had a think tank working to produce a large number of ways of teaching creativity in schools, and numerous papers and research projects on institutional creativity, employee creativity, structures for creativity, the creative environment, creativity as a way out of organizational failure, and creativity in education, to quote no more than a few. Ogunleye (2001) points out that there is no agreed definition of creativity, although it has been a concern of management theorists for fifty years. This book defines creativity as the development of a new kind of thinking, which is applied to solving problems, and generally dealing with working situations that are new, and perhaps not susceptible to conventional ways of thinking. Essentially, it depends on people learning and thinking, and applying the results where they work.

By and large, the book takes an unashamedly process-orientated, or even mechanistic, view of this area. Honey (2001) writes about the importance of tools and techniques in learning and development. He confirms that change can be accomplished in two ways: either by persuading people to believe in it, and so engineering long-term attitude change, or by changing their behavior first and allowing the belief to come later. Realistically, the behavior change route is the one to follow.

As a result, the book emphasizes the importance of organizational structures and development processes as a surer way of changing behavior. There is a critique of the failure of traditional structures to meet contemporary challenges in Williams and Yang (1999). They suggest that a concern for the effects of rigidity is not misplaced. The literature reflects a view that an enabling structure is a key element in fostering creative thinking, and learning in general. It has to underpin a breadth of learning, which comes from working in diverse situations with people from different backgrounds.

Creativity also depends on the universality of learning. This leads logically to the emphasis on self-development and learning from work in flexible organizations, as argued in part 2. These are proposed as the only realistic means of ensuring first that learning becomes embedded in the organization, and second that the learning processes that are already there are used to advantage. Libraries are now part of the knowledge economy, and we are beginning to see the potential of this for our profession. The question is whether we are ready to grapple with these ideas and really change our organizations. Parsloe and Wray (2001) confirm that work-based training, and coaching and mentoring taken together, are now in the top three of the most frequently used approaches. I think the first issue we face in libraries is the need to accept that learning from work and the associated techniques of coaching, mentoring, and team learning are not just desirable characteristics of development programs. They are the essential cornerstones of learning.

Goleman (1996), and Clutterbuck and Megginson (1999), have dealt with the idea of emotional intelligence, that Goleman calls "personal abilities." These are essentially part of the people-handling skills, which will become more and more important in our our knowledge-based and networked libraries. Equally important, we are now beginning to understand that how we feel about circumstances and incidents in work will affect the way in that we deal with them intellectually. Emotional intelligence covers:

- Analyzing and understanding our own emotions
- Doing the same for the other people with whom we interact
- Modifying and harnessing our emotions
- Motivating ourselves and others
- As a result, we improve our handling of other people.

What I am getting at in a roundabout way is that these techniques are vital, and they cannot be learned in classrooms or by any other more formal training techniques. They are personal. They involve behavior change, and they depend on models and on practice: in other words, coaching and mentoring and to a lesser extent group learning. This is why we need to make the leap forward and accept the centrality of the issues covered in this book.

I think this is related to the major challenge for learning in libraries. These are comparatively new ideas and, for some time, it has seemed to me that as a profession, and I include myself, we engage with theory in a very selective way. The most complex and abstruse ideas I have ever encountered are within the area of our new technologies, yet we accept them without demur. We are happy to take on board theories like Knowledge Management, where we think we can gain an advantage. Yet we do not always seem to grasp the fact that our library organizations have a huge amount in common with most other human enterprises. We have always paid attention to what managers outside the profession are doing. We seem to be slower to acknowledge, in practice not in theory, the possible relevance of ideas that point to the need for new organizational forms.

Unless we consider theory, we have no idea why we organize libraries in the way we do. This means we are handicapped when we consider the impact of change. We cannot really begin to look at the organizational implications of change unless we can assess the degree to which present practices might not be adequate for much longer, and find some reasons why. Even when we do consider theory, it sometimes leads us into the half-hearted and uncertain practical implementation of new features. This is true in a general sense. It is also true of learning theories specifically. We need to know how and why people learn in order to fashion organizations that support learning. We need to know of the link between organizational design, organization development, and learning, otherwise our development will be stunted and our organizations will not change. Chapter 1 tried to develop the argument that creativity in the workplace depends, in part, on a collision of ideas. To engineer this "big bang," we need to be more positive in how we look at ideas that are beginning to circulate outside the profession.

More precisely, in the area of learning and development, we need to take hold of the theories behind coaching, mentoring, and team learning. Because they are comparatively new to us, our definitions of them are fuzzy, and, in this instance, we are not helped by the fact that mainstream management theory suffers from the same complaint. These ideas need to be refined, and they will benefit from a sharper focus that is more appropriate for our organizations. Otherwise, we will become confused.

We also need the theory for confirmation. It may well be that most of library management on the ground, and most of the management of learning, is common sense. No one would dispute the sheer practicality of librarianship. Yet we need to be able to work back, and find a valid and tested basis for what we are doing.

I am also increasingly struck by the similarities between libraries and a whole range of institutions in other sectors. In organizational terms, I see less and less difference between libraries and many other ventures. Given the differences in scale, and the absence or concealment of the profit motive, globalization and the knowledge economy are affecting libraries as much as any other form of human organization:

> The point being made obliquely is that libraries face the same change problems as most other human enterprises: the massive challenge of technology; more complex and interrelated problems; shorter time spans; problem solving that has to be innovative because old solutions will not work; a need to build cross-boundary and cross-sector collaboration; a need for management styles based on identifying common interests and sharing; personnel who are willing to take responsibility for their own work and share some management responsibility; more discerning users who are also ready to exercise some control over how their needs are met; competition and the loss of a previously unchallenged position. This list does not include everything and while it is applicable to libraries it is actually taken from a global view of what is happening to business, industry, commerce, education, ecology, religion, politics, government and in the American parlance 'not-for-profit' organizations. (Lipman-Blumen, 1996, from Pugh, 2000)

The issue is that there are managers out there who are pushing forward with ideas to deal with the same problems we face. We can learn from them.

Paradoxically, I think the other major issue for development in libraries is our unwillingness to face the fact that development has to be subjected to a rigorous, concrete, even mechanistic system, if it is to work. There is no contradiction between arguing for a system, and arguing for the kind of wide-ranging and non-prescriptive learning this book champions. Whenever I lead a workshop on learning from work, I always begin by asking the participants if they would agree that learning from work, or learning from experience, is an instinctive and natural thing that happens all the time. I have never yet met anybody who, at the outset of a training session, disagrees with this. They are, of course, right, but only a little. Part of the problem is that we deal in concrete functions. We are less comfortable with the intangible things that go on under the surface of the library.

So it seems that there are two key issues. We have to become more adept at going into the theory: theory that comes from way outside the professional literature; theory that will assist our learning from others who face the same issues; theory that will help us understand our own learning processes and their relationships with our organizations. On the other hand, we need to accept that we have massively significant learning processes that are outside our formal approaches to development: These we need to systematize and bring within the structure. Only when we do these two things can we control, and own, our own development.

Bibliography

Allan, B. "From Library Assistant to Service Adviser: The Role of Competences in Staff Development at the University of Lincolnshire and Humberside." *Sconul Newsletter* 14 (Summer/Autumn 1998).

Argyris, C. *Personality and Organization.* New York, Harvard University Press, 1957.

Ashton, D. N., and M. J. Maguire. eds. *Young Adults in the Labour Market.* London, Department of Employment, 1986.

Atkinson, P. "Nurturing a Learning Climate." *Training Journal* (December 2000).

Attwood, M., and N. Beer. "Development of a Learning Organisation." *Management Education and Development* 19 (1988).

Ayres, F. "Empowerment: a Failure or Success in the Workplace?" *Training Journal* (September 2000).

Banwell, L., J. Day, and K. Ray. *Managing Organisational Change in the Hybrid Library.* Bath, U. K. Office for Library Networking, 1999.

Bateson, G. *Steps to an Ecology of Mind.* New York, Ballantine, 1972.

Beard, D. "Learning to Change Organisations." *Personnel Management Journal* (January 1993).

Beardwell, I. Address to the Institute of Personnel Development National Conference. London, Institute of Personnel Development, 1999.

Belbin, R. M. *The Coming Shape of Organisation.* Oxford, Butterworth Heinemann, 1998.

Blumer, H. *Symbolic Interactionism: Perspective and Method.* Boulder, University of Colorado, 1986.

Bowler, D. *Shanks: the Authorised Biography of Bill Shankly*. London, Orion, 1996.
Bruner, J. *Towards a Theory of Instruction*. Cambridge, Mass., Harvard University Press, 1966.
Branden, N. *Self–Esteem at Work*. San Francisco, Jossey-Bass, 1998.
Brundage, D. H., and D. Mackeracher. *Adult Learning Principles and Their Application to Program Planning*. Toronto, Ontario Ministry of Education, 1980.
Buckley, R. and J. Caple. *The Theory and Practice of Training*. 3rd ed. London, Kogan Page, 1995.
Burke, M. E., and H. Hall. *Navigating Business Information Sources*. London, LAPL, 1998.
Buttrick, R. *The Project Workout*. London, Pitman, 1997.
Child, D. *The Psychology of Learning*. 3rd ed. Houston, Holt, Rinehart, and Winston, 1981.
Clutterbuck, D. *Everyone Needs a Mentor: Fostering Talent at Work*. London, Institute of Personnel, 1991.
Clutterbuck, D. and D. Megginson. *Mentoring Executives and Directors*. Oxford, Butterworth-Heinemann, 1999.
Corrall, S. "Knowledge Management: Is it Our Business?" *Ariadne* (November 1998).
Daniels, H. ed. *Introduction to Vygotsky*. London, Routledge, 1996.
Dempsey, L. "Places and Spaces." in *Towards the Digital Library*. eds. Carpenter, L., S. Shaw, and A. Prescott. London, British Library, 1998.
Diane Bailey Associates. *The Training Handbook*. London, Gee, 2001.
Doyle, M. "Managing Development in an Era of Radical Change: Evolving a Relational Perspective." *Journal of Management Development*, vol. 19. no 7 (September 2000).
Dyson, G. Address to the 19th session of the International Olympic Academy. Athens, International Olympic Academy, 1979.
Edwards, V. "Self-Services: Transforming the Roles of Library Staff." *Sconul Newsletter*, 14 (Summer/Autumn 1998).
Engineering Employers Federation. *A New Millenium of Learning for Engineering*. London, EEF, 1999.
Erikson, E. H. *Childhood and Society*. 2nd ed. New York, W. W. Norton, 1963.
———. *Identity: Youth and Crisis*. New York, W. W. Norton, 1968.
Freire, P. *Pedagogy in Process: The Letters to Guinea-Bissau*. New York, Continuum, 1983.
Gatfield, J. *Teamworking*. Address to the BCCCA Biennial Conference. Harrogate, 1996.

Glass, N. *Management Masterclass: A Practical Guide to the New Realities of Business*. London, Nicholas Brealey, 1996.

Glynn, C. *The Management Agenda 2000*. Roffey Park Management Institute, 2000.

———. *Young People's Attitudes to Work, Careers and Learning*. Roffey Park Management Institute, 2000.

Goleman, D. *Emotional Intelligence: Why it Can Matter More Than IQ*. London, Bloomsbury, 1996.

Gouillart, F. J., and Kelly, J. N. *Transforming the Organisation*. London, McGraw Hill, 1995.

Hannabus, S. "Negotiating Meaning." *Library Management*, vol. 9 no 4. (1988).

Hargie, O., and D. Tourish. eds. *Handbook of Communication Audits for Organizations*. New York, Routledge, 2000.

Heller, F. *Organisational Participation: Myth and Reality*. Oxford University Press, 2000.

Hendry, C. "Corporate Strategy and Training." in *Training and Competitiveness*. eds. Stevens, J., and R. Mackay. London, Kogan Page, 1991.

Henry, G. *The X Factor*. London, Queen Anne Press, 1999.

Herzberg, F. *The Motivation to Work*. London, Granada, 1959.

Heseltine, R. "Beyond the Barriers: Access and Scholarship in the Digital Age." *MultiMedia Information and Technology*, vol. 26 no. 4 (November 2000).

Hill, W. F. *Learning: A Survey of Psychological Interpretations*. New York, Longman, 1997.

Hirshberg, J. *The Creative Priority: Driving Innovative Business in the Real World*. Harmondsworth, Penguin, 1998.

Honey, P. "Three Cheers for Tools and Techniques." *Training Journal*, (January 2001).

———. Address to the Institute of Personnel Development. London, 1999.

———. *You Are What You Learn*. Maidenhead, Peter Honey Publications, 1993.

Honey, P., and A. Mumford. *Using Your Learning Styles*. Maidenhead, Peter Honey Publications 1986.

Hudson, F. M. *The Handbook of Coaching*. San Francisco, Jossey Bass, 1999.

Inhelder, B. *Piaget Today*. Hillside, N. J., Lawrence Erlbaum Associates, 1986.

Johnson, I. M. "Where Will All the Flowers Grow?" *Library and Information Appointments* (January 2000).

Knowles, M. S. *The Adult Learner: A Neglected Species*. 3rd ed. Houston, Gulf, 1984.

Kohn, M. L., and K. M. Slomczynski. eds. *Social Structure and Self-Direction*. Cambridge, Mass., Blackwell, 1990.

Kolb, D. A. *Experiential Learning: Experience as the Source of*

Development. New York, Prentice Hall, 1985.

Kotter, H. *The General Managers.* New York, Free Press, 1982.

Leahy, T. H., and R. J. Harris. *Learning and Cognition.* 5th ed. New York, Prentice Hall, 1993.

Levy, M., and M. Delahoussaye. "Reg Revans: A Man of Action." *Training Journal,* (November 2000).

Lipman-Blumen, J. *The Connective Edge: Leading in an Independent World.* San Francisco, Jossey-Bass, 1996.

Mackay, R. ed. *Training and Competitiveness.* London, Kogan Page, 1991.

MacKinnon, D. W. *In Search of Human Effectiveness.* New York, Creative Education Foundation, 1978.

Maslow, A. H. "A Theory of Human Motivation." *Psychology Review* 50 (1943).

Mayo, A. *Creating a Training and Development Strategy.* London, Institute of Personnel Development, 1998.

McInerney, D. M., and V. McInerney. *Educational Psychology: Constructing Learning.* 2nd ed. Sydney, Prentice Hall, 1998.

Mintzberg, H. *Mintzberg on Management.* New York, Free Press, 1989.

———. *The Nature of Managerial Work.* New York, Harper and Row, 1973.

———. *The Structure of Organisations.* New York, Prentice Hall, 1979.

Mumford, E. "Only the Democrats Will Survive." *Observer,* 16th July 2000.

Myers, D. G. ed. *Psychology.* New York, Worth, 1988.

Nankivell, C., and M. Shoolbred. *Mentoring in Library and Information Services: an Approach to Staff Support.* London, British Library Research and Innovation Centre, 1996.

National Education Association Foundation for the Improvement of Education. *Creating a Teacher Mentoring Program.* Washington, D.C., NEA, 2000.

Norton, R., and J. Tivey. *Management Directions: Mentoring.* 2nd ed. London, Institute of Management, 1995.

Ogunleye, J. "Creative Training Techniques: How to Spell Success in Creative Organisations." *Training Journal* (January 2001).

O'Keeffe, J. *Business Beyond the Box: Applying Your Mind for Breakthrough Results.* London, Nicholas Brealey, 1998.

Owen, H. "Leading the Way in the Way of Leadership." *Western Mail* (27th January 2001).

Parsloe, E., and M. Wray. *Coaching and Learning: Practical Ways to Improve Learning.* London, Kogan Page, 2000.

Partridge, E. *A Dictionary of Catch Phrases.* 2nd ed. London, Routledge and Kegan Paul, 1986.

Pasternak, B., and A. J. Viscio. *The Centerless Corporation: a New Model for Transforming Your Organization for Growth and*

Prosperity. New York, Simon and Schuster, 1998.
Pearn, M., C. Roderick, and C. Mulrooney. *Learning Organizations in Practice.* London, McGraw Hill, 1995.
People Skills Scoreboard. London, Engineering Employers Federation and Engineering and Marine Training Authority,1999.
Pedler, M. ed. *Action Learning in Practice.* 2nd edition. Aldershot, Gower, 1997.
Perrow, C. *Organisational Analysis: A Sociological View.* London, Tavistock, 1967.
Piaget, J. *The Language and Thought of the Child.* London, RKP, 1997.
Pugh, L. *The Convergence of Academic Support Services.* London, British Library Research and Innovation Centre, 1997.
———. *Change Management in Information Services.* Aldershot, Gower, 2000.
———. *The innovative management of public sector higher education learning resources provision,* M.Phil thesis: Leeds Metropolitan University, 1990.
Randell, G. *The Skill of Leadership.* Holywell, Flintshire, Society of Headmasters and Headmistresses of Independent Schools Conference, 2000.
Redshaw, B. *Coaching for Managers.* Maidenhead, Peter Honey Publications, 2000.
Revans, R. W. *The ABC of Action Learning.* London, Lemos and Crane, 1998.
Rittel, H. W. J., and Webber, M. M. "Dilemmas in a General Theory of Planning." *Policy Sciences* 4 (1973).
Robbins, H., and S. Finley. *Why Teams Don't Work: What Went Wrong and How to Make it Right.* London, Orion Business, 1998.
Rogers, C. R. *Freedom to Learn: For the 80s.* Columbus, Ohio, Charles E. Merrill, 1983.
———. *On Becoming a Person.* Boston, Houghton Mifflin, 1961.
Sellars, C. *Mental Skills: an Introduction for Coaches.* Leeds, National Coaching Foundation, 1966.
Senge, P. *The Fifth Discipline: The Art and Practice of the Learning Organization.* Doubleday, 1990.
Skyrme, D. Knowledge management: making sense of an oxymoron. *Management Insight* series 2 no. 2 (1997).
http://www.skyrme.com/insights/22km.htm
Slavin, R. E. "Cooperative Learning" in *International Encyclopaedia of Education and Teacher Education.* ed. Anderson, L. W. 2nd ed. Cambridge, Cambridge University Press, 1995.
Smith, M. *Introducing Organizational Behaviour.* Basingstoke, Macmillan

Educational, 1982.

Tolman, E. C. *Purposive Behavior in Animals and Men*. Des Moines, Iowa, Appleton-Century Crofts, 1932.

Vygotsky, L. S. *Collected Works, vol 3. Problems in the Development of Mind*. New York, Plenum, 1997.

——. "Interaction Between Learning and Development." in *Mind in Society*. ed. M. Cole. Cambridge, Mass., Harvard University Press, 1978.

Wertheimer, M. *Productive Thinking*. New York, Harper Torchbooks, 1959.

Wertsch, J. V. "L. S. Vygotsky and Contemporary Developmental Psychology." in Daniels, H. ed. *Introduction to Vygotsky*. London, Routledge, 1996.

Whetherley, J. "When Only One to One Adds Up". *Library and Information Appointments* (February 2001).

Williams, W. L., and L. T. Yang. "Organisational Creativity." in *Handbook on Creativity*. ed. R. J. Sternberg. Cambridge, CambridgeUniversity Press, 1999.

Wills, M. *Managing the Training Process*. 2nd ed. Aldershot, Gower, 1998.

Withey, M. "Measures of Perrow's Work Unit Technology: an Empirical Assessment." *Academy of Management Journal* 25 (March 1983).

Wood, D. ed. *How Children Think and Learn*. Oxford, Blackwell, 1988.

Index

academic libraries, as learning organizations, 51-55, 69-75, 89-96; mentoring in, 181-83; problem solving in, 197-204; routines, improvement in, 113-17; self development in, 124-29
action learning, 203-204
adhocracy, 36-37
adult learning theories, 78-90, 135-37
andragogy, 80
appraisal schemes, 62-64, 72-73
behavioral change, 10-11, 20-22, 44-46, 223-27

Belbin's trapezium, 41-43
bureaucracies, machine, 36; professional, 36-37

change, and continuity, 11; and managers, 215-21; and problem solving, 197-204; behavioral, 10-11, 20-22, 44-46, 212-13; coaching as an instrument of, 139; cultural, 212-13; educational, 8-9; management of, 13-14, 44-46, 212-13; mentoring as an instrument of, 170-71; organizational, 1-30, 72-75, 163-64, 212-13; technological, 4-8;
coaching, xi, 131-57, 215-21; and assessment, 146-47; and attitudes, 138-39; and behavior, 149; and change, 139; and communication, 145-46; and development, 139, 142-43; and diagnosis, 142-43; and flexible learning, 136; and learning styles, 145; and managers, 132-34, 137-57; and mental skills, 140-41; and mental strength, 138-39; and practice, 148-49; and professional skills, 141-42; and self learning, 136; and self-worth, 135-36; and technical skills, 141-42; and the learning process, 144-47; and The Zone, 151-52; definition, 134, 136-37; for development, 142-43, 147; in libraries, 137-57; objectives, 147; planning, 147-48, 154-57; process, 146-50, 152-57; qualities required, 144-46; reassessment, 150; roles, 139-46, 143-44; teams, 150-52, 191; theories, 134-37
collaborative learning, 187-88

communication, and coaching, 145-46; management styles, 46;
creativity, 15-16; and thinking, 18, 89-96, 131-57; and innovative organizations, 17-20; and organizational development, x, 14-20, 29-30, 92-96, 131-57, 223-27; workplace, 17-20, 92-96, 131-57

development, and organizations, 1-75; and coaching, 139, 142-43; and mentoring, 159-83; and teams, 192-204
dialogue, and team learning, 192-94, 203-04
discussion, and team learning, 194
diversity, learning from, 188
divisional structures, 37
double loop learning, 20-21

educational change, 8-9
electronic libraries, and management, 6-8
emotional intelligence, 224-25
empowerment, and learning, 3, 10-11, 16, 20-21, 45, 59-60, 110-11, 169, 217-21
entrepreneurialism, 9, 25-30
equality, in learning, 87-88, 187, 193, 196
expectancy theory, and motivation, 208

flat structures, and learning, 2-4
flexible learning, 136
flexible structures, 41
formal learning, 113

Gestalt philosophy, and adult learning, 81
group dynamics, 112
group learning, 96, 189-90

hierarchies of needs, 207-10
hierarchies, and structural rigidity, 164-65; and team learning, 42
hygiene factors, and motivation, 207-08

ideas, creative, 15-16
incentive theory, and motivation, 206-07
inclusivity, in learning, 22-25, 87
individual learning, 3-4, 31-55, 47-48, 81, 97-104
informal learning, 105-06, 112-13
information delivery, processes, 39-41
innovation, in team learning, 196
integrative teams, 43-44
internalising, in learning from experience, 120-21

knowledge architecture, 47-48
knowledge management, 2, 49,

learning, ix,xi, 69, 223-37; action, 203-04; adult, 78-96, 223-37; and culture, 88-89, 92-96; and empowerment, 3, 10-11, 16, 20-21, 45, 59-60, 110-11; and flat structures, 2-4; and knowledge architecture, 47-48; and self-development, 99-104; and structural change, 2-3, 156-57; and the organization, 1-75, 169; as a strategic issue, 22, 39, 41, 57-61, 74-75; assessment, 8; cli-

Index

mate, and coaching, 146-47; and managers, 215-21; collaborative, 187-88; contracts, 64-65; cycle, 95-96, 118-19; double loop, 20-21; environments, 77-79; equality in, 87-88, 187, 193; flexible, and coaching, 136; formal, 113; from diversity, 188; from experience, 118-29, 122; group, 96, 189-90, 197-204, 215-21; in teams, xi, 34, 41-44, 65-66, 85-87, 173-83, 185-204; inclusivity in, 22-25; individual, 3-4, 31-55, 47-48, 97-104; informal, 105-06, 112-13; management of, 57-95; modeling, 136-37, 143-44; monitoring, 213-14; motivation, 85; peer, 188; process, 109-17; 120-22; skills, 132-33; structures, 31-55, 65-66, 88-89, 223-27; strategies, 35, 38-39, 59-60, 88-89; styles, 77-96; subsystems, 33, 35-36, 46-47, 49-50, 65-66; support for, 159-83, 212-13; systematic, 188-89; theories, 78-79, 85-89, 119, 135-57, 189-90, 206-21; transfer, 122; work-based, 105-29, 187; *see also* coaching; mentoring; teams

machine bureaucracies, 36
management, of learning in libraries, 57-75, 66-68, 79; of mentoring, 166-69; styles, 44-46, 188; theories, 1-4
manager-coach relationship, 132-137-57
managerial roles, 67-68

managerial support for learning, 215-21
manager-mentor relationship, 168-69
mental skills, and coaching, 140-41
mental strength, and coaching, 138-39
mentoring, xi, 159-83; and change, 170-71; and conservatism, 163-64; and favoritism, 166; and hierarchies, 164-65; and organizational change, 163-64; boundaries, 167; criteria for schemes, 166; definition, 162; exit strategies, 167; objectives, 166; process, 171-72; skills, 171; successful, 180-83;
modeling learning, 108-09, 136-37, 156, 211-12
motivation, and self-worth, 209; in adult learning, 85, 205-21; expectancy theory, 208; general theories, 205-10; hygiene factors, 207-08; in practice, 210; in team learning, 196; incentives, 206-07; personal construct theory, 208
multiskilling, 86-87

needs, assessment, 68-69; hierarchies of, 207-10
networking, 88

organizational change, 1-30, 72-75, 163-64
organizational complexity, 13
organizational design, 43-44
organizational development, 1-75, 169; and creativity, x, 14-20,

29-30, 223-27
organizational functions, 36
organizational learning, and knowledge management, 49
organizational processes, 36, 39-41
organizational structures, and teams, 43-44, 186; and technology, 4-8; and individual learning, 2-4, 31-35, 97-104; and innovation, 17-20; and learning, ix-xi, 1-75; and learning teams, 191; divisional, 37; flexible, 41-42; innovative, 41-42; people-centered, 3-4; problems, 51-55;
organizations, single loop, 87-88
ownership, in learning teams, 190-91
objectives, in mentoring, 166; in coaching, 147

peer learning, 188
people-centered organizations, 3-4
personal construct theory, and motivation, 208
policies for learning, 57-61
problem-solving, 15-16, 95-96, 193-94, 215-21; and coaching, 138, 193-94; in adult learning, 80-82, 193-94; in learning teams, 197-204
professional bureaucracies, 36-37
project management, 92-96
psychosocial development, 100

self-development, 77-130, 97-104, 202-03; and self esteem, 99-104; and specialization, 6, 86; and technology, 5-6; impact of, 122-29; in adult learning, 80, 118-29; in coaching, 147; definition, 98-99; theories, 100-101; process, 101-104; through work, 105-29
self-esteem, and self-development, 99-104
self-evaluation, 102-04
self-learning, 204
self-management, in adult learning, 84
self-managing learners, development of, 110-11
self-worth, and coaching, 135-36; and motivation, 209; and team learning, 196
single loop organizations, 87-88
skills, 11-13, 29-30, 86-87; deficits, 137-38; in learning teams, 192-95; learning, 132-33; mental, 140-41; of the coach, 141-42; of the mentor, 171; transferable, 132-33
staff development and appraisal schemes, 62-64, 72-73, 176-79

teams, and coaching, 150-52, 191; and innovation, 196; and performance improvement, 196; building, 195-96; composition, 190; in libraries, 42-44, 65-66, 69-75, 173-183; integrative, 43-44; learning, xi, 34, 41-44, 52-55, 65-66, 85-87, 173-83, 185-204; motivation, 196; learning skills in, 192-95; objectives, 190; structures, 44, 50, 64-47, 65-66; value, 195-204
technical infrastructure, 49

technology, and organizational structure, 4-8, 12; and self-development, 5-6
training needs analysis, 61-62

unlearning, 20-21, 45

work, and creativity, 17-20, 29-30; and learning, x-xi, 82, 88, 105-29, 156, 187, 196-97, 213-14, 226-27; and self-development, 105-29

About the Author

Lyndon Pugh has been a library manager in the academic sector, and a trainer and teacher of librarians, for thirty-five years. For a little over half of this time, he was Head of Learning Resources at the University of Wales Institute in Cardiff. Educated at the University of Wales Aberystwyth, he has a B.A. degree in English Literature, and for his M.A. degree he researched the poetry of R. S. Thomas. His M.Phil. research was on the topic of innovative management in libraries and learning resources. He has worked as a trainer and consultant throughout Europe, and since 1994 has been heavily involved in delivering management training for librarians in Eastern Europe and the former Soviet Union. He has written training material for a number of organizations, and has carried out research into organizational change in information services. He has also written on this topic and many other library management issues. Formerly the managing editor of *Ariadne*, a parallel print and Web journal that reports and comments on the development of electronic and digital libraries; he is now managing editor of *MultiMedia Information and Technology*.